PEACE IN BELIEVING:

A MEMOIR OF

ISABELLA CAMPBELL.

G. L. AUSTIN & CO. PRINTERS, WILLIAM-STREET.

PEACE IN BELIEVING:

A MEMOIR OF

ISABELLA CAMPBELL,

OF

ROSNEATH, DUMBARTONSHIRE,

SCOTLAND.

By Robert Story

WITH A PRELIMINARY ESSAY,

BY

AN AMERICAN CLERGYMAN.

"No nourishment is here for worldly minds;
But for theirs who of the world are weary."

From the last English Edition.

New-York:
JONATHAN LEAVITT, 182 BROADWAY.

Boston:
CROCKER & BREWSTER,

MDCCCXXX.

PRELIMINARY ESSAY.

lass of modern religious biographies, this work
..—peculiar from its destitution of all interest, ex-
founded in religion. There were no incidents,
......ue of Isabella Campbell to excite interest, and
.he lived in the midst of natural scenery, both wild
.utiful, there is no attraction given to the Memoir
...at, or indeed any other incidental circumstance.
... .alue of the biography consists in the peculiarity of
..ious character displayed; and on this account it is
of the most attentive and studious perusal. I
opinion, that the nature of personal religion has not
..ufficiently studied among us; and while the press has
eeming with religious controversy, with biblical cri-
.., with missionary intelligence, and with plans and
uasives pertaining to benevolent enterprise, compara-
'v little has been written upon religion, as a mode of
as a course of action, as the perfection of spiritual ex-
.ce. And because it has not been thus studied, the
rch in our land, is very deficient in eminent examples
living piety;—examples that throw a holy radiance
..ut them, which warm and animate all within the
here of their influence. It bodes ill, that we have so
.any, in the high places of our Zion, who rather give us
.. light .. .intry sun, than those golden rays, which
..e p.. .aturity to our fruits.
R... .g been studied, as a system to be ex-
.... .ed to reigning opinions on intellec-

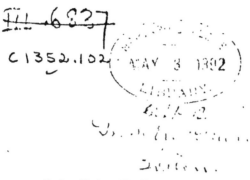
Southern District of New-York, ss.

BE IT REMEMBERED, That on the tenth day of September, A. D. 1830, in the 55th year of the Independence of the United States of America, JONATHAN LEAVITT, of the said district, hath deposited in this office the title of a book, the right whereof he claims as proprietor, in the words following, to wit:

"Peace in Believing: a Memoir of Isabella Campbell, of Rosneath, Dumbartonshire, Scotland. With a Preliminary Essay, by an American Clergyman.

> "No nourishment is here for worldly minds;
> But for theirs who of the world are weary."

In conformity to the act of Congress of the United States, entitled "an act for the encouragement of learning, by securing the copies of maps, charts, and books, to the authors and proprietors of such copies, during the time therein mentioned," and also to an act, entitled "An act, supplementary to an act, entitled an act for the encouragement of learning, by securing the copies of maps, charts, and books, to the authors and proprietors of such copies, during the times therein mentioned, and extending the benefits thereof to the arts of designing, engraving, and etching historical and other prints."

FRED. J. BETTS,
Clerk of the Southern District of New-York.

PRELIMINARY ESSAY.

In the class of modern religious biographies, this work is peculiar—peculiar from its destitution of all interest, except that founded in religion. There were no incidents, in the life of Isabella Campbell to excite interest, and though she lived in the midst of natural scenery, both wild and beautiful, there is no attraction given to the Memoir from that, or indeed any other incidental circumstance. The value of the biography consists in the peculiarity of the religious character displayed; and on this account it is worthy of the most attentive and studious perusal. I am of opinion, that the nature of personal religion has not been sufficiently studied among us; and while the press has been teeming with religious controversy, with biblical criticism, with missionary intelligence, and with plans and persuasives pertaining to benevolent enterprise, comparatively little has been written upon religion, as a mode of life, as a course of action, as the perfection of spiritual existence. And because it has not been thus studied, the church in our land, is very deficient in eminent examples of living piety;—examples that throw a holy radiance about them, which warm and animate all within the sphere of their influence. It bodes ill, that we have so many, in the high places of our Zion, who rather give us the light of a wintry sun, than those golden rays, which give perfection and maturity to our fruits.

Religion has too long been studied, as a system to be explained and conformed to reigning opinions on intellec-

2

G. L. AUSTIN & CO. PRINTERS, WILLIAM-STREET.

PEACE IN BELIEVING:

A MEMOIR OF

ISABELLA CAMPBELL,

OF

ROSNEATH, DUMBARTONSHIRE,

SCOTLAND.

By Robert Story

WITH A PRELIMINARY ESSAY,

BY

AN AMERICAN CLERGYMAN.

"No nourishment is here for worldly minds ;
But for theirs who of the world are weary."

From the last English Edition.

New-York:
JONATHAN LEAVITT, 182 BROADWAY.

Boston:
CROCKER & BREWSTER,

MDCCCXXX.

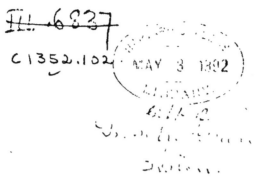
Southern District of New-York, ss.

BE IT REMEMBERED, That on the tenth day of September, A.
D. 1830, in the 55th year of the Independence of the United States of
America, JONATHAN LEAVITT, of the said district, hath deposited in this
office the title of a book, the right whereof he claims as proprietor, in the
words following, to wit:

"Peace in Believing: a Memoir of Isabella Campbell, of Rosneath,
Dumbartonshire, Scotland. With a Preliminary Essay, by an American
Clergyman.

"No nourishment is here for worldly minds;
But for theirs who of the world are weary."

In conformity to the act of Congress of the United States, entitled
"an act for the encouragement of learning, by securing the copies of maps,
charts, and books, to the authors and proprietors of such copies, during
the time therein mentioned," and also to an act, entitled "An act, supplementary to an act, entitled an act for the encouragement of learning, by securing the copies of maps, charts, and books, to the authors and proprietors
of such copies, during the times therein mentioned, and extending the benefits thereof to the arts of designing, engraving, and etching historical and
other prints."

FRED. J. BETTS,
Clerk of the Southern District of New-York.

PRELIMINARY ESSAY.

In the class of modern religious biographies, this work is peculiar—peculiar from its destitution of all interest, except that founded in religion. There were no incidents, in the life of Isabella Campbell to excite interest, and though she lived in the midst of natural scenery, both wild and beautiful, there is no attraction given to the Memoir from that, or indeed any other incidental circumstance. The value of the biography consists in the peculiarity of the religious character displayed; and on this account it is worthy of the most attentive and studious perusal. I am of opinion, that the nature of personal religion has not been sufficiently studied among us; and while the press has been teeming with religious controversy, with biblical criticism, with missionary intelligence, and with plans and persuasives pertaining to benevolent enterprise, comparatively little has been written upon religion, as a mode of life, as a course of action, as the perfection of spiritual existence. And because it has not been thus studied, the church in our land, is very deficient in eminent examples of living piety;—examples that throw a holy radiance about them, which warm and animate all within the sphere of their influence. It bodes ill, that we have so many, in the high places of our Zion, who rather give us the light of a wintry sun, than those golden rays, which give perfection and maturity to our fruits.

Religion has too long been studied, as a system to be explained and conformed to reigning opinions on intellec-

2

tual philosophy, rather than something to be believed ; to be believed, not as a chain of arguments, of which, about as much may be said on the one side as the other, but believed as in itself furnishing the sustenance of the soul—that from which its daily life comes, and in which it consists. Many a weary battle has been fought with Motives, and Voli- tions, and Tastes, and Moral Power, and Moral Tendency, and no very perceptible advantage gained, because the parties had forgotten that the victory that overcometh the world is our FAITH. Religion is a system of truths to be be- lieved. And if BELIEF does not express enough to thought- less minds, then, I say religion is a system of TRUTHS, in which our moral life is to have its being. Here is the suste- nance, the peace, the purity, the happiness, of the soul. Life and immortality are here ; joy and bliss are here. By argu- ments, a variety of things may be made known ; but not life and joy ; these must be felt to be known. Many, many things may be said of the why and the wherefore in reli- gion, the cause and the reason abundantly stated, without the least advance in the knowledge of religion *as a life*. And yet it is only as a life, that God has condescended to speak of it to us ; and he that would be godlike must contemplate it, and speak of it ; nay, and should teach it only as a life. O! how full of folly are those, who are wasting their time, and their temper, and their energy in pulling down and building up the ungainly scaffolding of the Christian tem- ple, which men as full of folly as themselves, have hereto- fore erected to the marring of its beauty, and the utter de- struction of its imposing grandeur.

Isabella Campbell treated religion as a life. She lived in it. It was the life of her life. And she received it not from the arguments of man, nor from the opinions of man, nor from any source in man, but from God. But she had not seen God, and as the only possible way, she received it by *Faith*, adopting it, as she received it, to her necessities ;

feeding upon it, living upon it, hoping in it, rejoicing in it. She went about to establish no righteousness of her own, to form no notions of her own, to seek no path of her own, to lean on no strength of her own, but submitted herself to the righteousness of God in Christ. *She believed God.* In that belief, she found all her wants more than supplied. Her soul was filled with peace; yea, it overflowed with love; it brake forth in joy, it shouted in thanksgiving, it continually uttered praise, it did exalt and magnify the Lord our Saviour.

To these unusually clear and distinct views, Isabella's peculiar situation doubtless contributed in some degree. She was not placed in circumstances where any object, calling for the active exertion of her own mind, had seized upon it, with controlling power. Her health and her constitution were delicate, which withdrew her still more from the bustling thoughts and feelings of active employment, and which seemed to give a kind of serene calmness—a pure and lovely abstraction to her whole conversation and manner, that exhibited *her faith* in bold relief, more prominent perhaps, than the same measure of faith would have been, had she been compassed with the cares of life, and dwelt amid the din and bustle of active business. In this way, she became a more transparent medium for the transmission of the light of truth, than she would otherwise have been. The sustaining principles of her mind are more apparent, at least to the superficial observer, than they would have been in different circumstances. Her experience, however, is only the natural and legitimate effect of receiving Religion as a life, and the making of faith the continuous act by which the principle of life is sustained. *We live by Faith,* says the Apostle. We live so, because there is nothing of the spiritual life, which our souls demand in this world. It is required, therefore, in the outset, that we draw our sustaining strength from something above and beyond

G. L. AUSTIN & CO. PRINTERS, WILLIAM-STREET.

PEACE IN BELIEVING:

A MEMOIR OF

ISABELLA CAMPBELL,

OF

ROSNEATH, DUMBARTONSHIRE,

SCOTLAND.

By Robert Story

WITH A PRELIMINARY ESSAY,

BY

AN AMERICAN CLERGYMAN.

———

"No nourishment is here for worldly minds ;
But for theirs who of the world are weary."

———

From the last English Edition.

———

New-York:
JONATHAN LEAVITT, 182 BROADWAY.
Boston:
CROCKER & BREWSTER,
MDCCCXXX.

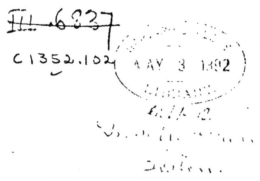
Southern District of New-York, ss.

BE IT REMEMBERED, That on the tenth day of September, A. D. 1830, in the 55th year of the Independence of the United States of America, JONATHAN LEAVITT, of the said district, hath deposited in this office the title of a book, the right whereof he claims as proprietor, in the words following, to wit:

"Peace in Believing: a Memoir of Isabella Campbell, of Rosneath, Dumbartonshire, Scotland. With a Preliminary Essay, by an American Clergyman.

"No nourishment is here for worldly minds;
But for theirs who of the world are weary"

In conformity to the act of Congress of the United States, entitled "an act for the encouragement of learning, by securing the copies of maps, charts, and books, to the authors and proprietors of such copies, during the time therein mentioned," and also to an act, entitled "An act, supplementary to an act, entitled an act for the encouragement of learning, by securing the copies of maps, charts, and books, to the authors and proprietors of such copies, during the times therein mentioned, and extending the benefits thereof to the arts of designing, engraving, and etching historical and other prints."

FRED. J. BETTS,
Clerk of the Southern District of New-York.

PRELIMINARY ESSAY.

In the class of modern religious biographies, this work is peculiar—peculiar from its destitution of all interest, except that founded in religion. There were no incidents, in the life of Isabella Campbell to excite interest, and though she lived in the midst of natural scenery, both wild and beautiful, there is no attraction given to the Memoir from that, or indeed any other incidental circumstance. The value of the biography consists in the peculiarity of the religious character displayed; and on this account it is worthy of the most attentive and studious perusal. I am of opinion, that the nature of personal religion has not been sufficiently studied among us; and while the press has been teeming with religious controversy, with biblical criticism, with missionary intelligence, and with plans and persuasives pertaining to benevolent enterprise, comparatively little has been written upon religion, as a mode of life, as a course of action, as the perfection of spiritual existence. And because it has not been thus studied, the church in our land, is very deficient in eminent examples of living piety;—examples that throw a holy radiance about them, which warm and animate all within the sphere of their influence. It bodes ill, that we have so many, in the high places of our Zion, who rather give us the light of a wintry sun, than those golden rays, which give perfection and maturity to our fruits.

Religion has too long been studied, as a system to be explained and conformed to reigning opinions on intellec-

2

thrones, dominions, principalities, powers, things in heaven
and earth ; this is my Christ. He that is the Alpha and
Omega, the first and the last, the Lord God Almighty.
He that was dead and is alive again, and lives for evermore, and hath the keys of Hell and Death. This is my
Christ. The name Christ fills such a man's soul with light
and glory, even in that very instant when he believes this
Jesus to be the Christ ; so as that admitting him into the
mind under this notion, it insensibly admits a Deity in his
all-comprehending fulness. He doth not believe a trivial
thing concerning this Jesus, when he believes him to be the
Christ, but believes him to be all in all. This is my all,
and the universal all unto whosoever they are that shall
come to partake felicity by him at length. This is nothing
like the mock faith of the multitude, that think themselves
well if off-hand they answer the question when you ask,
Is Jesus the Christ ? Yes—But they neither know nor
consider what Christ means, nor what they attribute to
this Jesus, in calling him the Christ."

It is the habit of many to say, that their religious indifference is the result of unbelief, and want of Faith ; but they
seem not to understand *how* it is so, and *why* it is so. It is so
of necessity, because the objects of Faith, which the soul
requires for her joy and strength, are kept entirely out of
mind, or if occasionally thought of, are not placed in the
attitude, in which they appear in the Bible. Suppose the
soul contemplating Christ, in the method and spirit of the
above extract, and any thing but doubt and indifference
will be its state. And this is both the *how*, and the *why*, that
there is such criminal indifference to the life of Faith among
professed Christians. The natural consequence of such
a state of mind is practical infidelity, living without hope,
and emphatically without God in the world. But the conscience will not permit this. The semblance of religion
must be kept up to the view of the inner man, and this

is very commonly done by turning the mind in upon itself, and asking the state of the heart, the condition of the affections; as though a Metaphysical Analysis of all possible states of moral feeling, was the preliminary to a belief that God had spoken the truth, and that the truth was to be obeyed. And because this analysis, or examination, usually leads to no definite conclusion, the mind comes short of those lucid results, which are necessary to peace and joy, or to vigorous and purifying obedience. In this point of view, I think "the treatise on Religious Affections," by Mr. Jonathan Edwards, to be of injurious tendency. I am aware of the peculiar circumstances that called for that book. But it seems to be forgotten, that the state of religious feeling was deemed, by the author himself, to be peculiar, and he wrote it for an exigency. An exigency which, to be sure, the human mind is always liable to, but in no such way as demands a deviation from the method God has given for us to ascertain whether we are true disciples of Jesus Christ—viz. A LIFE OF FAITH; not a life of examination—a life drawing its vitality from God in Christ, and not from the weak, and wavering, and earthly affections of the human heart. I would not be understood to say, that the Christian duty of self-examination is useless. Far from it, it is in the first degree salutary; but the examination is to proceed on the assumption, that faith in God is the sustaining power of the Christian, that the way to glorify God is not to be in doubt and uncertainty, but to be so strong in the FAITH as not to stagger at the promise, Rom. iv. 20. The examination is not to find the state of our affections or feelings, and as we happen to find *them*, rise to joy or sink to despondency. And that for the simple reason that we are not justified by the state of our feelings, but by FAITH—that the strength of our hope lies in Christ, and not in ourselves, and that the glorious and ever-living light cometh from above, and not from

within. " Who would ever," said Isabella, in the language
of an old divine, " who would ever cast an anchor within
the ship to hold it secure ? so there cannot be safety found
for any soul in itself, but just as it is standing on the rock
of ages." How often is this forgotten, and we find one and
another speaking of their indifference to religion, their
want of feeling, when to an attentive observer, their mind
looks only in upon itself, and expects to find peace, and joy,
and ardency of affection, while the object, in view of which
alone these can exist, is excluded from the contemplation.
There is joy in what ? looking at the state of the heart ? No,
in believing, in looking to Jesus and in trusting in him.
While the soul turns in upon itself, it may, and it often does
examine, and watch, and excite itself to a constant wake-
fulness, until it shrinks, like the sensitive plant, from duty
and from hope. Or perhaps, stung with a sense of spiritual
danger, it rolls itself in agony, and calls up the most har-
rowing and terrifying conceptions of its eternal state. O !
when will Christians remember that their life comes not
from themselves, but from Christ ; and then look, not to
their own guiltiness for consolation, but to him, who is
the chiefest among ten thousand !   When will they keep in
memory, that howsoever aggravated may be their guilt,
there is but one way of return to God, and that is through
Christ !

The readers of Mr. Edwards's work on the " Religious Affections," I have usually found in one of two states of mind.
Either baffled by its abstract acuteness, and incapable of
fully comprehending it, or left in a state of doubt and in-
quietude respecting their own piety. The doubt sometimes
leads to a farther examination of the Word of God, and in
that way, a purer and stronger kind of religious feeling is
elicited. And thus has the Treatise often been indirectly
useful ; but, in a majority of cases, the doubts predominate,
and the individual believes it impossible for him to acquire

any satisfactory proof, that he is a child of God. And this is precisely the result that should have been anticipated. Who, from sounding the depths of his own heart, and comparing it with the law of God, can presume that he would find ground of hope? How can he, in looking at broken resolutions, and ineffectual efforts, and feeble prayers, and in constant feelings, and variable love—how can he build up from such materials a hope that maketh not ashamed? How can he find so much of purity and holiness, as to give him peace? And if he is inquiring how many forms deceptive hope may assume, and in how many ways ill-founded joy may spread itself over the soul, when will he be able to settle the question? and especially, if he is seeking with the acuteness, and the discrimination, and the earnestness of one, who feels that his eternal peace is connected with the decision. There is, literally, no end to the possible states he may not suppose his mind to be in, without being truly a child of God. Does our heavenly Father intend to leave us in this hopeless state? Does he shut us up to such sorrowful contemplations, and overwhelm us in a sea of doubt? And is the liberty of the gospel, only a constant entanglement? No, I believe it is not; and this Memoir shows it is not. There is peace, and joy, and hope *in believing*. But it comes from *believing*, and not from doubt and uncertainty.

Much as I admire, and even reverence the religious character of Brainerd, and the affecting humility of Edwards himself, I think their manner of self-scrutiny, particularly the former, spread too dark a tinge of melancholy over their private religious history. And the same remark is applicable to many of our American specimens of religious biography. Nor do I think, that this is at all accounted for by saying, as has been said of Brainerd, that they were of a melancholy temperament. The fault lay not in a constitutional habit, but in neglecting to fix the eye steadfastly upon the Saviour, as the sole, entire ground of justification. They did not make a false estimate of them-

selves as sinners, but the eye was kept fastened upon their
sins, until they rose like mountains shutting out light from
their horizon, rather than as lofty and dark eminences, defined and made manifest in the radiant glory of a heavenly
Faith.   There are exceptions, we are sorry they must be
called exceptions, as in the account of William Tennant,
the Memoir of Mrs. Graham, and particularly the last days
of the late Dr. Payson of Portland.   " The Sun of Righteousness," says the latter in a letter dictated to his sister,
" has been gradually drawing nearer and nearer ; appearing
larger and brighter, as he approached ; and now he fills the
whole hemisphere ; pouring forth a flood of glory, in
which I seem to float, like an insect in the beams of the
sun, exulting, yet almost trembling, while I gaze on this excessive brightness, and wondering with unutterable wonder,
why God should thus deign to shine upon a sinful worm."
To Mrs. Payson he says, " It seems as if the soul dis-
dained such a narrow prison, and was determined to break
through with an Angel's energy, and, I trust, with no small
portion of an Angel's feeling, until it mounts on high.   It
seems as if my soul had found a pair of new wings; and
was so eager to try them, that in her fluttering she would
rend the fine network of the body in pieces."   And what
was the foundation of these joys ?   " I find no satisfaction
in looking at any thing I have done.   I want to leave all
this behind—it is nothing—and fly to Christ, to be clothed
in his righteousness. *All my joy comes from looking at him.*
I have done nothing of myself.   It seems as if I had not
fought, but Christ had fought for me—I had not run, but
Christ had carried me—that I had not worked, but Christ
had wrought in me.   Christ has done all."

These are the spontaneous feelings of a soul which has
learned its utter sinfulness and its infinite weakness, and
for its righteousness and its strength, looks only to the Saviour.   Here it finds its highest conceptions more than
realized ; its present hopes, more than gratified, and its lof-

tiest faith more than substantiated. O ! why is it that Christians will turn away from this anchor of their souls ? why will they neglect this fountain of unutterable blessedness—this ever-flowing river of divine consolations ? Here they may feast on the food of Angels, and be nourished as the Spirits of the just made perfect. Here they may partake of the living streams that flow out from the throne of God. Here they may behold those pure and dazzling glories that fill all Heaven with wonder and with joy, and which, radiant in beauty and in majesty, spread over the works of God, giving to holy hearts the light of his countenance and the joy of his salvation. The joys of this life may depart, but the unspeakable joys remain ; the honour that cometh from men may have passed away, but here is a dwelling-place with the King of kings. The end of all things may be at hand, but it is a day of victory for the soul, and of its triumphant admission into its own appropriate Mansion ; and it shall live, and its life flow on, and flow on, in a pure, clear, ever-deepening channel of eternal blessedness.

Growth in grace is not precisely defined, by saying it is a perception of growing purity of heart, though this is a very common opinion, where any definite opinion is entertained. It consists often in an increasing strength of conviction, that we are accepted through Faith alone—this conviction, as the foundation of hope, and with it, a perception, or rather a realization of how Faith operates to sustain the heart in all possible trials, and gives it strength as it is shaken by the temptations of the world. It is growth in attachment to the Saviour—growth in confidence in Him—growth in submission to Him—growth in reliance upon Him. It is not the being free from sin, not the sensible increase of purity of heart ; not these, as *treasured attainments.* But it is an increasing attachment to spiritual things ; the soul living more by Faith on the truths of the Gospel—it is their becoming more and more the Life of its

3

Life. Sin may be daily developed, as having great power
in the soul, and often bringing it into captivity; but there
is increasing strength of Faith in Christ, by which sin loses
its depressing and killing power, and the soul becomes
free in the liberty of Christ. Free, because its burdens are
upon Him who was wounded for its transgressions, and who
has borne the burden of us all. O! when will Christians
learn to reason with the blessed Apostle in the 8th chapter
of Romans—"Since God spared not his own Son, but delivered him up for us all, how shall he not, with Him, also
freely give us all things?" Who, then, shall lay any thing
to our charge? Shall God? Why, He justifies us. Who shall
condemn us? Shall Christ? Why, "He died for us; yea,
rather is risen again, who is even at the right hand of God,
who also maketh intercession for us." These are the immense, the inconceivable pledges of God's love, on which
the Apostle placed his undoubting confidence. And behold
what spiritual might they wrought in him. Having these
pledges, he breaks forth, "Who shall be able to separate us from the love of Christ? Shall tribulation, or
distress, or persecution, or famine, or nakedness, or
peril, or sword; though we be killed all the day long,
and be counted as sheep for the slaughter? Nay; in
all these things we are more than conquerors, through
him that hath loved us." Nay; neither the world, nor
death, nor hell shall get the victory; " For I am persuaded, that neither death, nor life, nor Angels, nor principalities, nor powers, nor things present, nor things to come,
nor height, nor depth, nor any other creature shall be able
to separate us from the love of God, which is in Christ Jesus our Lord." O brethren! brethren! what more can
we ask, than such glorious promises and pledges of
God's love; and such blessed examples of their powerful
efficacy.

It has been my object, in this Essay, to speak of Religion

as a Life ; of that Life as begun and sustained in Faith ; and of the evidence of that Life as springing mainly from the definiteness and strength of our Faith, as applied to the truths of the gospel, which are the objects of Faith. And the views I have advanced, are, I think, enforced in a most beautiful and living manner in the Memoir of Isabella Campbell. This I have done without meaning to say, that there is no propriety in the different course which has been so much and so long urged among us ; which demands, that we should look mainly at the evidence of Regeneration, making this evidence to consist in the examination of states of feeling, as such, which I think often leads to deceits, fears, despondency, and the destruction of the life of God in the soul.

I have been urged to write this from my own sad experience, and from a desire to deliver others from a state of spiritual thraldom, which the mode of my Theological Education imposed upon me. I have said little of the influence of the Holy Spirit, for all who will believe my remarks, admit that as *a fact*—a fact necessary—necessary as the connecting link between a state of entire sinfulness, and a state of a progression to entire holiness—a link without which the *conclusion never can result from the premiss.* A fact, too, not to be *understood*, except as it is *seen*, and not to be *comprehended*, except as it is *felt.* And in these respects, so far forth as objections can be urged, it is like all the other works of God. Having said this, I have said enough to induce the children of men to apply themselves to the work of Faith, and to the Life of Faith, nothing doubting that God, who spared not his own Son, will give them his Spirit also. And I do most earnestly pray that some of our Writers and Ministers may take this view. For many of them seem to me, in their discussions on the means and motives necessary or useless in Regeneration, to be using words like unknown quantities in Algebra, with the hope that before the Treatise is finished, or the Review completed, a full and definite meaning will be evolved, with this difference, however, that, from the nature of the subject, the desired knowledge never can be obtained. O! could one poor Minister, from his closet and his knees, lift up his voice, and be heard for Christ, amid the hum of benevolent enterprise, and the noise of polemical discussion, he would say, cease your operations of Science ; stop a moment in your onward career, and examine yourselves, *whether ye be in the faith* ;. whether ye are living in the Faith, and whether, living in the Faith, ye are dying daily to the world ; whether ye do count all things but loss for Christ, that ye may be found in Him ? In my lone closet, how poor does all our boasted Philosophy appear ; but how glorious does Christ appear, and the Life of Faith in Him—how weak and vapoury do the thousand appeals to the spirit of the age, to the genius of the nineteenth century, to the mighty engines of Colleges, and Seminaries, and Presses, and Periodicals, seem, but how Almighty the simple influence of God's word. Here, with my Bible open, I ask, where is the FAITH that " subdued kingdoms, wrought righteousness, obtained promises, that out of weakness was made strong ; waxed valiant in fight, turned to flight the armies of the aliens;" where is it ? My table groaning with its religious Periodicals from the four corners of the world, echoes, where ! where ! With eyes suffused with tears, I turn within, and lift up my soul to God !

O Thou who seest the end from the beginning, and who knowest our weakness and short-sightedness, keep us in the FAITH. Let not thy people trust in an arm of flesh ; let them not trust in themselves ; fill their minds with love, and peace, and confidence in believing ; and, through Faith, make them mighty to the pulling down of strongholds. O ! accomplish this, that the purposes of Redemption may be fulfilled, and the Ransomed of the LORD be brought home with songs and everlasting joy, Even *so*, come, LORD JESUS. Amen.

PREFACE

In constructing this memoir, I have had no other end in view, but to present a true delineation of Isabella's character, that those who behold it may glorify God in her. My study, therefore, has been to keep her continually before them, avoiding whatever might turn away their eyes from the contemplation of so holy an example : and intermingling with the narrative none of the discussions which, however natural, could only have indulged those feelings of literary ambition, which so often tempt memorialists, in doing justice to the dead, to estimate too highly the applause of the living.

To those, who must be amused or excited by what they read, I have provided no gratification and no stimulant ; but whosoever thinks, that of all histories, that of a soul delivered from conscious guilt and fear is the most intensely affecting, will find in this record of peace and joy, of holy living, and triumphant dying, abundant occasion for solemn and delightful meditation.

The materials, which I procured from the most authentic sources, I have arranged, so far as could be ascertained, in chronological order ; and regarding them, more is not needful to be said, than that nothing has been recorded but after the severest scrutiny of its genuineness. In reference to the letters indeed, which, it is possible, (from the language in which they are clothed, irrespective of the subjects they treat of,) may attract peculiar notice, I may

3*

mention, that although the daughter of a retired officer of
the army, unless in very early childhood, when there was
a teacher in the family, Isabella had no advantages of education, but such as were afforded in the school attended
by the children of the contiguous farmers and cottagers.
The religion of the Gospel, however, elevated her mind,
and polished her taste ; and habitually conversant, as she
was, with its great and glorious things, she easily found fit
expressions for her thoughts, often, as may be seen, not a
little memorable for their sublimity and beauty.

For various reasons, I have adopted the form in which
the Memoir appears. It has had its disadvantages, which,
I fear, may be felt by many : but I found, from the nature
of my materials, I could best preserve the interest of the
narrative, by moulding it into the form of an address to my
own people.

                                ROBERT STORY.

INTRODUCTION.

WELCOME, great guest, this house, mine heart,
    Shall all be thine;
  I will resign
  Mine interest in every part:
  Only be pleased to use it as thine own
  For ever, and inhabit it alone :—
    And, by thy light,
    Possess my sight
  With sense of an eternal day.

IT has been beautifully said, by an old Divine,* that "to replenish this desolate world, with temples every where, and with the divine presence," is the design of God in the gospel. He follows out the metaphor, in a large dissertation, with great ingenuity, often with consummate eloquence; and somewhere, in the course of his meditations, observes, that the method, which God has devised for its accomplishment, is exceedingly expressive of his love; for he has not merely told of what materials these temples must consist, which, of itself, would have been a great blessedness to men so darkly ignorant, through their apostacy; but, in pitiful consideration of their weakness and incapacity, he has made manifest to our very eyes "a primary and original temple, animated with his own glory, replenished with his own fulness, of pure and holy life and vigour," as the model of them all; an exemplary temple, " the fair and lovely pattern of what we were, each of us, to be composed and formed unto, imitating us, for sweeter insinuation and allurement, in what was merely

* John Howe.

natural, and inviting us to imitate him, in what was, in a communicable sort, supernatural and divine." By this device of God, we see how these materials are composed and put together ;—surveying at once " the beautiful frame in every part, the lovely imitable glory of the whole, the divine excellencies that beautify this original, exemplary temple."

In all this may be seen how tenderly God adjusts to our condition, the means he employs for our recovery from sin and misery ; for, from whatever cause, we unquestionably cannot see or feel the power of truth in the abstract, in the same way as we do, when it comes home to our convictions and bosoms, in the form of example. This weakness must have been obvious to the very earliest teachers of our race, obtruding itself on their notice, while framing any scheme of tuition fitted to their capacity. Even in the first family of human beings, the father of us all must have had reason for regarding as true, what, in all ages, has been expressed in the form of a proverb, " Example is better than precept." He might have attempted to teach his offspring the principles of religion and morals ; unfolded, to the extent of his own knowledge, the character of God, his government, and his laws ; the blessedness of obedience to his will, and the misery of apostacy from his service : but, all that he could say, howsoever powerful and impressive in itself, would derive tenfold energy from the vicissitudes of his own eventful history, and the illustrations which it afforded of the retribution of divine Providence, during the brief period of his joyful innocency, and the intermediate years of his sinful and sorrowful life.

From the beginning God knew what was in men ; that, in addition to this incapacity, there was a disinclination to understand the abstract truths of religion, averse as they had become to holiness, the original end and purpose of their creation. He does not, therefore, in the Bible require them to believe as true of him, or his providence, any thing unillustrated by facts of easy comprehension.—It is not, for example, by demonstrations of his necessary exist. ence, or of his possessing all possible perfections, but by individual manifestations of his power and wisdom, his pu. rity and goodness, he reveals to them his character, and draws forth their veneration and homage. In the promul- gation of his laws also, he rests his claim to the obedience of the Israelites, rather upon the deliverance which he had wrought for them, than upon any abstract consideration of his omnipotent sovereignty ; while generally it may be af- firmed, that the obligations of holy living are enforced, by the contrasted experience of the righteous and the wicked, rather than by any announcement, as of an immutable de- cree of his government, of the necessary connexion of vir. tue with happiness, and vice with misery.

He knew, that they could judge of a fact, when they could not comprehend a principle ; like one of their own infants, capable of feeling the kindness of its mother, while deriving nourishment from her breast, although without any general notion of the constraining power of the in- stincts and tendernesses of nature. By facts, therefore, did he from the beginning attempt to raise them to the knowledge of himself ; and by this knowledge, to conform them to his likeness, according to the original end of their creation. All these, however, had reference, and were preparatory to the manifestation of that great device of his wisdom,—the final and most perfect token of that love which yearned to rescue their souls from their debasement and misery, the erection of the holy temple of Christ's humanity. Now made visible in the frame of one like unto themselves, the possibility of any erroneous judgment of his character seemed to be taken away ; and in the life of Jesus, showing how he wished his laws to be obeyed, none could remain in perplexity how to serve him.

To creatures so utterly destitute of the very first elements of divine knowledge, and averse to the acquisition
of the art of holy living, or, in other words, the construction of a temple for the habitation of God, how merciful
(independent of all other considerations and purposes) is
the manifestation of the Lord Jesus! For, in the knowledge
of God's character which his life gives, in erecting a temple after this model, beaming with all possible excellencies,
is realized the true felicity and glory of their nature. He
might have lived and died elsewhere; they might have
heard only with the hearing of the ear, of his unspotted holiness, unequalled sufferings, and mysterious death; but, what
would have then been the power? or rather what would
have been the weakness of the gospel, without the visible
events of his history, to accomplish the ends of God's love,
which it professes to unfold, " in the filling of this desolate
world with temples every where, and with his own presence?" To this exemplary temple the eyes of all men
must be directed in obedience to the counsel, "Behold
mine elect in whom my soul delighteth;"—"Look unto
Jesus,"—and to the voice that proceeds from the sanctuary of the temple itself, "Learn of me."

If men look in other directions, they make void the
decree of God's wisdom, and cannot possibly experience
or inherit the blessedness which it has in store for them;
nowhere else will they see the brightness of the Father's
glory, and the express image of his person; and let their
eyes wander where they may, they will see no excellency
possessed of any attractiveness to withdraw them from their
own evil and wretchedness; or in any way to raise, and
purify, and make beautiful their nature.—" Look unto this,
all ye ends of the earth, all ye kindred of the people," is
imperative upon all who would be conformed to the holiness in which God's soul delighteth; and to those who do
so look, will it be known, how this temple, full of divine

vitality, and power, is capable of multiplying itself into innumerable forms of moral loveliness and beauty,—holy temples destined to constitute the new Jerusalem, the city of the living God.

As the contemplation of this temple is far better fitted to excite an admiration and love of all excellency, than abstract and general discourses of virtue and goodness, which are of little power to affect minds so deeply oblivious of God, and so obstinately averse to all that God loves, so also, the imitations of such a temple meeting our eyes, are more likely to affect, or excite us, than any cold lessons of religion or morality. Here is apparent the use of religious Biography, which professes to present these imitations of the primary temple, by portraying the lives of holy men and women, in whom dwelt the Spirit of God. For, should a doubt of the possibility of realizing any similitude of Christ's loveliness exist in depraved minds, regarding it merely as what ought, although it could not be ; these show what is, or has been in earthen forms, and that, amid infirmities, and sin, and death, of some of Adam's children, it may be said, without any violent use of Scripture language, " Ye are the temples of the living God." In those who have already seen the original in its beautiful glory, and experienced as they beheld the blessedness of admiring love, such portraitures are fitted to excite the most exquisitely pleasing sympathies; and in those who have not yet, in their darkness, seen that great sight, an impatience of their ignorance, and unquenchable curiosity may arise from such feelings, as were once expressed by a visiter of Isabella in the days of her suffering,—"I thought how glorious a being Jesus must be, when his image is so lovely, under a body of sin and death !"

The Hymn.

Lord, what is Life ?—'Tis like a flow'r
  That blossoms, and is gone;
We see it flourish for an hour,
  With all its beauty on ;
But death comes like a wintry day,
And cuts the pretty flow'r away.

Lord, what is Life?—'Tis like the bow
  That glistens in the sky ;
We love to see its colours glow,
  But while we look, they die.
Life fails us soon : to-day 'tis here,
To-night perhaps 'twill disappear.

Six thousand years have passed away,
  Since life began at first;
And millions once alive and gay,
  Are dead and in the dust.
For life, in all its health and pride,
Has death still waiting by its side.

Lord, what is Life?—If spent with thee
  In duty, praise, and pray'r,
However long, or short it be,
  We need but little care,
Because eternity will last
When life and death itself are past

The Scripture.

Now Samuel did not yet know the Lord, neither was the word of the Lord revealed to him.

Then shall we know if we follow on to know the Lord.

When I was a child, I spake as a child; I understood as a child,—when I became a man, I put away childish things.

Little children, keep yourselves from idols.

Remember not the sins of my youth, nor my transgressions: according to thy mercy remember Thou me, for thy goodness sake, O Lord.

CHAPTER I.

—— There are strange movements in young souls;
Fears, hopes, aversions, loves, conspire to wean
From things they see; and in a viewless world,
Excursive oft they search for anodynes
Of unallayed desires. But whence are these ?

IN presenting you, therefore, with a memoir of our young friend, you cannot but be aware of the motives that have prompted me. A temple has past away from the visible world ; and I am anxious that its loveliness should be held in everlasting remembrance among you and your children, and all to whom the story of her life and death shall be made known.

The prayers of all the faithful I entreat, that the glory of God may be promoted, while you look upon his workmanship, and that each contemplation may lead you to think of the perfect pattern, the exemplary temple, so that you may be changed into the same image from glory to glory. For this purpose, I shall tell you what I know of her history, from her own declarations, from what I observed myself, and from the authentic testimony of others, during the early vanity and sinfulness of the years that past away, without any right apprehension or feeling of divine love, while her heart was carnal and ungodly, till the time when the Lord, by his mighty power, snatched her from conscious condemnation and misery, as a brand plucked out of the burning ; as well as when with tenderness he trained her soul, amid sufferings and disease, to the knowledge of his own holy loveliness, to tastes, which now most assuredly, are blissfully gratified; to habits, without which heaven could furnish no felicity, because she could have had no relish for the society of those who, clothed with the Saviour's untainted righteousness, in grateful adoration, live in the presence of the eternal majesty.

According to the language of men, she was, as you know, from the earliest childhood, blameless, and of good report, of singularly mild and gentle manners, full of affection and tenderness, beloved by all who knew her, because so lovely, and worthy of love. About thirteen years ago I first saw her, and although a very young girl, only about eight years old, I was struck with her appearance. Her countenance had a gravity very unusual at so early an age, combined with a most delicate sweetness of expression; while her manner was very diffident and retiring, so much so, that I still remember the shrinking sensitiveness, and blushing confusion, manifested by her while replying to any of the questions I might put to her among the other children. She was among the most early attendants in the Sabbath-school, which, shortly after this, was instituted; and although from the remotest house in the parish, was always present, when the weather would permit, or when her movements depended upon herself: often indeed, she appeared in her place even on stormy days, when the children of the contiguous villages would not venture beyond the threshold of their cottages; and her delicate frame, for more than five miles along the open shore of the Gairloch, would be beat upon by the winds and the rain, when the most robust of the people, shrinking from the exposure, came not up to the solemn assembly. When in the school, her demeanour was singularly decorous and solemn; her diligence most assiduous, and her intelligent discernment of the meaning of what she would utter, was very apparent from the mode and emphasis of her expression. In all this she was a model for your children. Indeed, many of her class companions of that time, although without such opportunities of observation as I myself enjoyed, so far as their recollections go, can bear witness of these things, of which I have a very vivid remembrance.

I have said, she was in this a model for your children; but you must not be deceived. Something far more than I have described must be earnestly supplicated from God for them, as you regard their well-being, and would not entail upon them a curse instead of a blessing. All that I have described, as characteristic of Isabella's early years, in connexion with her religious history, may, or may not be regarded, according to people's views, as preparatory to her reception of the grace of God, and her subsequent advancement in the divine life : in her own opinion, her early youth was a period of utter vanity. Any concern she had about the state of her soul was light and trivial, consisting merely of transient emotions that terminated in nothing— productive of no results, because growing out of no seed planted by the hand of the Eternal. That form of godliness which seems desirable for your children, may adorn *them*, as it did *her*,—without any knowledge, or experience of its power. Your anxieties, therefore, regarding those objects of your affection must extend beyond their outward comeliness of demeanour ;—far, far deeper than meets either the ear, or the eye of man. Had she then died, it was her fixed persuasion, (when the light of truth took possession of her mind,) that she must have gone to a place of torment, entirely ignorant, as she was, of her God reconciling in Christ her rebellious heart unto himself; and consequently without any of those feelings that fit for the society of the heavenly Jerusalem. I, you, or any other, looking upon her outward frame, saw only the loveliness, simplicity, and innocence of childhood—a beautiful form of an interesting age. But what was it in reality ? If her own conceptions were correct and true, a lovely mansion

4*

of all levity and unholiness, an object of meritorious wrath, equally with the most infamous receptacles of pollution and impiety.

The decorum, the services of her childhood, indeed, she saw, as she believed God saw them, only as varying manifestations of error and of guiltiness. Do not then in this deceive yourselves, ye fathers and mothers of my people, by resting on the seemly behaviour of your children any hopes of their safety. I tell you, the worm that never dieth may be nourished by the heart's blood of the loveliest and most decorous among them. Clasp them to your bosoms, as you may, in the transports of parental tenderness, but let not your fondness stifle the anxiety which prompts the awful question, "What are they? Holy and blessed of God, or reprobate through their own perversity; or whither are they going? To the peaceful mansions of joyful hallelujahs, or the dark prison-house of ungodly blasphemers, whose smoke ascendeth for ever and ever?" O then, from the earliest age, press upon them to seek for newness of life, and let your yearnings be breathed in continual prayers, that their pollutions may be washed in that blessed fountain opened in the smitten heart of the Lord, for the young and the old;—to which the infant may go with as much freedom, because its necessity is the same, as the hoary sinner, groaning beneath the accumulated guilt of an hundred years. Be not satisfied, I beseech you, as well as all parents who shall read this record, with occasional manifestations of seriousness in your children, or with even frequently expressed desires of holy living, if, in reality, you are anxious that they should imitate Isabella's example; for, she exhibited not merely that outward decorum which we have described, but many serious thoughts of God and of her condition; many a scheme of righteousness, framed in much anxiety, occupied her mind; and many breathings after holiness would agitate her heart.

Often did she ponder, even at an earlier period than that I speak of, on the awful interests of eternity; when the thought, or prospect of dying more especially, was pressed upon her attention, its irrevocable results would fill her with alarm, while uncertain what these might be. When only five or six years of age, during thunder storms for example, which seemed to increase the probability of such an event, she would pray most fervently for a continuance of life, till better prepared to meet her God. Occasionally also, at this time, she was vividly impressed with the necessity of loving her Creator; but such feelings very soon faded away before reasonings like these, suggested by a rebellious heart, whence even in childhood are the issues of impious thoughts. " I ought, perhaps, but how can I love God better than my father?" she would say, " I cannot see him, his face is hid from me, he does not come and twine his arms round me; how then can I love him better than my father?" Often in after-life she alluded to these infantine feelings, when death had lost all its terrors in her mind, looking upon it in the light of eternity, when its agonies were hailed as prelusive of a glory on which she had set her heart: when she had indeed seen her Creator, the King, in his beauty, felt his love, while its expressions were multiplied before her eyes, as her soul had found rest within the blessed enclosure of his everlasting arms.

These little notices are given, not for the purpose of proving that, in her childhood, she was habitually occupied about the things of religion, but as indications of a spirit of seriousness, which indeed was visible in her appearance and manners. What is generally interesting to children, seemed to attract but little of her attention. She seldom engaged in the ordinary gambols of little girls, and when she did, there was still a solemnity about her, which was far from according with the hilarity and sportiveness of her

companions. As she advanced to the age of about eight
or nine, this seriousness increased, and she would occupy
herself in a way which most of you, it is probable, would
regard as decisive of Christian feeling and experience;
and indicating a mind already devoted to the employment
of a religious life. Her prayers were regular and frequent.
Besides, when any event occurred that excited her anxiety, she would engage in extraordinary exercises of devotion. If her father, for example, went from home, at any
time, she would pray long and repeatedly for his safe return; vowing upon these occasions, in the spirit of Jacob,
that, if God granted a favourable answer, she would offer
him her sacrifice of thankfulness, and acknowledge him
with increasing gratitude, as the author of all her blessings.
Nor was she in the habit of forgetting her vow. Whenever she heard of the arrival of her father, or saw him
coming, eager as she was to meet him, she made a point
of first retiring to some secret place to give glory to God
for having fulfilled the desire of her heart. Long afterward, when accustomed to try the character of past and
present feelings by the true standard which the divine Spirit, by the wisdom there is in his word, had given her, she
saw nothing in this practice decisive of willing homage and
resignation to God. Selfishness prompted her prayers,
while it pervaded also the spirit of her thanksgivings.
The former were long and importunate; the latter, brief
and hurried, exhausting, as it were, in one short acknow-
ledgment, her gratitude: while often expressed, only lest,
if neglected, her prayers should not again be answered.
The dread of evil to an object she loved, and in loving
whom she found her happiness, constrained her to propitiate the almighty Disposer of events, while the joy of possession, without immediate anxiety, or apprehension, soon,
like a spring-tide, bore away from her thoughts the remembrance of him whose providential care and kindness had so
blessed her.

Although we have no very minute record of her feelings, the anecdote here inserted, is sufficiently presumptive of her having deep and serious anxieties about her own safety, as well as that of others. The very fact of her thus imploring God's favourable interposition, in any emergency, must have led her to think of the blessedness there is in the conviction and knowledge of his love for time and for eternity. Accordingly, it appears that, at various times, the necessity of being religious, (a condition which she identified with safety,) thrust itself upon her thoughts. Her vague impressions concentrating, as it were, into sudden convictions of the peril of her state, and darting through her mind, would excite most painful agitations. One evening, for example, when returning with her eldest sister from a meeting of the Sabbath scholars at Barem-men, as if seized with a sudden anguish, she knelt down by the way-side, and with many tears, deplored their want of religion. " O, let us pray," said she, " let us pray to God that he would make us religious, at least before we die; that he would tell us, since we know not, how to be so !" Her look, and voice, and gesture, were expressive of extreme emotion, while a certain tone of awful solemnity in what she uttered, terrified Mary.

Her first impulse was to leave her, and proceed on her way ; but, anxious as she felt to go, she was riveted to the spot, awed, as in the presence of the Invisible." " She could not but feel," she said, "as if Isabella was approaching Him ; although unable to comprehend what kind of intercourse she could have with one that inspired herself with such fear." Isabella prayed for a long time, in the presence of her trembling and agitated sister, and when she arose, seemed as if her mind had been lightened of a heavy burden. They proceeded homewards, often weeping as they went, conversing upon the absolute necessity, and forming together various plans of a religious and holy life. One resolution after another they laid down, to which they vowed most faithful and scrupulous adherence.

For several days there was a decided change in Isabella's appearance, and she seemed to feel and act as if she were a new creature. She was most regular in her private devotions; her whole demeanour was more than usually decorous and solemn, while, in her intercourse with all around her, she was more civil, and tender, and affectionate than ever before.

Although her impressions at this time were very vivid, they did not continue long so to influence her. They would often recur, however, to her memory, and excite her, but with decaying power, to a temporary seriousness, not without considerable anxieties. Thus it appeared, that she had not heard as she ought, nor rightly interpreted the voice of the divine Spirit in what she had experienced; and the door of her heart remained shut, excluding him, who had, amid her violent emotions, given unquestionable tokens of his gracious presence and intentions. For whence arise at any time those mental anxieties, however transient, regarding the great concerns of religion? From the earth, or from under the earth? from the evil heart, or from him that practises upon it his delusions? Do they not all originate in heaven, proceeding from the bosom of God, as from an ever-living, ever-flowing fountain, in which compassions are continually moving and "kindling together," toward the miserable children of men?

She was about eleven years of age when the incident here recorded occurred; and for more than two years afterward, no remarkable variation of feeling seems to have taken place. Generally, it may be said, that during that period, her Bible was read, her prayers offered up, the church attended, and the lessons of the Sabbath-school prepared, without awakening any other emotions in her mind than those which a conviction of the becomingness and propriety of such practices inspired.

The Hymn.

Lord, come away;
  Why dost thou stay?
Thy road is ready; and thy paths, made straight,
  With longing expectation wait
The consecration of thy beauteous feet.
Ride on triumphantly: behold, we lay
Our lusts and proud wills in thy way.
Hosannah! welcome to our hearts: Lord, here
Thou hast a temple, too, and full as dear
As that of Zion, and as full of sin :—
Nothing but thieves and robbers dwell therein.
Enter, and chase them forth, and cleanse the floor;
Crucify them, that they may never more
  Profane that holy place,
  Where thou hast chose to set thy face ;
And then, if our stiff tongues shall be
Mute in the praises of thy Deity,
  The stones out of the temple wall
  Shall cry aloud and call
Hosannah! and thy glorious footsteps greet.—Amen.

The Scripture.

Thus saith the High and Lofty One, who inhabiteth Eternity, whose name is Holy: I dwell in the high and holy place, with him also that is of a contrite and humble spirit, to revive the spirit of the humble, and to revive the heart of the contrite one.

Ye are the temple of the living God; as God hath said, I will dwell in them, and walk in them, and I will be their God, and they shall be my people.

He that defileth the temple of God—Him shall God destroy.

CHAPTER II.

LAND of Eternity! what shadowy hosts
Mantle thy dim interminable shore?—
All voyagers from life's tempestuous sea.
Shore of Eternity!—Wave after wave
Influent, to thy mighty bosom bears
Successive generations. Our faint eyes,
Aching with vain surveys of the vastness,
Do find a sweet repose, on spots suffused
With mellowy light of pitying Hope,—the bournes
Of voyagers we loved.

SUCH as has been described was the condition of Isabella's mind, when, her affectionate anxieties strongly excited by domestic affliction, she engaged with greater earnestness and frequency than ever before, in the performance of such religious services, as she thought were fitted to influence in her favour the will and purposes of God.

To Dugald, one of her brothers, she was attached with more than ordinary fervour and tenderness, their character and habits being very similar; for he was a youth of great gentleness of manner, of meek and tranquil dispositions, with very strong affections. She often spoke to me of the enjoyment which she had in his society. He was some years older indeed; but he took great interest in whatever seemed to engage her attention, and availed himself of every opportunity of doing what promised to gratify her feelings. Her delight was in retirement, for example, and he made a little garden for her in a sequestered spot, overhanging one of the waterfalls formed by the rivulet flowing down the hill, at the foot of which Fernicarry stands. It is only a few stone-casts from the house, but almost entirely concealed from it, by the encircling rocks and intervening trees. It continued for years her favourite spot, and so long as she was able to walk,

5

she spent in it a portion almost of every day,—a secluded oratory, well fitted for meditation and prayer; more especially, as the dashing of the waters along their precipitous and rocky channel sheltered its privacy from the invasion of the ear, while its position concealed it from the eye of man.

Their intercourse, so very pleasing, was soon to come to a close; for Dugald had contracted a cold, which fixing upon his lungs, it became obvious to all, that a virulent consumption was carrying him down to the grave. Her conduct and feeling, during his illness, it was deeply affecting to witness. She almost never left his room; and exhausted all her ingenuity in devising whatever seemed likely to promote his comfort. When I visited him, I uniformly found her by his bedside; and remember very well, how carefully she seemed to avoid whatever might tend to distress or alarm him. When near him, or looking in the direction where he lay, she appeared always to smile; but when out of his sight, to be filled with deep and solemn anxiety; and although silent, she seemed like one engaged in earnest prayer. I have understood, that whenever she ceased to sustain the assumed cheerfulness of which I have spoken, she would rush from his room, and give vent to her feelings in sobs and tears; and then, as if disburdened of the accumulations of her heart's bitter grief, again resume, with a cheerful countenance, her little labours of love by the pillow of her dying brother. Upon one occasion only, according to her mother, when in his presence, her fortitude failed her.

He had requested her to look in his trunk for something he needed, and seeing there different objects which had interested him, such a conflict of feeling occurred in her mind, from joyful remembrances and dismal forebodings, that she could no longer conceal her grief; and she wept bitterly. When he asked the occasion of her sorrow, "Oh, I cannot think of our being parted; I cannot endure it," she unguardedly exclaimed : but, by some kindly and soothing expressions of her brother, such as, if they were parted they would meet again, (for he was piously disposed,) she regained, and never afterward lost her tranquillity.

But her anxious love was not merely manifested in watching by his pillow; it vented itself also in frequent and importunate intercessions for his life, before the throne of the great Disposer and Numberer of our days. Not to mention her brief ejaculations, prompted continually by her vehement anxieties; she set apart various seasons in the day, for retiring to some secret place, chiefly to her little garden; where she might pour out the burden of her soul's anguish into the sympathizing bosom of God. Often she would fast, even for a whole day, that her mind, as she conceived, might be fitter for devotion; and the devotion itself, as she fondly hoped, more acceptable to the witness of his children's necessities. In all this, as she has sometimes told me, she persisted, from an idea that God would not continue neglectful or insensible, but would at last yield to such earnest and incessant prayers.

As her brother's malady increased, and her hopes were diminishing, still these exercises, with strong cryings and tears, were not intermitted, but rather multiplied, even to the close of his life; the spirit which prompted them, gathering strength and fervour as it were, from the very despair that threatened to extinguish all prospect of recovery.

In the retrospect of this period of her life, she failed not to see the sin of her devotions; unmarked, as they were, by any resignation to the will of God, or any knowledge of his character as a being more willing to grant, than his creatures are to ask what is needful to their true happiness. The importunate widow in the Parable, she took for her example; and her recorded success stimulated Isabella's exertions: but when the result in her own case was different, she was led to form harsh judgments of him to whom she had presented so many entreaties. This was sufficiently apparent from the effect which her brother's death had, for some time, upon her mind. She had loved him very tenderly, and she now felt, that her heart was indeed laid waste and desolate; and the more so, because she could not pray for resignation : the fact of his death seeming decisive of God's indifference to her desires and necessities; and therefore precluding the privilege and freedom of entreating from him any comfort or consolation. The prolongation of Dugald's life was all she had desired, or hoped for; and now, that a deaf ear had been turned to her prayers, her abstinence, her fasting, to which she had attached such importance and efficacy, she could discover nothing in his love or tenderness which seemed to justify such a blasting of her past hopes; and therefore, was not prepared to see in his character, or feelings towards her, any thing to relieve the desolateness of her bereavement. At this period she certainly had no pleasure in living; for this she used to say was the habitual language of her feelings after Dugald's death, " Well, I'll lie down and die too ;" thinking with painful sympathy of Jonah, when murmuring, " it is better to die than to live." She now very seldom prayed, although for months she had so intensely engaged in exercises of devotion. Indeed the necessity which urged them had ceased; for it argues a singular state of mind, that while praying so repeatedly for her brother, so far as she remembered, she never at that time prayed for herself.

Defeated in her struggles for an object so deeply interesting, such apathy and indifference succeeded, that, according to her own expression, all idea of God, as the hearer of prayer, seemed for some time to have faded from her mind. This state, however, was not likely to last very long. Such feelings of loneliness, when she mourned the departure of her beloved brother, constrained her, at last,

to look to God for comfort and relief. Her thoughts of
that eternity, the unseen, mysterious, unchanging condition upon which he had entered, involved considerations of
his relationship to God, and naturally excited anxieties
about her own. Frequently, she now pondered upon the
probable safety of her soul, beseeching light and comfort
from God, while engaged in devotional exercises, and in
reading the Scripture. Her health had been considerably
injured by her attendance on her brother, so that, for some
time, she had been unable for the exertion of walking to
church; but now she resumed her regular appearance
there, and manifested an increasing depth of interest in the
exercises of the Sunday-school. Such were her feelings
and employments, when her father, previously in delicate
health, became very ill, exhibiting symptoms of a disease
resembling that which had terminated the life of her brother, whose death she had not yet ceased deeply to mourn.
She was called upon to repeat the performance of those
duties which, in the preceding year, had so engrossed her;
and the same incessant watchfulness, so tender and unwearied, I witnessed by the pillow of her dying father, as was
manifested during the sufferings of her departed brother.
The prospect of his death filled her with great apprehension and grief of spirit; but she did not attempt those exercises, and intercessions, and fasting, with which, formerly,
she had hoped to subdue the divine sovereignty to a com-
pliance with her wishes : for these having totally failed to
draw forth in any degree, as she conceived, the compassion
of God, she was induced to regard them as utterly vain;
while she recoiled from their repetition as a presumptuous
interference with the irrevocable decrees of the Giver of
life and death.

Her father died, and there does not appear to have been
in her feelings and views, at such a crisis, any thing peculiar, but such as a girl of strong and tender affections expe-

5*

riences when bereaved of a kind-hearted and indulgent parent. As she had not recovered entirely the exhaustion induced by her anxiety during the illness of her brother, what she had again experienced seems to have seriously injured her health. Her frame, indeed, naturally feeble and delicate, was thus so weakened as to prepare the way for that malady, which, at an early period, was appointed to dissolve it. This new bereavement, although it produced no decided effect upon her mind, was not fitted to diminish her serious thoughts regarding God and eternal things. She appears indeed to have commenced gradually the searching of the Scriptures more diligently, in the hope of light; and various passages would excite temporary interest and anxiety. The state of her health, the absolute poverty in which the death of her father had left the family, and other circumstances, combined to teach, in an especial manner, that this world had only broken cisterns for her; and that there was only one fountain which could contribute to her happiness. This she was constrained from time to time to think of and seek after; but, as yet, her spirit was not truly awakened to see clearly her necessity or its remedy, or what station she was occupying in the universe of God.

In "dim uncertainty" she remained, ignorant of her relationship to him who is the prince of life, the first-born and head of a living family—that "peculiar people," that "chosen generation," who, amid a perverse and polluted world, are predestinated to be conformed to the image of his own living piety and virtue. Yet in what did she differ from the great majority of Christian professors, both old and young, who, through this dark ignorance of what alone can give to all they do, a holy life and vigour, manifest merely a form of godliness, while performing their round of duties in listless servility of spirit; or attending, with scrupulous exactness, to some ritual of a prescribed devotion.

The Hymn.

O WHITHER shall I fly ? What path untrod
Shall I seek out, to 'scape the flaming rod
Of my offended, of my angry God ?

No, sea, nor shade, nor shield, nor rock, nor cave,
Nor silent deserts, nor the sullen grave,
What flame-eyed fury means to smite, can save.

'Tis vain to flee; 'tis neither here nor there,
Can 'scape that hand, until that hand forbear ;
Ah me! where is He not, that's every where?

'Tis vain to flee, till gentle Mercy show
Her better eye; the farther off we go,
The swing of justice deals the mightier blow.

I know thy justice is thyself; I know,
Just God, thy very self is mercy too ;
If not to thee, where, whither shall I go?

The Scripture.

———

WHEN thou with rebukes dost correct man for iniquity, thou makest his beauty to consume away like a moth.

O my God, my soul is cast down within me:—Deep calleth unto deep at the noise of thy waterspouts: all thy waves and billows are gone over me.

I am desolate and afflicted; I am like a broken vessel.

Thy arrows stick fast in me: Thy hand presseth me sore. There is no soundness in my flesh, because of thine anger; neither is there any rest in my bones, because of sin: for my iniquities have gone up over my head as a heavy burden:—they are too heavy for me. I am troubled. I am bowed down greatly. I go mourning all the day long. I am feeble and sore broken, by reason of the disquietness of my spirit.

O that I had wings like a dove, for then would I fly away, and be at rest.

CHAPTER III.

—— As a tame dove's,
Grasp the dread whirlwind's stormy wing;
Or, with thy lullaby, like sleeping babe,
Hush the great deep's billowy thunders:—Then
To a spirit wounded, speak of repose.

At last, however, several months after her father's death, she was excited, as she had never been before, and filled with new emotions. While reading Walker of Truro's 'Christian,' a condition of the immortal soul was made known to her, without which she saw there could be no comfort or blessedness. " She would do something, would do any thing," yet knew not what to do to secure it. " Some eternal nerves were now waked within her ;" passionate longings to be what that book described, that now took all quiet from her mind. The new creature there set up before her, she felt she was not ; while it seemed, as she looked on it, death to all peace and happiness in any other condition. At this crisis I do not know how her feelings could be better described than in the eloquent language of Gambold's Sermon " On the reasonableness and extent of religious reverence." " A tame and feeble bird that accidentally has hatched an eagle's egg, and is afterward affrighted at the strength and impetuous tendency of what has been fostered under its own wings, cannot find itself in a more critical case than a man when holding dialogue, like Adrian, with his own soul. He perhaps hath been an indolent, unmeaning thing ; but that immortal part within him carries a keener edge than has ever yet been unsheathed ;

and how its edge is likely to be employed in a long here-
after, he has but either bad omens of, or at least must be
in a trembling suspense till grace gives a competent deter-
mination."

So roused now was Isabella. Every new conversation
she held with her soul occasioned only anguish. Such a
feeling, indeed, was progressive, not immediate, in all its
depth and energy; but at this period it originated, gathering, from time to time, power, and terror, and agony, which,
as we shall see, unless the compassions of God had interposed, must have rendered her existence one dark, desolate, unmitigated misery. What, however, hastened its
progress was the manner her mind was impressed, or rather startled suddenly, by the words—" This is the accepted time, this is the day of salvation; to-day, if ye will hear
my voice."

Two great facts were thus at once before her : the necessity of a certain condition which Walker had portrayed, and the peril of delay. She was truly in a sore extremity, conscientiously alien from God, and helpless in her
ungodly misery; while she felt the essence of that misery
to consist in hatred of that which alone could make her
happy. She recoiled from the unholiness of the new creature as the image of him who is holy; while unbelief of
his power to change her would not allow her to enter into
the rest he has prepared for the most miserable and impious human rebels. In this state, she at last turned to the
Bible, in search of counsel; but, although in every age it
has been full of light, to her it was all darkness. The field
of the word, where the Spirit of the Lord had, from the beginning, led believers by a river of life, spread before her as
the valley of the shadow of death. She began reading the
gospels, in the hope of finding something suited to her ne-
cessitous condition; but as she proceeded, in every declaration *there*, she seemed to see only the record of her own

condemnation. Successive blasphemies filled her mind;
as the word condemned her, she hated it; and in a tumult
of despairing anguish, as if the arrows of the Almighty
Avenger were all piercing her spirit, she would cast it from
her, fearing, lest in reading more, she should perish as she
read, although she felt, *that* would have been a blessing.
Yet again, without the word, her desolation seemed intole-
rable. She would snatch it up again and read; but such
blasphemies would return, stirring up unspeakable distrac-
tions of soul, that in her ignorance of any refuge from such
sore misery, she would in mute and motionless amazement,
sit as if within the grasp of final despair. That some heavy
sorrow possessed her soul, was obvious to those around her;
although not one word had yet indicated what she felt. At
midnight, however, all was revealed : yet why should I say
all ; for what words can tell to the ear of man, the deep
things of the spirit; the anguish and the bitterness felt,
when it knows and sees itself engaged in terrible warfare
with its Maker :—but, in the dead of night, when all in the
house was silent, a voice was heard from the apartment
where Isabella lay—a voice of lamentation and anguish,
and of bitter wailing :—" O Lord, I can see nothing but
the blackness of darkness for ever : I feel that I am far
from thee, and that is misery." It awoke Mary, and made
her sore afraid. She would have fled beyond the reach of
its sound, but she could not ; while once and again she
heard from the sister she loved so tenderly, these awful
and solemn words—" O Lord, I am far from thee : I can
see nothing but the blackness of darkness for ever."

From this period, her sorrows multiplied beyond all expression, and often as if beyond endurance. From time to
time her mind was torn and buffeted by such suggestions
as only seemed fit to confirm the utter hopelessness of
her condition. The sin against the Holy Ghost, for example, was charged upon her conscience with resistless

energy. Long she struggled and toiled beneath this fearful burden; but, at last, God in mercy gave her deliverance, while reading the following passage in the works of Erskine, one of the first seceders from the church of Scotland: "But thou mayest consider, that Satan cannot know thou art a reprobate: was Satan, think you, in God's council when he made his eternal decrees? Satan, who is not so much as one of God's hired servants, but a slave and a malefactor kept in chains? He is so far from being of God's council, that he is not so much as one of his family: if thou sayest, thy conscience tells thee, that thou art a reprobate, know that no man living can tell who are reprobates, nor can any man know himself to be a reprobate, except he hath committed the sin against the Holy Ghost, which no man hath committed, who is sorry to think he hath committed. For it is impossible that such a one should be renewed either by, or to, repentance."

When this suggestion had exhausted its power of tormenting, doubts of her election rushed into her mind. She was long tossed by this agonizing anxiety; and no light seemed to dawn upon the counsels of God.—These remained in thick darkness; or rather, a terrible light from the Most High, as a consuming fire, seemed to reveal to her the decree of her own reprobation in the records of eternity. Such passages as these were ever recurring to her mind, "He hath blinded their eyes, and hardened their hearts, that they should not see with their eyes, nor understand with their hearts, and be converted, and I should heal them." "Hath not the potter power over the clay, of the same lump to make one vessel unto honour, and another unto dishonour? What if God, willing to show his wrath, and to make his power known, endured with much long-suffering the vessels of wrath fitted to destruction." And the example of Pharaoh stood forth meeting her eye continually, as a visible symbol of God's capricious sovereignty which had fore-ordained her own rejection. God, however, of whom she judged so unrighteously, mingled mercy with her great affliction; for another passage from the work I have mentioned, by the teaching of his Spirit, checked her profane prying into his secret decrees, and quieted her mind. "I must say, it is presumption in you to inquire into your election.—What God hath folded, no man, no angel, no devil, no creature, can unfold till God himself do it. If an angel from Heaven should come to you, before you come to Christ, and say, you are an elect person, you ought not to believe him; for it is a lie to tell you what he does not know; if the devil from Hell should come, and tell you, that you are not elected, you ought as little to credit him; but tell him he is a liar, for telling you what he does not know, for *that* is the folded leaf which no creature can unfold. It is like the book you read of, Revel. v. 1—6, and it is not lawful for you to pry within the folded leaf. It is not the first object of your faith to believe your election; secret things belong to God, but to us, the things that are revealed, the things that are written within the open leaf; and till you read, and subscribe what is written there, it is not possible for you to know if your name be written within the folded leaf; nor are you concerned to know. If it were possible for you to know your election, before you come to Christ, it would do you no service, but real hurt: it would make you secure in your natural state, and therefore it is in infinite wisdom and mercy, both, that it is hid from your eyes. Some are hardened with the very fancy of it, saying, if I be elected I will win to heaven, and so neglect God's call; but now the open leaf of Christ's commission is before your eyes."

But although Isabella's mind ceased to be agonized in this particular way; either from conceiving that she had committed the sin against the Holy Ghost, or, in vainly

6

attempting to ascertain her election; yet, peace seemed
as far away and hopeless as ever.—Although not distracted by the imagined commission of an unpardonable
sin, or the terror of irrevocable reprobation, she felt in her
soul an utter incapacity of happiness.. Neither any idea
of the sovereignty of God wrathfully regarding her, nor
any fear lest the fountain of his mercy was sealed, now
distressed her; but the enmity of his glorious excellencies
pervading and stimulating her entire soul, still was the
source and element of all her misery. The dread of punishment comparatively little affected her mind; her conscious vileness was the burden of we under which she
groaned. For at this period she had most clear conceptions of the holiness of the divine law—the transcript of
God's own glorious and loveable excellency; and her
conscious non-conformity to what she saw ought to be
loved and embraced, (which her desire of happiness made
her long for, notwithstanding the recoilings of her hostile
and carnal heart,) constituted that moral condition of her
soul, which, to use her own words to a venerable father
of our church, she felt to be "a very hell of pollution and
of torment."

The passage you have read having effectually rescued
her mind from the terrible thought of eternal reprobation,
she now saw no reason, why she might not, like other miserable sinners, lay hold of the great salvation in Christ
Jesus, through whose blood there is redemption from sin.
Yet, so long as she felt that she could not believe, the
agitation and misery of her mind continued. The all-sufficiency of Christ's mediatorial labours she seemed to see;
of which, indeed, she could not but admit from Scripture,
the guiltiest sinners were warranted to avail themselves,
in securing their eternal peace: she, however, for herself,
could not realize this blessedness, although what he had
done equalled in virtue all that could be imagined of the

necessities of depraved souls; for here she regarded as a
peculiar case, not to be judged of by the analogies of guilt,
or by any thing hitherto recorded of the feelings of dark
souls searching after truth.

In such a state of mind, it may easily be imagined, how
all representations of Christ's power to save would fail to
affect her heart, or communicate any comfort. The imagined peculiarity of her case, obviously rendered impossible the appropriation of her completed salvation; and she
seems to have indulged in exaggerating to herself her guilt,
so as to justify the putting away from her that which cleanseth from all sin. As an illustration of this, the following
incident may be selected from many that might be recorded:—While listening one morning to her brother and a
stranger conversing about a person who had been guilty
of some infamous profligacy, she said to herself, "O did
they but know how much more abandoned and depraved I
am! would they allow me to remain in their presence?"

To those who know little of the workings of the soul,
panting to be delivered from the conscious dominion of
sin; or of those temptations of Satan fearful lest he should
lose his prey, which suggest such views either of God or
of itself, as perpetuate its misery, by continuing its unbelief; these feelings of Isabella will be regarded as the
result of a morbid delicacy and tenderness of conscience:
but in those, who have sounded the depths, where awakened souls find no rest, nor hiding place from the requirements of that inexorable law which demandeth, in all
thoughts and feelings, holiness to the Lord, they will excite
a deep interest, and draw forth many kindred sympathies.

They know how natural it is, when the needed redemption seems never to be drawing nigh, to think that
some peculiar guiltiness occasions the delay; while delusions, fostered in the evil heart of unbelief, multiplying
every moment, and darkening more deeply on the mental

vision, conceal the mighty power of him who hath abolished death, and is the destroyer of all sin.

Isabella was still the prey of those delusions. She wandered into the fields, on the side of the mountain, or along the solitary shore, seeking rest, but finding none. She fasted and she prayed. Her soul, as it were, "abhorred all manner of meat." "Wearisome nights" were appointed to her. No sooner did she lie down in her bed, than she would rise again, venting her agonies in piteous moanings; or, if she found herself falling asleep, she would start from her pillow, terror seizing upon her, lest her awakening should be in a place of torment.

Her bodily strength decayed; while her mind seemed to retain its strength, only for the endurance of greater suffering. But no words can more fitly express her condition, than those which she herself once used in her sister's presence. One of her cousins had been observing "how miserable Isabella is! What can be the matter with her? she has a look of such great anguish;" and Mary a little afterward approaching where she was, heard her thus mournfully express herself, rather in the way of soliloquy, than in the form of an address to her, "O sin! sin is just hell. I can understand well *that* which David said, 'the pains of hell took hold of me.' For one to experience a little more of this awful enmity against God would make life insupportable. I feel it to be so almost as it is," and she turned away her face, and groaned deeply.

She began now to think that it was sinful in one with so much conscious hatred to God and all things holy, to dare to hold communion with him, or to examine the revelations of his will. She seems, accordingly, at this time, to have abandoned altogether the reading of the Bible, and refrained from intercessory prayer; although she continued to deplore and confess her guiltiness.

It may be recorded also as very remarkable, that the

passages of Scripture, which she had got by heart, entirely faded from her remembrance. She seemed to have no kindred thought, or feeling, none that corresponded or sympathized with the sentiments they contained;—so that her mind, as it were, lost the power of retaining them. It is scarcely necessary to observe, that she likewise absented herself from church, were it not for the purpose of alluding to the reason, which she assigned for doing so, illustrative amid all her anxieties and distresses, of the integrity and conscientiousness of her mind. "Had she felt otherwise able for such an exertion," as she expressed herself, "she would have recoiled from any such outward profession of piety," while her enmity against God was unabolished, and reigning with all its virulence in her mind.

Were you to regulate your attendance on public worship by the severe righteousness of feeling, which, at this time, prevailed in Isabella's mind, how many of you would be present in the solemn assemblies? Although God loves the gates of Zion more than all the dwellings of Jacob; who among you would be worshippers there? Alas! it is a strange delusion, as it is a bold presumption in men, to appear in holy places, presenting with their bodies a visible reverence to the Eternal Father, while their spirits riot in unnatural rebellion against his holy sovereignty; confessing with their lips Jesus to be the Son of God,—the good Shepherd who laid down his life for the sheep; although their haughty and unbroken hearts wreck upon that most blessed of all truths—unbelieving scorn. Constrained to regard as hypocrisy, the assumption of the least appearance even of the form of godliness, poor Isabella was thus bereft, by her own conscientious feelings, of whatever comfort she might have found in social devotion. But was she less happy, than those have a right to be, that worship with worldly or careless minds in the presence of Him, who, in the wilds of Midian, cried to Moses, "Draw not nigh hither, put off thy shoes from off thy feet, for the place whereon thou standest is holy ground?"—of Him, who, by the dead bodies of Aaron's sons, that had profaned his altar with unconsecrated fire, thus vindicated his sovereignty, in the infliction of so sudden a judgment—"I will be sanctified in them that come nigh me, and before all the people I will be glorified?"

The Hymn.

Why dost thou shade thy lovely face? O why
Does that eclipsing hand so long deny
The sunshine of thy soul enliv'ning eye?

Mine eyes are blind and dark, I cannot see;
To whom, or whither should my darkness flee,
But to the light, and who's that light but thee?

My path is lost, my wand'ring steps do stray;
I cannot safely go, nor safely stay:
Whom should I seek but thee, my path, my way?

O, I am dead: to whom shall I, poor I,
Repair? to whom shall my sad ashes fly,
For life? and where is life but in thine eye?

If I have lost my path, great Shepherd, say,
Shall I still wander in a doubtful way?
Lord, shall a lamb of Israel's sheepfold stray?

Thou art the pilgrim's path, the blind man's eye,
The dead man's life: on thee my hopes rely;
If thou remove, I cry, I grope, I die.

Disclose thy sunbeams, close thy wings, and stay;
See, see, now I am blind, and dead, and stray,
O thou that art my light, my life, my way?

The Scripture.

WHY standest thou afar off, O Lord, why hidest thou thyself in time of trouble ?

How long shall I take counsel in my soul, having sorrow in my heart daily? Consider and hear me, O Lord my God; lighten mine eyes, lest I sleep the sleep of death.—Hold not thy peace at my tears.—O spare me, that I may recover strength before I go hence and be no more.

While I suffer thy terrors I am distracted.

Out of the depths have I cried unto thee, O Lord. My soul waiteth for the Lord more than they that watch for the morning—I say more than they that watch for the morning, for with him is plenteous redemption.

O Jerusalem, how long shall thy vain thoughts lodge within thee ?

——They cried the more, saying, " Have mercy on us, O Lord, thou Son of David"—So Jesus had compassion on them.

CHAPTER IV.

My soul, being spent, for refuge, seeks to thee,
But cannot find where thou, my refuge, art;
Like as the swift foot hart doth wounded fly
To the desired streams, ev'n so do I
Pant after thee, my God, whom I must find, or die.

In such a state, it is obvious no peace could be enjoyed. Indeed it had very much the aspect of a fixed despair; as if all hope of its attainment had vanished. It continued for some months, but it was not permitted to last for ever. Passages of scripture now gradually rising to her remembrance, excited dormant feelings; and new resolutions were formed, and plans devised to secure, if possible, what was necessary to render existence desirable. She now became more diligent than ever in the performance of religious duties. She prayed, and read the Scriptures; repeated her fastings; adhered at all times to the severest abstinence; took only what was barely necessary to sustain nature, and that, of the coarsest food she could find; persuaded at this time that something on her part was necessary to merit what juster views would have shown God freely, and without reluctance, bestows. Every day beheld her more assiduous in her work of righteousness than before. While she was anxious to do all that the law required, she was most scrupulous in avoiding what it forbade, even to the least appearance of evil. She would not, for example, exchange the ordinary salutations with any person she met on the road, lest she should be tempted to utter vain words, or expend foolishly one of those moments upon which eternal results seemed to depend. When in society she was generally silent and thoughtful, listened eagerly to any religious conversation; and when she did speak, it was with great earnestness and solemnity; while at all times, she seemed to regard with sacred horror, any approach to cheerfulness and gayety.

At this time, however, she enjoyed comparative tranquillity of mind; and, in religious exercises, she appears to have had considerable enjoyment. The complacency with which she regarded the righteousness she was labouring to frame for her justification in the sight of God, and the deceptions which a beautiful ritual of devotion and perfect formulary of holy deeds practise upon the feelings; can easily account for her temporary quietude, or the absence of agonizing emotion.

She resorted, at regular seasons, to her sequestered garden, for reading, and meditation, and prayer. I have before me an interesting letter from a young divine, descriptive of an incident, which illustrates this habit of her life. One morning, at sunrise, in the month of May, 1824, he had walked from Garelochhead, a hamlet in the immediate neighbourhood; for the purpose of ascending the hill behind Fernicarry, to enjoy the glories of that scene, which contains more of the sublime and beautiful, than is to be found in many regions. As he pursued his way by the margin of the rivulet, a book, lying outside the wickerwork, which, with the rocks, formed the enclosure of Isabella's garden, attracted his eye; and, at the next glance, he saw a young female engaged in devotion. He naturally felt inclined to enter into conversation; but dreading to interrupt her by a rash intrusion, he retired softly, and ascended the mountain, in the full persuasion of meeting her on his return, as he took her for the girl tending some cattle in the contiguous field. Nearly an hour elapsed before he came back; when he found her in the same attitude, and obviously engaged in the same exercise. He again retired to a little distance, and, in a short time, he saw her rise from her knees, and sit down to read.

He then approached, and found that she had with her the Bible and two catechisms: he learned from her that she often spent the morning, when the weather permitted, in that manner; preferring the retirement of her little garden to any other place. "She seemed," he adds, "to be duly impressed with a sense of the goodness of God, in allowing her to enjoy such a privilege; and to be more alive to the value of the soul, and the preciousness of the gospel, than any young person I have conversed with."

The agonies which she had formerly endured, were decisive of the value she attached to her soul; and how precious she estimated the gospel to be. Had she underrated either, like the careless multitudes of a dark and unregenerated world, she might, like them, have spent the days of her youth without disquietude or pain; but she had seen so much of truth as to make her restless, until she knew the whole truth needful to seal the peace of a believer's mind. The tranquillity which, at this time, she enjoyed, her subsequent experience proved, was greater, than the quantity of truth she in reality knew, could possibly warrant.

One of those books, which she had with her Bible, must have been a sacramental catechism, which the young people of this parish study, and upon which they are examined, previous to their admission, for the first time, to the holy communion; for now Isabella had resumed, among her other holy sevices, attendance in the Sunday-school; and at the time of the interview described, must have been occupied in such exercises as were prescribed before partaking of the Lord's Supper.—Indeed, the prospect itself of this solemn act of devotion may have contributed to the temporary repose of her mind. The Saviour, as she must have heard, has made himself known in the breaking of bread ; and her hopes naturally would fix upon the altar of communion, as the place where substantial and permanent blessedness was most probably to be found in the presence of a crucified Redeemer. She had been reading Doddridge's ' Rise and Progress of Religion in the Soul,' and examined with the deepest interest that history of the divine life. Whatever other effect resulted from the perusal of this work, it fixed her resolution, should she be found qualified according to the ordinary rules, of becoming a communicant.

Although she could not say that Christ was her Saviour, or that she had felt him to be the author of peace to her soul ; she was actuated by the hope, that in this service it might at last be found, and in obeying his dying command, sin might at last be destroyed.

She prepared herself most diligently, according to the rules prescribed by Doddridge ; and more particularly in devoting herself to God in the manner he enjoins. The following form of self-consecration, upon his own model, was found among her papers, which, from the date it bears, must have been constructed a day or two before the Sabbath of communion :—

Fernicarry, July 11, 1824.

" Eternal and ever-blessed God, I come to present myself before thee with the deepest humility and abasement of soul ; sensible how unworthy such a sinful worm is to appear before the holy Majesty of heaven, the King of kings and Lord of lords ; and especially on such an occasion as this, even to enter into a covenant transaction with thee. But the scheme and plan is thy own. Thine infinite condescension hath offered it by thy Son, and thy grace hath inclined my heart to accept of it. I come, therefore, acknowledging myself to be a great offender, smiting on my breast, and saying with the humble publican, God be merciful to me a sinner. I come invited by the name of thy Son, and wholly trusting in his perfect righteousness, entreating that for his sake

thou wilt be merciful to me, and wilt no more remember my sins. Receive, I beseech thee, thy revolted creature, who is now convinced of thy right to her, and desires nothing so much as that she may be thine. This day do I with the utmost solemnity surrender myself to thee. I renounce all former lords that have had dominion over me: and I consecrate to thee all that I have, the faculties of my mind, the members of my body, my time, and my influence over others, to be used entirely for thy glory, and resolutely employed in obedience to thy commands, as long as thou continuest me in life, with an ardent desire and humble resolution to continue thine, through all the endless ages of eternity ; ever holding myself in an attentive posture to observe the first intimation of thy will, and ready to spring forward with zeal and joy to the immediate execution of it. To thy direction also I resign myself, and all I am and have, to be disposed of by thee in such a manner as thou shalt, in thy infinite wisdom, judge most subservient to the purposes of thy glory. To thee I leave the management of all events, and say without reserve, not my will, but thine be done ; rejoicing with a loyal heart in thine unlimited government, as what ought to be the delight of the whole creation. Use me, O Lord, I beseech thee, as an instrument of thy service : number me among thy peculiar people : let me be washed in the blood of thy dear Son ; let me be clothed with his righteousness ; let me be sanctified by his Spirit. Transform me more and more into his image ; impart to me through him all needful influences of thy purifying, cheering, and comforting Spirit ; and let my life be spent under those influences, and the light of thy gracious countenance as my Father and my God. And when the solemn hour of death comes, may I remember this my covenant, well ordered in all things and sure—all my salvation, and all my desire.

"And do thou, O Lord, remember it too. Look down with pity, O my Heavenly Father, on thy languishing, dying child; embrace me in thine everlasting arms : put strength and confidence into my departing spirit, and receive it to the abodes of them that sleep in Jesus ; peacefully and joyfully to wait the accomplishment of thy great promise to all thy people, even that of a glorious resurrection, and of eternal happiness in thine heavenly presence. And if any surviving friends should, when I am in the dust, meet with this memorial of my solemn transactions with thee, may they make the engagement their own ; and do thou graciously admit them to partake in all the blessings of thy covenant,

7

through Jesus, the great mediator of it. To whom, with thee, O Father, and thy Holy Spirit, be everlasting praise and glory.— Amen. "ISABELLA CAMPBELL."

With such solemnity did she thus approach to pay her vows before the holy altar of God. All seemed to promise well. She had done what was deemed necessary by a wise and holy man; and she had good hope of at last attaining what she had long so intensely desired, that her parched soul might be as a well-watered field, which the Lord had blessed. She ate, however, the body, and drank the blood of the Lord, without realizing what she had been anticipating; so that she might have said to the promises of her deceiving hope, " where is the blessedness ye spake of?" At the same time, while, from the holy sacrament itself, no essential benefit was derived, she had enjoyment in some of the accompanying services; and one sermon, in particular, she held, till the day of her death, in grateful remembrance.

During the preceding period of comparative tranquillity, she had been perplexed and harassed by other troubles than those of a spiritual nature. Her family were in the lowest and most desolate poverty; the creditors of her father having claimed whatever worldly substance he had possessed. She was, besides, extremely delicate; unable, by her own exertions, to provide for her support; and the fear of want distressed her, when her mind, somewhat relieved of its anxiety regarding eternal things, was more alive to worldly interests and cares. At such moments, she had not faith to lay hold of the promises of him, who is a father to the fatherless, the stay of the orphan, and who considereth the case of the destitute; in great compassion declaring, " when the poor and needy seek water, and there is none, and their tongue faileth for thirst, I the Lord will hear them; I the God of Israel will not forsake them."

The sermon alluded to was preached by the Rev. Dr.
B., from the words, "Stand fast in the liberty wherewith
Christ maketh you free." The train of thought which
pervaded it, communicated to her mind great comfort : but
in a passage where believers were exhorted, amid their
trials, to lay hold of the divine promises, the declaration
"your bread shall be given you, and your water shall be
sure," came home with such power to her soul, that, from
that moment, worldly cares never excited the most transient anxiety, or the want of visible means of support, distrust of the providence of God.

Her state at this time cannot fail to be regarded as peculiarly interesting. Nothing is more certain than that she
had not yet "received and rested upon Christ alone for
salvation," in whom all the promises are "yea and amen."
Yet, in a sermon addressed to believers, and from a promise quoted for the consolation of believers, she found what
terminated, in one large field of temptation, all her disquietude. Sometime before, at the sale of her father's effects,
when a relation was weeping and lamenting over the entire desolation of the household, she had said to her sister,
"we would need to have a more durable portion than any
thing this world can afford, if we would be happy," without appropriating, however, any of those promises which
are intended, even in man's utmost need, to prevent dejection of spirit, or distrust of God. She now, in all uncertainty about her portion in another world, lays hold of a
declaration which she considered as a sufficient pledge of
her enjoying a portion in this.

Her portion in another world indeed seemed further from
her grasp than ever ; for the services of that solemn season were no sooner at a close than new anxieties and sorrows possessed her soul. She now saw that she had laid
her hands on the broken body and shed blood, in entire
ignorance of her relationship to the crucified Redeemer.

Wo's me, for I am undone! she was ready to cry, feeling
as if with those wicked hands she had crucified the Lord
afresh, and put him to an open shame. That blessed or-
dinance, in which so many have experienced such consolation and joy, she felt she had presumptuously profaned;
remorse for her rash boldness seemed to re-open all the
fountains of her former agony, and her heart was bowed
down with a most oppressive dejection. So many beautiful
hopes had sprung up in her soul, in the prospect of the
holy communion, now so quenched in utter despair, that
she felt like Job when he cried, " Wherefore is light given
to him that is in misery? or life unto him that is bitter in
soul?"   " O, that my grief were thoroughly weighed, and
my calamity laid in the balance for ever! for now it would
be heavier than the sand of the sea; therefore my words
are swallowed up, for the arrows of the Almighty are within
me, the poison whereof drinketh up my spirit—the terrors
of God have set themselves in array against me." All her
confidence seemed to have given way, and her righteous-
nesses she felt were indeed as filthy rags, too short a covering for her soul, beneath the eye of him who was making
inquisition for holiness.

I remember at this time, about two weeks after she had
taken the sacrament, meeting her one morning very early,
when on my way to Arrochar, wondering but not knowing
the reason why she had been so soon abroad.—Her appearance was that of desolateness and depression; but I
was not aware till afterward, that during the whole of that
night she had been wrestling in prayer, crying for relief
from God; yet without any such answer as suited her
great necessity. No words could more faithfully portray
her condition, than those which the patriarch used as descriptive of his own:—" I am made to possess months of
vanity; wearisome nights are appointed unto me. When
I lie down, I say, when shall I arise, and the night be gone;

and I am full of tossings to and fro, to the dawning of the
day."—Speaking in the anguish of her spirit, complaining
in the bitterness of her soul, scared with dreams, and terrified through visions, there seemed reality only in eternal
things, and they alone she could not but judge worthy of
her pursuit, otherwise she must have chosen strangling and
death, rather than life. Still, however, through some
strange delusion, she did not yet find her way to the only
sure consolation, though agonizingly restless in its pursuit.
Isabella slept at this time with her mother, and the account
she gives of her condition and practices is very affecting.
Groaning and lamenting, night after night, she literally
watered her couch with her tears—the house continually
resounding throughout the silent watches with the voice of
her weeping. Long would her mother lie sleepless, listening to expressions of grief, for which she had no remedy
or comfort; or when awakening from slumbers, which,
through weariness of nature, she could not avoid, finding
Isabella absent, she would thus be filled with alarm, lest
some new calamity should visit her beloved child. Thus,
at dead of night, had she to rise and leave the house, and
search for her in the fields, or where she often found her,
and that during the depth of winter, careless of any of its
storms, weeping and praying in her little garden. "O
then it was pitiful to see her," she has said to me, "not
like an earthly creature. I could give her no help, and
she could find none where she was seeking it. She looked
so pale and wo-begone, it was easily seen that her misery
could not be told."

What a contrast the mental anxieties of the same individual sometimes present! You have seen how Isabella,
when the life of her brother was in hazard, prayed only for
his deliverance and safety, without permitting, even for a
moment, any necessity of her own to become the subject
of her devotions: now, she was her own absorbing anxiety.

7*

Of kindred, or of friends, she thought not in her attempted communion with God. What she herself felt and desired, formed the exclusive burden of her prayers. She could not, however, but believe that peace was somewhere to be found, although hitherto it had been as far off, and concealed from her view; for she felt as one not born for this world and its enjoyments; while, at the same time, the realities of eternity had not filled up the void in her soul. She looked upon all things under the sun, and such was the language of her feelings—" Ye are not for me; and although I have nothing besides, and as yet, lacking all I desire elsewhere, ye are not for me."—In such a state, without interest in time, and without hope in eternity, she has said to me, that she seemed to know well what the feeling of the disciples had been, when the Saviour found them sleeping for sorrow. Repeatedly, however, texts of Scripture would convey to her mind a temporary relief, and raise up her soul, ready to bow down and die. Thus from time to time sustained, she would multiply her labours of righteousness and piety more sedulously than ever, in the hope of obtaining from God what she desired.—Not only in private, but in the presence of others, although without any pharisaical reference to their opinion, would she frequently engage in protracted devotional exercises. That this attracted attention is obvious, from the remark of a little boy, of sufficient simplicity indeed, but affording a very graphic description of her practice: " Isabella makes as long prayers as would save a kingdom."—All, however, she found unavailing. In whatever way she exerted herself, whatever form of righteousness she attempted, howsoever eagerly her spirit strove to secure God's favour; still she remained in toils—only wearying herself with vain devices, each, in succession, attesting the more strongly, her utter helpessness to mitigate her own misery.

The Hymn.

Rock of ages, cleft for me,
Let me hide myself in thee;
Not the labour of my hands
Can fulfil thy law's demands:
Could my zeal no respite know,
Could my tears for ever flow,
All for sin could not atone—
Thou canst save, and thou alone.

To that sacred cleansing flood
Of thy freely flowing blood,
I, a helpless sinner, fly,
Wash me, Saviour, or I die;
Nothing in my hand I bring,
Simply to thy cross I cling;
Rock of ages, cleft for me,
Let me hide myself in thee.

While I live my fleeting day,
When I sigh my soul away;
When I soar to worlds unknown,
See thee on thy judgment throne;
Still, O Lord, be thou my stay,
Cast not thou my soul away:
Rock of ages, cleft for me,
Let me hide myself in thee.

The Scripture.

THE Lord hath heard the voice of my weeping.

Speak ye comfortably to Jerusalem, and cry unto her, that her warfare is accomplished; that her iniquity is pardoned.

He brought me up also out of an horrible pit, out of the miry clay; and set my feet upon a rock, and established my goings. And he hath put a new song in my mouth, even praise unto our God: many shall see it, and fear, and shall trust in the Lord.

Jesus saith unto her, Said I not unto thee, that if thou wouldst believe, thou shouldst see the glory of God?

I had fainted, unless I had believed to see the goodness of the Lord in the land of the living.

I will sing unto the Lord, as long as I live: I will sing praise to my God, while I have my being.

CHAPTER V.

Lo! from the fearful depths of guilt and wo,
Incumbent on her Saviour's arm ascends
A ransomed spirit, filled with one vast thought
Of grateful love ;—inhaling from each glance
Of the great Conqueror's gracious eye, life's joy,—
The joy of sins forgiven.

It must have appeared to you very obvious, that Isabella, in all the variations of her mental suffering and agony, had, as yet, imperfect and obscure views of the freeness of the salvation contained in the gospel; a persuasion being ever present, that something was to be done to deserve it; something in her own strength, and by her own wisdom, apart from the power and counsel of the Spirit of God.

She was not, however, permitted to die under so manifest a delusion. Long, indeed, it had continued; but he, who is always doing great marvels, in bringing good out of evil, and light out of darkness, and leading the blind by a way which they know not, rescued her from its influence ; when bitter experience had sufficiently taught her the hollowness and vanity of every device of that self-righteous spirit, which cannot brook the reception of any gift from God, without, in the pride of its independence, attempting to render him some equivalent compensation.

She had traversed, as it were, the whole world of its legal inventions; left nothing in it unexamined, none of its arts untried; and all she now intensely felt to be, but travail and vexation. She was thus, however, made thoroughly aware, how impossible it is for the creature to secure, or enjoy solid peace, by attempting, of itself, to propitiate the offended Creator. Her progressive experience of this truth was a record, as we have seen, of darkness, perplexity, and suffering, reducing her to the very lowest point of conscious helplessness.

There, however, light, at last, began to dawn upon her; and this desolate child, so long "tossed, and afflicted with tempests," seemed to have some prospect of repose to her weary and troubled spirit. Passages of Scripture would now recur to her mind, obviously designed by her Heavenly Father to open her eyes to just views of all his dispensations; and persuade her, that his compassions were unfailing; that he afflicted not willingly, nor grieved the children of men. One, however, in particular, her thoughts dwelt, and doted on :—" He shall not break the bruised reed, nor quench the smoking flax." That gave her such encouragement and hope, as her disquieted and fearful soul had never felt, nor cherished before. "Surely," said she to herself, "if ever there was a broken reed, I am one. I do, indeed, feel wounded and bruised, broken-hearted, ready to perish. Am I not just in such a condition, as warrants me taking comfort from this description of the Saviour's character and agency ?"

Words cannot tell, how much of refreshment her soul derived from this prediction of the prophet regarding him. She had long felt her misery, while spending her money for that which was not bread to her undying soul; and her labour for that which did not satisfy its longings after happiness. To her spirit, drooping in her forlorn desolateness, it was like the springing up of a stream in the desert, like the descending of the dew upon a parched wilderness; when she saw, for the first time, the tenderness of the Saviour, which this passage so sweetly portrayed. All helps had failed; all her resources dried up; she had looked every where; and whatever seemed to promise fulfilment to the desires of her heart, had " dealt deceitfully with her as a brook, and as a stream of brooks that passeth away." All that she had been striving to accomplish by her prayers, and fastings, by her holy deeds, of whatever form or kind, seemed now but to have increased the sum of her misery; making her feel only more needful than ever of such a friend as the prophet describes in the words which her soul had fixed upon,—" a bruised reed shall he not break, and the flax dimly burning shall he not quench."

She now saw one, whom the most miserable might love for his tenderness,—a good Samaritan, not likely to turn away from suffering and sorrow like the Priest, or the Levite; but ready to heal diseases, to sooth sorrows, to relieve necessities;—the blessed one, "who gathereth together the outcasts, who healeth the broken in heart, who bindeth up their griefs."

About this period, when engaged in the contemplation of the compassion of the Saviour as fitted to her miserable estate, she seems first to have communicated to Mary her peculiar feelings. What she had previously witnessed of Isabella's sufferings and anguish is well described in the following extract from a letter of hers; while a deep and solemn interest cannot fail to be excited by the fact which it discloses, of two sisters under the same roof, companions from their infancy, so intent, each for herself, on the important transaction of securing an eternity of happiness, and avoiding an eternity of sorrow, as to have suspended, by mutual consent, or in delicacy to each other's feelings, all the confidential endearments of sisterly love.

"For about two years previous to my beloved sister's reception of the gospel, her agony of mind was truly affecting: though suffering much in my own mind, at the same time, I was often obliged to conceal it, that I might not be the means of deepening her anguish; which, to use her own words, was almost insupportable. The change in her manner and appearance soon became manifest to all who knew her; though, I believe, for the most part, ill health, rather than mental suffering, was assigned as the cause. Often she used to go about, wringing her hands, and uttering the following words :—'How can thine heart endure, or thine hands be strong, in the days that I shall deal with thee?' &c. Frequently, at midnight, was the cry of lamentation and wo heard to issue from her chamber. So very strong were her cries for mercy, that sometimes you could distinctly hear what she said in any corner of the house. I have known her run through the room, almost in very despair, exclaiming, ' I am lost ! I am ruined for ever ! the pains of hell have taken hold of me ! What shall I do ? whither shall I flee from his presence ? Nowhere, nowhere; there is no place where the Almighty is not. O ! that I could tear this awful heart from within me, or escape from myself.'—At other times, she would retire to her little garden, and there remain for hours, searching the Scriptures, and pouring out tears unto God. We had often to send for her to meals; for, by this time, she had begun to endeavour to better her heart by fasting ; and continued the practice, for such a length of time, adding to it the want of sleep, until she became almost a skeleton. This spirit of legalism increased so much, that I have seen her, if calling at any place, and if offered any thing to eat or drink, occupy eight or ten minutes in soliciting a blessing, ere she would venture to take any of it. The enemy of souls was also busy with her. At one time he would torment her fainting soul with election; at another with the blasphemy against the Holy Ghost; and not unfrequently he has tempted her to believe that her day of grace was past. For some months, she was dreadfully harassed with atheism ; especially when ministers were spoken of in her presence. I have sometimes, at such seasons, seen her attempt to stop her ears. If, at any time, she seemed more composed, worldly conversation, or the least expression of mirth, threw her again into the most inexpressible misery; and often made her run away to mourn in secret places. Very often, after having ate any thing like the quantity of food necessary to support her, she appeared very unhappy, and would say, ' Why need I feed a body to burn for ever in hell ? O that the Lord would have mercy upon me !' For eight or nine months, before she informed me of her joy and peace in believing, she occasionally felt some composure, as she afterward told me, from seeing, in some passages of Scripture, the possibility of her being saved. By this time, she had some imperfect view of the work of Christ. She knew he had done something ; but had no definite idea of what it was. This ignorance, as she afterward said, was most awfully remarkable : for almost all her

Sabbath School hymns testified of him; and she had, besides, been in the habit of learning passages of Scripture, which had reference principally to his death and resurrection. But all was now obscured; so much so, that she sometimes spent hours in crying to God, without making mention at all of the power of Jesus. I left her in the April of 1823. Then, for the first time, she told me she saw more and more the possibility of her salvation. She said, ' God can save me for what Christ has done, if he WILL !' "

For some time, the mere knowledge of such a tender-hearted Saviour existing, seemed to have soothed all her disquietude. Previously she had not understood, although she had heard of him, with the hearing of the ear. The possibility, therefore, of finding the sympathies she needed, was a wonderful relief to her harassed and vexed soul. But while she saw the suitableness of the compassionate Jesus to her condition, she knew not whether God had permitted him to compassionate her. It is obvious, there was still something wanting, and that the mere possibility of relief from his sympathies, could only for a season tranquillize her mind.—Such a discovery was, indeed, a great contrast to her former ignorance ; and although the light was faint that thus dawned upon her mind, she ceased to be full of such gross darkness. After such struggles, however, such throes and anguish of spirit in the pursuit of happiness ; after such perplexing and sickening disappointments, she was not likely to be satisfied, but by something real and tangible ; something, at all events, more definite than a mere possibility, she felt, was necessary to her peace and blessedness.

Thus a new fountain of bitterness was soon opened in her mind. " True," said she to herself, " he shall not break the bruised reed, nor quench the smoking flax ; but how shall I know, that he will not break nor quench *me* ?" The possibility of obtaining a good, excites a delightful feeling in seasons of despair, or of dejection ; but it is not needful

8

to show, how soon hope deferred sickens the spirit. Just in proportion to the estimate we form of its importance to our happiness, is the uneasiness or pain of uncertainty; and this rule will be found, in an eminent sense, to obtain in the great matters of salvation and eternity. So felt, at least, Isabella: but, having suffered so much, she was not afflicted beyond what she was able to bear. God having begun, proceeded in the perfecting of his good work in her soul; and she was not, for a long season, permitted to remain in this condition of doubt and fear. The suspicion she had entertained of the willingness of God to extend to her case the compassion and sympathy of the Saviour, was rebuked by her attention being directed to various passages, descriptive of the comprehensive love of God; but more especially, by her being enabled to hear, and understand in some degree, the blessed invitation, "Come unto me, all ye that are weary and heavy laden, and I will give you rest. Take my yoke upon you, which is easy, and my burden, which is light; and ye shall find refreshment to your souls." The multitude of her thoughts concentrated, as it were, around these words. While in the knowledge, she had previously obtained, of her Saviour's character, connected with the unlimited compassion which the invitation expressed, she seemed to discover a sufficient warrant for that hope which maketh not ashamed, that hope which is as an anchor of the soul, sure and steadfast in the darkest seasons; even when "deep calleth unto deep," when all the waves and the billows of God threaten to go over the soul.

She was now satisfied, that the necessities of her miserable case were not excluded from the commiseration of Jesus, or his Father; since the words which he uttered, were addressed to all that are weary and heavy laden; and this conviction soothed and quieted her amid the misgivings and doubtings that still would disturb her mind. Her condition was now that of comparative enjoyment;

which indeed was visible in her outward demeanour, still
grave and serious, but not sad and melancholy, as during
the long season of her sorrowful estrangement from peace
of soul.

She could, now, take interest in the happiness of others ;
as we find expressed in a note written, at this time, to her
sister, who had communicated some pleasing information
regarding her own condition. It is studiously evasive of
any distinct statement of her views or feelings at the time ;
although this might have been expected from the nature of
their parting interview, as well as the character of her sister's letter ; but Isabella was very cautious, and she was
yet without the consolation of any certain faith or hope.

"My dear, dear Sister,—I may safely say, that the comfortable
intelligence your letter contained, has filled my heart with joy
and gladness. I have felt more dull, for some days past, than when
you first went away; but all is right. I hope you are happy;
finding, though separated from earthly friends, that yours is a
friend that sticketh closer than a brother. May it be your delight,
my beloved sister, to glorify Him, and may you ever enjoy his
sweet smiles.—Adieu, may the best of heaven's blessings rest upon
you."

Still it is obvious, that a mind like hers, so excited by
protracted and varied anxieties about her eternal interests,
could not remain satisfied merely with the negative comfort, arising from the persuasion, that she was not excluded from the compassion expressed in the all-comprehen-
sive invitation of the Saviour. The voice is to all, " Come
unto me." " Unless I go, how do I secure the rest and refreshment spoken of by Jesus ? Have I gone?" she would
ask herself. The absence of a real blessedness rendered
impossible a reply in the affirmative. " Can I go ? How
am I to ascertain whither I go ?" and similar questions and
ponderings kept her mind from time to time restless and
disquieted, because still toiling to do something ; till, at last,

the words, "Whosoever will, let him take of the water of life freely," terminated the long period of darkness, and doubt, and fear for ever; being brought home and effectually blessed to her soul by the tender-hearted Spirit of God.

In the day of their power, she was made willing to go; and she found refreshment in drinking of that fountain, of whose living waters, if a man taste, he will never thirst again.

Her agitation had now subsided, her struggles were at an end, the terrors that had distracted her were rebuked; the elements of her frame ready to melt in the fervent heat of her combat with the powers of darkness, in seeking for glory and immortality, if I may be allowed so to express myself, were moulded into a new and happy creation; and at the feet of her deliverer, the first-born of all new creatures, she now sat, meekly rejoicing in conscious security; believing, that Christ Jesus had died to take away sin; the Spirit witnessing with her spirit, in so believing, that she was a child of God.

She was now able to sing, "I love the Lord, because he hath heard my voice and my supplications. The sorrows of death compassed me, and the pains of hell got hold upon me. I found trouble and sorrow; then called I upon the name of the Lord, O Lord, I beseech thee, deliver my soul. I was brought low, and he helped me. Return to thy rest, O my soul, for the Lord hath dealt bountifully with thee. Thou hast delivered my soul from death, mine eyes from tears, and my feet from falling." Truly she had found that peace, which the world's friendship cannot give, nor the world's enmity take away. For she was at last acquainted with God. The light of a glorious knowledge had arisen upon her mind, disclosing his love to miserable sinners; and in that one blessed contemplation, her soul found refuge from all perils, and repose from all disquietude. The poet beautifully says ;—

" I'm apt to think the man,
That could surround the sum of things, and spy
The heart of God, and secrets of his empire,
Would speak but love ; with him the bright result
Would change the hue of intermediate scenes,
And make one thing of all theology."

And certainly at this time divine love, to Isabella's eye,
seemed every where, and was that which made all things
new in her, and around her.

Then would her heart thus give vent to her feelings, (as
she expressed herself to an intelligent friend, who has preserved notes of their conversation,) in the review of all that
had passed. " O blessed be his holy name, he did not leave
me to seek in vain. He heard the voice of my cries ; in
the depth of my distress I found the object of my anxious
solicitude—I found the Saviour : I was led to look to him
at last : I embraced him : I obtained the pardon of my sins :
and was given to enjoy a sweet and delightful assurance,
that God had accepted me in the beloved. The cloud which
had hung over me so long, was now dispelled ; and all my
fears of the Divine wrath taken away, and my soul was
filled with love to my gracious Saviour. O yes ! Jesus
now appeared to my mind as the chief among ten thousand ;
I felt that old things were passed away, and that all things
were become new. I could take delight in nothing else,
than in thinking and speaking of the glory of the Redeemer,
and of his wondrous love, which he had manifested to a
guilty world in pouring out his soul unto death." " No,
(she continued,) I could not find language to express my
sense of obligation to the blessed Redeemer, for the love
wherewith he had loved me, in calling me by his grace out
of a state of ignorance and condemnation, into a state of
safety and peace. From that time till now, I have been
enabled to live by faith in his precious blood, to glory in the
riches of his grace, to confide in him for a complete victory
8*

over sin and all my enemies. Yes, through the merits of his glorious atonement and prevalent intercession, I look for final acceptance at his throne."

Soon after this crisis in Isabella's history,—the attainment of what she had hoped for, she received a letter from her sister, descriptive of certain changes that had also passed upon her views and feelings, after a similar period of darkness, of doubt, and of perplexity. It is unnecessary, perhaps inexpedient, to detail what these changes were; suffice it to say, they were such as gave to Isabella great delight; and the more especially, since she now knew how to value and how to sympathize with the peace and joy that are found in believing.

The following letter to Mary, contains a very interesting and simple exposition of the now tranquil, and happy state of her mind.

"I am very unwell just now with a bad cold; it is almost a month since I caught it, and I think it is still increasing. A cough and severe pain in my side trouble me much. But, Mary, I am happy. Jesus enables me to feel quite contented under all this, and would, I am persuaded, although my sufferings were twice as severe. Yes, I can cheerfully say, the will of the Lord be done, and trust him for strength to bear his dear will.

"It gives me unspeakable joy, my dearest sister, to know that you are now clothed in the splendid robe of our Redeemer's righteousness, that you are delighting in his sweet smiles. You wish me to assist you in praising and glorifying our God and Father, for what of his love and mercy he hath manifested to your needy soul. I have done it with my whole heart; I trust, I shall ever continue to do so.

"You tell me, if I have still any remaining doubts, to throw them aside, and believe in the everlasting love of God recommended to a perishing world, in the offer of a free and adequate salvation by his dear Son.—My Sister, I have done so; the Holy Spirit hath pointed my weeping eyes to Calvary, and the awfully glorious sight has chased away my fears. Yes! Mary, with his stripes I am healed—surely he hath borne my griefs, and carried my sorrows;—yet I still weep. But O! it is just because I shall never

come into condemnation, and because I cannot love my risen
Lord. O Jesus, whom have I in Heaven but thee! and there is
none in the whole earth that I desire besides thee,—thou art fairer in my estimation than any of the children of men—yea, the
chiefest among ten thousand, and altogether lovely. O Mary,
Mary! let it be our delight to confess and glorify him; in the
midst of a wicked and gainsaying world, may we rejoice to be
counted fools, that he may be honoured and extolled. Dear Mr.
—— has preached here several times since you went away, and
also once or twice in Glenfroon. I am sure you would have much
pleasure in hearing him now, he is so rarely earnest. Much seed
has been sown by him here; pray, my dear, that the Lord would
water it with the rich influence of his holy Spirit, and produce a
shaking among the dry bones.

"In conclusion, I solicit you will not be uneasy respecting me;
just leave me in the hands of him who hath redeemed your spirit.
Adieu, I weary much to see you, and to talk with you of our
matchless refuge. Your dear loving

"ISABELLA."

Long had weeping endured; but this letter you have
read attests sufficiently, that joy unspeakable had come in
the morning of the glorious day of her believing on him,
who was a light to lighten the Gentiles, and the glory of
his people Israel. The confidence which this letter expresses, according to her own statement already recorded,
was no temporary or occasional feeling; nor was it in any
way allied to that presumption, which often is founded on
the rash conclusions of partial and limited views of God,
and his relationship to his creatures; for grace and peace
were rapidly multiplied to her, "through the knowledge of
God and of Jesus her Lord, according as his divine power
had given to her all things that pertain to life and godliness, through the knowledge of him that had called her to
glory and virtue, her life was now a life of joy. Her soul
walked as a child of light, proving what is acceptable to the
Lord, giving continual thanks unto the Father, who had delivered her from the power of darkness, and translated

her into the kingdom of his dear Son. For he who commanded the light to shine out of darkness, had shone into her heart, to give the light of the knowledge of the glory of God, in the face of Jesus Christ. She was now in a different world of thought and feeling; for the barrier which had enclosed her spirit, and against which she had so long vainly struggled, was removed, and she enjoyed the great freedom with which Christ maketh his children free. She could, indeed, fix upon no particular time, with such precision as to say, that on such a day or at such an hour, she received the truth, by which this great moral revolution was effected in her soul: but she knew that she had once been blind, and now saw; that old things had passed away, and all things had become new. As the morning, from its earliest dawn, is spread upon the mountains; so the light of the Sun of Righteousness upon the dark mountains of error, and doubt, and fear, gradually diffusing, the shadows flee away; and her soul, full of the bright realities of blessed truth, reposes beneath the great day spring, that had visited her from the Most High.

During the whole of the process, which has been briefly detailed, the agency of the Holy Spirit is exclusively apparent. Generally, religious conversations, impressive sermons, or striking incidents are employed, as instruments to excite a concern in careless and unbelieving minds about divine and eternal things. But Isabella, in solitude and silence, avoiding confidential communion with every human being, travelled alone, through depths of sorrow, and fear, and anguish, in pursuit of that, without which she felt it was misery to live: and while so occupied, whatever light or consolation she occasionally enjoyed, it flowed without any human instrumentality directly from the spirit of truth into her afflicted soul. " Did you not think of revealing your mind to any one during this gloomy season, that by Christian advice and instruction, you might be led to look to the Lamb of God for peace, and pardon, and life?" she was once asked; and she replied, "No, sir, I did not; I could not prevail with myself, at that period, to reveal my mind to any one. I continued, as before, to address God in prayer, and to plead for deliverance in the name of his dear Son, from sin, and from the wrath which I saw impending over me." The transaction was, indeed, between God and her soul alone; and from him alone she received what she needed.

This, in truth, more or less, is the experience of all who believe in Jesus,—that God, by his Spirit, is the only teacher, although, in most cases, instruments and occasions are selected, by which may be made manifest his purposes of mercy. She, however, when the friend alluded to, quoted, "all thy children shall be taught of thee, and great shall be the peace of thy children," could, with peculiar propriety, as she did, thus express herself, her eyes filling with tears of joyful gratitude: "Yes, yes, I know from experience, that blessed is the man whom the Lord teacheth, and whose eyes are enlightened by his grace and Spirit: he first subdues and melts the heart with his love; and then, as I have felt in my own case, he keeps alive and cherishes in our souls the sacred flame."

The Hymn.

No more with trembling heart I try
  A multitude of things ;
Still wishing to find out the point,
  From whence Salvation springs.
My anchor's cast ; cast on a rock,
  Where I shall ever rest
From all the labour of my thoughts,
  And workings of my breast.

What is my anchor ? if you ask,
  A hungry, helpless mind,
Diving with misery for its weight,
  Till firmest grace it find ;
What is my rock ? 'Tis Jesus Christ,
  Whom faithless eyes pass o'er ;
Yet there—all sinners anchor may,
  And ne'er be shaken more.

The Scripture.

I WILL be glad and rejoice in thy mercy, for thou hast considered my trouble; thou hast known my soul in adversities—I will greatly rejoice in the Lord, my soul shall be joyful in my God: for he hath clothed me with the garment of salvation, he hath covered me with the robe of righteousness.

What shall I render unto the Lord for all his benefits towards me? I will take the cup of salvation, and call upon the name of the Lord. I will pay my vows unto the Lord in the presence of all his people. Come and hear, all ye that fear God, and I will declare what he hath done for my soul.

God hath called us to peace.

For the Lord taketh pleasure in his people; he will beautify the meek with salvation. Let the Saints be joyful in glory, let them sing aloud upon their bed.

The Lord is my shepherd. He leadeth me in the paths of righteousness for his name's sake. Surely goodness and mercy shall follow me all the days of my life. I will dwell in the house of the Lord for ever.

CHAPTER VI.

WHAT! are the jealous cherubim asleep?
Their swords, ceasing to wave o'er Eden's gates,
Quench'd in their scabbards? Lo! the holy ground,
Where blooms the guarded tree, so lonely once,
Echoes with songs of exil'd Adam's race,
Free from the grave. The Prince of life, they sing
His love—his triumphs; one whom angel hosts,
Ere Eden was, hosanna'd as their Lord.
Could flaming sword of jealous cherubim
Daunt in its path, or from th' immortal fruit
Awe the most timid soul—cheered by the smile
Of such a brother?

THE season for the annual celebration of the holy sacrament of the Supper in the parish was now at hand, which
excited in Isabella, as may well be supposed, far other prospects and feelings, than those which occupied her mind the
year before. She had then looked forward to communion
simply as a means of grace; or, as the performance of a
duty, in the hope of attaining what her soul panted for, of
seeing in the breaking of bread, and in the pouring out of
wine, what she had not yet beheld, the crucifying of the
Lord of Glory for the remission of her sins. It proved, as
we have seen, a vain expectation; the end of that ceremo-
nial observance was vexation of spirit; for she had found in
it no life-giving power, nothing of comfort, nothing of joy;
all was dead, as the elements she had been handling. She
found not the Lord; and had her feelings been vented in
words; in the disappointment that saddened,—that laid
waste and desolate her heart, she would have been saying,

9

" from these elements they have taken away the Lord, and
I know not where they have laid him."

Now, however, believing she had found him whom her
soul loved; being risen with him; conscious of kindred
spirit and affections, she joyfully anticipated communion
with him, wherever he had promised to be present.—Persuaded, as her heart burned within her, while he had talked
with her already in the way, and opened to her the Scriptures, that he would also be known to her, in the remembrance of his love, and the showing forth of his death; she
did not now look forward doubtfully, or in the mere hope of
meeting with her Saviour; but felt as by a sure word of
prophecy, to which she was impelled to take heed, that at
his holy table, he would be most certainly present, and re-
deem all his pledges, by fulfilling all his promises.

It was indeed, though from great bodily weakness little
able to attend, from such a distance, the various services, a
season blessed of the Lord to her soul. I remember to
have spoken with her on the Sabbath evening; and urged
her not to think of returning to Church on the Monday,
since she seemed so feeble; while her cough and breathlessness excited my apprehensions of any exertion that
might increase the malady, which, it was too obvious, had
fairly begun its ravages upon her frame. She returned,
however, on the day of thanksgiving, to give glory to God;
and to worship for the last time in your solemn assemblies.

The state of her health, as well as of her mind, excited
in her sister a strong desire of seeing her, to ascertain precisely the extent of her malady, and examine more clearly
the great and wonderful things which the Spirit of God had
done for her soul; that she might be able, still more inti-
mately, to sympathize with her sufferings and her joys.

Accordingly Mary returned home, and the two sisters met
as they had never met before.

For two years they had had no confidential intercourse

regarding the state of their minds; by conjecture only,
they judged of each other's feelings; each, in her own way,
toiling for deliverance from the greatest of all miseries,
feeling, that the secret of her sorrows could be reposed
only on the bosom of God.

They met; and words can give but little idea of the joy
they felt. They wept, and they sung together. The day
was exhausted in making mention of the righteousness and
love of God. Their mouths were opened to show forth
his praises; while their hearts were filled with a rapture of
blissful gratitude, to which they felt they could give no adequate utterance. They retired to rest, but they could not
sleep. All that night, in prayer and praise, their souls
were poured out like a stream of living water before the
God of their salvation. Truly, in the language of Scripture,
"they fulfilled each other's joy;—being like minded, having the same love, being of one accord, of one mind; having such consolation in Christ, such comfort of love, such
fellowship of spirit, such bowels and mercies together," as
in this world the most tender-hearted sisters but seldom
know; and to which the bosoms, even of the most loving
and devoted, must be strangers, till warmed into the same
ecstacy, by the contemplation of the same King of Glory,
in the beauty of his holiness drawing forth their admiration
and love.

For two years, as has been stated, they had been estran-
ged from each other; although, from childhood, they had
slept in each other's bosoms. They were not so separated
by distance, or occupied by worldly pursuits and cares,
as to have no opportunity of confidential communion; but
the mighty realities of an unseen world, which they were
determined to see, engrossed their thoughts, when awake
and when asleep; and although they loved each other,
they knew that the ties of sisterhood, howsoever dear and
tender, if to be dissolved by death, or consumed by the

fires of the last day, could promise, or secure to them, only a precarious felicity.

The joy of their love, they felt, could only be perpetual, amid all changes of their being, by their knowing that they shared the love of God. Till *that* was attained, they seem to have avoided such confidential intercourse, as by endearing themselves to each other, might have added only bitterness to the affliction of their uncertainty, while harassed and agonized by the fearful possibility of an eternal separation.

Now, however, the fountains of sisterly tenderness so long sealed, were opened; and in the confluence of those waters, so to speak, their souls were refreshed beyond all expression. They felt, as if they had never known before what it was to love. Their affection seemed to have within it an undecaying energy; and while its endearments were purified by an incorruptible principle, its joy was perfected by the blessed hope of uninterrupted and ever increasing rapture of communication amid the beatitudes of eternity.

From that time, they walked in love; in sisterly love preferring one another, as Christ also, they were persuaded, loved them. Amid their various cares and sufferings, they bore each other's burdens; and so fulfilling the law of Christ, remembering the words of the apostle, "Blessed be God, even the Father of our Lord Jesus Christ, the Father of mercies, and the God of all consolation, who comforteth us in all our tribulation, that we may be able to comfort them that are in trouble, by the comfort wherewith we are comforted of God."

With united hearts they now searched the Scriptures together: repaired to them for counsel in all emergencies,—for the solution of all difficulties, and found such delight and refreshment in pondering these true sayings of God, as we may conceive David to have felt, when he thus beautifully expressed himself: "Thy testimonies are my delight, and my counsellors. O how love I thy law! it is my meditation all the day. Thy statutes have been my songs in the house of my pilgrimage."

Upon one occasion, either from some of those misgivings of spirit natural to the soul possessed of an extraordinary felicity, or from some conversation with a Christian friend, who attached undue importance to those dark experiences so often detailed in the lives of believers, as if they were the most decisive tokens of the presence of the Divine Spirit, she was anxious to know, whether the existence of such painful feelings really indicated, or was inseparable from a state of salvation. She was joyful in the believing contemplation of the finished work of her Redeemer, and now unwilling to return to " the spirit of bondage unto fear" and sorrow ; or be again entangled in that yoke, from which she had been so blessedly set free. To the Bible, therefore, she, with her sister, went for counsel, and finding there the fruit of the Spirit, declared to be " love, joy, peace," her soul henceforward magnified the Lord, and rejoiced in God her Saviour, since against her feelings there was " no law."

From this she seems to have concluded, that in all instances unbelief, or want of a realizing faith, must precede spiritual terrors, capable of existing only in the absence of a just view of truth, or entire trust in the all-sufficiency of the remedy, which God has provided for diseased and miserable souls.

With regard to her own case, her judgment was very decided. For example, she, had occasionally kept a diary during the season of her darkness and agony. This, after the knowledge of the truth had filled her soul with light and joy, she committed to the flames, from a persuasion, as she afterward declared, that it was a mere record of sin and unbelief. Her sister expostulated with her, entreating her to save it ; but her resolution was fixed, and with great

9*

solemnity of manner, she thus justified its destruction:—
" Why should I preserve what is so dishonouring to God ?"
There was nothing now, indeed, in her experience, similar
to what it detailed. All was different. The sequestered
garden, so long the scene of mental conflicts, of sore temptations, of agonizing devotions, now witnessed other feelings and exercises. Isabella, solitary, fearful, and miserable, by day and night, had often been there, without comfort in prayer, without light from Scripture, careless of
human sympathy, and ignorant of God's ; but now, with a
companion of kindred views, confident in the faith of the
gospel, glad with its hopes ; on the very spot of so many
awful remembrances, is anointed with the " oil of joy for
mourning," and clothed with the " garment of praise for the
spirit of heaviness."

Her health having rallied a little, she accompanied her
sister to Falkirk, for the purpose of acquiring some knowledge of millinery, in the hope that she might, with Mary,
be able to do something for the support of her destitute
mother and family, should God add to her days. She had
always been of industrious habits ; and now that she had
received the gospel, and laid hold of eternal life, she felt it
more incumbent upon her than ever, to do with all her might
whatsoever her hands found to do. Delicate as her frame
was, " feeble and sore broken by reason of the disquietness of her heart wounded within her," her strength having
gone " like the shadow when it declineth," she was peculiarly alive to the obligation of labouring, however faintly,
and more especially, with such a holy profession, of avoiding the reproach of eating the bread of idleness. She remembered the words of Paul, " We command and exhort
by our Lord Jesus Christ, that with quietness they work,
and eat their own bread :" and when she looked upon her
mother and her sisters, the words of another apostle, " But
if any provide not for his own, and especially for those of

his own house, he hath denied the faith, and is worse than an infidel."

Immediately upon their arrival, however, the prospect of being in this way useful to her family was almost entirely blasted ; for she was taken alarmingly ill, and for some days suffered great agony : so that a speedy death was more probable than a continued life of exertion—that she should never see her mother again, rather than that she should be able to contribute to her comfort.

Since the reception of the truth and enjoyment of its peace and freedom, this was the first crisis, so to speak, of her religious experience; the first trial of that foundation upon which she had rested all her soul's interests for time and eternity : and the foundation, because of God, was not removed nor shaken, but continued steadfast and sure. Her feelings were those of the most triumphant joy. Her mouth was continually filled with the "high praises of the Lord." Often she would say to her sister, "Oh how I long to speak to sinners of the love of Jesus ; I now see this world to be a real desolation ; all men say, what shall I eat, or what shall I drink, or wherewithal shall I be clothed ? O it is painful to think, that men are rolling among God's gifts, and serving the devil. It is painful too that my tongue has been so little employed in telling them of this thing.— Through grace strengthening me I will be silent no long- er. No, I will testify against the abominations that abound. I will tell those around me they are not giving glory to him that made them." She would then repeat the words of John the Baptist, " what he hath seen and heard that he testifieth, and no man receiveth his testimony ; he that hath received his testimony, hath set to his seal, that God is true." " O I cannot live," again she would exclaim, " with- out speaking to sinners of the love of God ; for to-day I feel his words as a fire within my heart ;" she seemed thus to realize somewhat of the feeling of the ancient Prophet, whenconstrained to deliver his burden from the Lord, "His word was in mine heart as a burning fire shut up in my bones, and I was weary with forbearing, and I could not stay;" or of a still more ancient servant of the Lord, " I am full of matter : my spirit within me constraineth me, I will speak that I may be refreshed.—I will open my lips and answer; let me not, I pray thee, accept any man's person, neither let me give flattering titles unto man, for I know not to give flattering titles; in so doing, my Maker would soon take me away."

These are remarkable expressions and sentiments from the lips of so youthful a person, from her earliest childhood diffident and retiring in her manners, and through long mental suffering, still more cautious and reserved in the disclosure of her feelings. What was it that gave her such boldness and zeal? such deep interest in the condition of others?—She had seen a great and wonderful sight, —the love of God in Christ Jesus, " which the angels themselves desire to look into ;" a great salvation she herself had received, and her fellow-mortals, she saw, to the hazard of their everlasting well-being, scorning and rejecting the manifestations of God's glory. Her spirit was stirred up within her, constrained by the love she bore to sinners for her Redeemer's sake, and the value of the good they were despising ; and the diffident and reserved girl felt prepared to speak in the spirit of the Prophets and Evangelists in presence of all the people.

Even at this early period of her religious life, she was deeply impressed with the low state of true piety among the people, notwithstanding the ostentatious bustle and activity of what is called the evangelical world of this country. Young converts are apt to be easily deceived ;—the knowledge, and the reception, and the love of the truth, being creative of singleness of mind, and great charity of feeling, high profession and talkative zeal are laid hold of

without very narrow scrutiny, as presumptive of entire consecration of soul to the cause of truth and God.

The sufferings of Isabella, however, her successive disappointments, her varied delusions, through so long a period of mental darkness, seem to have sharpened her spiritual sagacity and discernment; and fitted her in a peculiar
manner for winnowing the professions and feelings of re-
ligionists.

She knew, from varied experience, how the soul could
be deluded by what seemed its own religious and godly
doings; and thus imagined how much more easy it might
be for the most eloquent even of Biblical or Missionary
Orators, to advocate the cause of their societies than fight
the good fight of faith, in struggling to chain some besetting sin, or to extract from its deepest root of bitterness
some secret corruption. Her heart, indeed, sunk within
her, notwithstanding what she read in Registers and Chroni-
cles; or heard from others of what seemed to be going on
throughout Christendom. To her feelings, one day, she
thus gave free vent, and exclaimed when sitting by her
sister, "O that the Lord would pour out his Spirit upon
this land, for it is a land of darkness and deceit! Men think
themselves alive, and they are still dead in trespasses and
sins. All think themselves Christians, but alas! few there
are who worship God in the spirit, rejoice in Christ Jesus,
and have no confidence in the flesh. O that God would
raise up another Whitefield, to testify boldly to the truth
as it is in Jesus, one who would glory in being conformed
to Christ in reproaches and in persecutions. Something
must be wrong, things cannot be right, when people, in
general, are so well pleased with what is told them concerning their state.—This is a subject, since I knew the
Lord, which has occupied me very much, viz. Why were
men so enraged at the preaching of Christ and his apostles,
and so well pleased with the preaching of the present day?

Is it because there are more Christians now than there were
then ? Is it because men's hearts are now better ? That
cannot be. Is it because smoother things are prophesied.
O that the Lord would glorify himself in Israel !"

It was indeed very natural for her so to meditate ; and
the questions she propounded to herself, are well worthy
of the grave consideration of the fathers and teachers of
Christian wisdom, who lift up their voices amid crowds of
admiring hearers, and whose ears are familiarized from
day to day to idolatrous eulogiums. Is it because true
things are spoken ? because God is glorified and man
abased ? In ancient times what did the people say ? " To
the seers, see not ; to the prophets, prophesy not ; speak
unto us smooth things ; prophesy deceits." Is the world
changed ? Have the people renounced their love of error ?
Are they deceived ? or do they understand what they hear ?
The judgments of charity are very pleasing, but often very
false. The greatest of all teachers was crucified for saying what was true ; and the men that constrained Paul to
receive divine honours, on account of his eloquence, stoned
him almost to the death on account of his doctrines. Can
the truth of God excite the admiration and love of carnal
hearts ? Judge ye.

The state of the world, at this time, and the little real
godliness manifested in any rank or condition of life, did,
with intense interest, engross her mind. Her anxiety for
the salvation of souls, radiating, so to speak, from her own
family and kindred, embraced all of the same flesh and
blood. Often during the night she would say to her sister,
" Arise, dear, and pray : it does not do for you to take rest
all night, when immortal souls are perishing around you.
I have been pleading for hours, and do not feel much weakened ; such an influence of God has been poured into my
soul as constrains me to plead for sinners, and more especially for unbelieving relations, with strong crying and

tears. O that I could weep day and night, until I see them
all relinquishing the service of Satan for the sweet blessed service of God!" Thus she expressed herself, for
she felt that however outwardly correct and moral any of
them might be, an inward spiritual change, as she herself
had experienced, was alone decisive of the life of God ;
for, as she said to her sister, "We were long esteemed
Christians when we were no Christians. Now we are in
very deed begotten to a lively hope by the resurrection of
Jesus Christ from the dead ; let us see that we walk as
Christians. I am often troubled, lest either of us should
give occasion to the enemies to blaspheme. O it is well,
that God has promised to walk in us and dwell in us, else
we should stumble and fall. Hold up our goings, Lord."

Such was the state of her mind during her short residence at Falkirk with her sister.—Her bodily suffering did
not affect her mental joy. While her joy was chastened
by such godly jealousy of herself, and intense anxiety for
others, as attested how far she had advanced already in
the Divine life ;—how much of wisdom as well as of love,
of humility as well as of joy, characterized her habitual feelings; for, while she often exclaimed, "O the riches of
divine love! my Creator, my Redeemer, my Sanctifier,
my All ; I am lost in Thee !" language expressive of the
most triumphant assurance ; she would likewise frequently
urge upon Christians the necessity of being sober, filled
with gravity ; seeing there was so much within and without them, to create and perpetuate a lowly broken-heartedness of spirit : thus manifesting the utmost caution, and
humility, and self-abasement, although feeling consciously
secure in her holy condition. Indeed, from the beginning
of her confidence towards God, there was apparent in her
mind a continual jealousy, lest she should be betrayed even
into a momentary indifference to the requirements of his
holy law, or by any inconsistency, in appearance or reality,

cast reproach upon that blessed relationship, which she scrupled not now to declare existed between God and her soul.

Having somewhat recovered, it was deemed expedient that she should return home,—a trial to both sisters after a season of such holy and happy communion. She had completely overcome her reserve, and by day and night had poured into Mary's bosom, most confidentially, the knowedge of all her feelings both of sorrow and joy. At all fit and convenient seasons, she spoke of the great things that had been done for her soul; and often during the night watches she could not sleep for gladness,—her heart wakeful with melody to the Lord. She rose from time to time to vent it in hymns and spiritual songs : mingling, as we have seen, vehement and importunate prayer for others, for the progress of the truth, for the diffusion of the knowledge of salvation among all for whom Christ died. While her soul was anointed with the oil of gladness, her bodily disease, although its virulence seemed somewhat rebuked, was continuing its progress; and return to her native air was considered necessary, both by her sister and herself. The night before they parted, notwithstanding the trial, she felt pretty strong, and prayed much for Mary; and particularly, that she might be holy in all manner of conversation and conduct. Almost the whole night was spent in devotion by the sisters. At breakfast she appeared deeply solemn, while she spoke of their parting with much composure. She said among other things to Mary, "I must tell you in much love, that there are many things about you that I could wish different. These I have prayed God to remove, and believe he will remove them. One of them I must particularly mention, for I conceive it to be of much importance. The other night I saw you much distressed to find out the meaning of a passage of Scripture, and instead of retiring, and soliciting the Lord to reveal it

to you by his Spirit, you struggled to understand it yourself.
Now be humbled when I tell you, you are depriving God
of his glory, and yourself of much happiness." She then
bade her farewell, adding with much tenderness and affection the apostolic benediction, "May grace be multiplied
unto you." The intercourse of these few weeks, of such a
kind as has been described, would, in itself, at any time,
and under any circumstances, have been productive of much
blessedness. The confidential intimacy of two sisters who
love each other in the bonds of the gospel, even the most
exquisite tenderness of mere natural affection can give no
idea of. They love not merely in health and sickness, in
joy or sorrow, in poverty or riches, in life or death—but
for eternity. These two sisters so loved; and the contrast
of their present condition with so long a period of reserve,
of distance, and of mystery, added unspeakably to its blessedness. Each formerly had her doubts, and fears, and
anguish, without daring to entreat the other's sympathy.
Now, their thoughts, their feelings, their desires, mingled
with each other; and seemed to flow onward in one de-
lightsome path of love and joy, beneath the holy smile of
their heavenly Father, not imputing to them their trespasses; and looking away, so to speak, by his very graciousness, the darkness that had so long and deeply settled on
their minds.

I happened to be on the Greenock quay when she landed from the steam-boat. I was struck with her changed
appearance, from the time I had seen her last, although
then she had seemed so weak and emaciated. We only exchanged a few words. I saw she was under the influence
of emotion, of which, however, till afterward, I did not
know the cause. Within a few paces stood the Minister,
whom God, when she was first admitted to the communion,
had honoured, as the instrument of so much peace to her
mind. When she saw him, as she afterward said, she
10

could have clasped him to her bosom; nor did she ever feel, as she then felt, so strong and vehement a desire to speak to any human being, and make known to him the joyful gratitude of her soul, for having received from his lips such a word of consolation,—which the Spirit had so effectually sealed. He knew not whither, or into what heart, the words which he had uttered had been carried; but this shall not have been recorded in vain, should any servant of the Lord, heavy and sorrowful of heart, because he sees not his Master's work prospering in his hand, take good courage, and cease not to believe, that not one word which he utters, in the name and by the authority of God, although he see it not, will return void, or without accomplishing " that whereunto it is sent."

Isabella remained some days at Greenock in the house of a religious friend, to whom she had brought letters of introduction from a devout lady at Falkirk. At this season she experienced peculiar enjoyment; she had found one to whom she could unbosom most confidentially her feelings, because apparently possessed of a kindred spirit glowing with love to the Redeemer. With the exception of her sister, she had not yet found a believer to whom she could fully unfold her mind.—But the frank and affectionate manner of Mrs. ——— induced a disclosure of her previous history, of the ways by which her Father had led her from death to life, and opened her eyes upon the glories of the truth, as it is in Jesus. She portrayed to her, with great depth and tenderness of feeling, the workings of her mind from her earliest age; her general indifference, her occasional convictions and anxieties, her conflicts, trials, and agonies, her peace and joy in believing. Her shyness and diffidence were laid aside, her eyes beaming as with divine light, and her whole countenance full of emotion, she burst forth into the most eloquent expressions of joy and gratitude, in reviewing the wonderful love of God to her

soul. Mrs. ——— describes her disclosure more as be-
interesting, more especially, as it was obvious that there to
emotions which filled her soul constrained her as by restless energy ; so that she could not but magnify the Lord,
and rejoice in God her Saviour. It surpassed her own conceptions of religious joy, even although her experience had
not been very limited among a believing people ; while to
herself it was a blessed refreshment in the land of her pilgrimage, so to see and hear of the marvellous doings of the
Lord. From that evening they were in possession of each
other's secrets ; and although they had never been together
before, their intimacy was like that of an ancient friendship ; and why ? because beings and things not of time, but
of eternity, gave interest to their intercourse, in the knowledge and love of which originate those intimacies which
are not affected by the vicissitudes of life and nature.

Isabella enjoyed, while with her friend, opportunities of
seeing many who seemed to delight themselves in the
Lord ; to whom the glory of their Redeemer's name appeared an object of the deepest interest, and who professed
to have, amid a crooked and perverse generation, a kindred joy in tracing his power and love in the manifestations
of redeeming grace.

The night before she left Greenock, she spent with a
relative. Next morning she called upon Mrs. ———, to
bid her farewell. Her words, although expressive, were
but feeble signs of what reigned, and shone, and enraptured
within. " O what a night," said she, " have I spent, meditating on the precious truths we heard last evening, (alluding to the religious exercises she had engaged in with some
other Christians,) and particularly on the Paraphrase with
which we concluded. I have been feasting on it all night."
The hymn she spoke of is very beautiful. I insert it, and
the more particularly, as ever afterward it was more pro-

could ha... *intensely great*... as a... ...er mind, of dilightful and con-

...ese glorious spirits shine,
...heir white array ?
...y to the blissful seats
...ing day ?

...are they from sufferings great,
...me to realms of light;
... blood of Christ, have wash'd
Those robes which shine so bright.

" Now with triumphant palms they stand
  Before the throne on high ;
And serve the God they love amidst
  The glories of the sky.

" His presence fills each heart with joy,
  Tunes every mouth to sing ;
By day, by night, the sacred courts
  With glad hosannahs ring.

" Hunger and thirst are felt no more,
  Nor sun with scorching ray ;
God is their sun, whose cheering beams
  Diffuse eternal day.

" The Lamb that dwells amidst the throne,
  Shall over them preside ;
Feed them with nourishment divine,
  And all their footsteps guide.

'Mong pastures green he'll lead his flock,
  Where living streams appear ;
And God, the Lord, from every eye
  Shall wipe off every tear."

She then spoke of the realities of eternity, and of the
blessedness there, in entire freedom from sin, in being for

ever with the Lord. She spoke also of her departure as being at hand; while her whole soul burned with desire to be conformed to the divine image of him whom she had found, to her soul, the chief among ten thousand. She seemed, as if willing to exhaust her whole strength in descanting upon these topics; still another thought would spring up; still a new burst of feeling would swell from her heart. Her state is well expressed by the friend, with whom she had this interview, in the following extract from her letter.

"Although her time was expired, she could not go away, her heart was so full of the subject. By faith she entered within the veil, and was unfolding the glories of the upper sanctuary; drawing largely from the fountain head of spiritual life. She seemed almost to forget her connexion with earth, and left me, saying, We shall not meet in all likelihood, till we meet around the Throne; there will be no separation in those holy regions. How different then our exercises; then singing with new and increased delight, 'Worthy is the Lamb that was slain, to receive all glory and blessing.'"

She crossed the Clyde from Greenock, never again to return. Although she conceived her decease to be at hand, she was not, however, so soon to die. For many days, she was still to live to the glory of her heavenly Father; and in the peaceful solitude of Fernicarry, to advance from one degree of grace and glory to another, in conformity to the holy image of Him who is the first-born among many brethren.

The following account of her feelings is from an extract of a letter, written to Mary a few days after her arrival, dated 7th September, 1825.

"My dear, dear sister, I arrived here on Wednesday. I have enjoyed pretty good health since. My cough still troubles me a little; but I think it will soon wear away. I cannot, my dear sister, inform you how kind the Lord has been to me, since I left you. Did we trust more implicitly to him, what peace of mind

10*

would we enjoy amid all our perplexities! O may it be our meat
and our drink to glorify him; for surely he hath done great things
for our souls. Yes, while others are allowed to follow after the
perishing vanities of the world, he enables us to live in some measure above them. He hath disclosed to us the beauty and comeliness of Jesus. O may our mouths be filled continually with his
praises, and may we glory in nothing but the cross of Christ. O
praise the Lord, praise his name for all his kindness to unworthy me,
who am always grieving him, and straying from him. Adieu; my
kind love to all my Christian friends. Praying that you may enjoy
much of the heart-reviving presence of your glorious Redeemer, by
abiding in the light, I remain, my dear, dear sister, your loving
sister,   ISABELLA CAMPBELL."

The view which this gives of her health is rather favourable; but I am persuaded, she had been led so to express
herself, partly to sooth her sister's anxieties; for when
I first visited her, which must have been shortly after the
date of the letter, the malady had obviously fixed itself too
deeply in her system to admit any probable hope of recovery.—She coughed frequently, and her pale emaciated
countenance, occasionally brightening with hectic bloom,
seemed as an index of the will of God, that she was not
long to linger in the house of her pilgrimage : at all events,
it was not likely that her days should have been so multiplied before her translation to glory. Nothing particular
occurred at this, or even at a subsequent interview; for
the secret history of her mind, as has been already detailed,
was then unknown to me. Circumstances had prevented
those disclosures necessary to confidential intercourse;
and we parted, after some brief devotional exercise, and
general conversation on the importance of a religious life.
It was about the end of October, when her disease had
so increased as to confine her chiefly to bed, that she first
unfolded to me the condition of her soul; making known
to me her confidence towards God, which, as on a sure
foundation, she rested on the knowledge and belief, that

the blood of Jesus was shed for the remission of sins; and the gratitude which engrossed her in contemplation of the gift, so unspeakably precious! of his own eternal Son.

I remember my own impressions at this time more distinctly then Isabella's details: how such maturity of faith, —such enlarged knowledge of divine things,—such delicate holiness of feeling,—such weanedness from worldly interests,—such longings for the heavenly blessedness and glory, as her whole conversation and demeanour expressed, inspired me with no small surprise and joy. I had known of her seriousness, and attention to the things of religion; but I was not prepared for the disclosures of a spirit, although dwelling in a decaying tabernacle, so possessed by the powers of the world to come, as to feel habitually its only joy in the contemplation of the invisible realities of eternity.

I have said that I was joyful: indeed, when one disclosure after another only unveiled a greater beauty of holiness,—a still more wonderful work of the grace of God, I had a joy with which a stranger could not intermeddle. I could not help, in returning along that sequestered shore, giving glory to God in her; feeling, as if I knew not sufficiently, to adopt the words of Paul, how "to render thanks to God for her, for all the joy, wherewith I joyed for her sake before God." But, my beloved people, what a scene would any parish exhibit in this dark, and polluted world, were the minister and *all* his flock to interchange those blessed and holy sympathies, so beautifully expressed by the same apostle to the Philippians, "I joy and rejoice with you all, for the same cause also do ye joy and rejoice with me."

The Hymn.

That "I am thine, my Lord and God;
Sprinkled and ransomed by thy blood,"—
  Repeat that word once more!
With such an energy and light,
That this world's flattery nor spite
  To shake me never may have power.

Yes, my dear Lord, in following thee,
Not in the dark uncertainty
  This foot obedient moves;
'Tis with a Brother and a King,
Who many to his yoke will bring,
  Who ever lives, and ever loves.

Now then my Way, my Truth, my Life!
Henceforth, let sorrow, doubt, and strife,
  Drop off like autumn leaves;
Henceforth, as privileged by thee,
Simple and undisturbed be
  My soul, which to thy sceptre cleaves.

Let me my weary mind recline,
On that eternal love of thine,
  And human thoughts forget;
Child-like attend what thou wilt say;
Go forth and do it while 'tis day,
  Yet never leave my sweet retreat.

The Scripture.

BLESSED is the man unto whom the Lord imputeth not iniquity, and in whose spirit there is no guile.

Blessed is the people that know the joyful sound; they shall walk, O Lord, in the light of thy countenance ;—In thy name shall they rejoice all the day: and in thy righteousness shall they be exalted.

With my whole heart have I sought thee : O let me not wander from thy commandments. Thy word have I hid in my heart, that I might not sin against thee

My heart is fixed, O God; my heart is fixed.

The mountains shall depart and the hills be removed : but my kindness shall not depart from thee, neither shall the covenant of my peace be removed, saith the Lord that hath mercy on thee.

Doubtless thou art our Father—our Redeemer ; thy name is from everlasting.

To whom shall we go ? thou hast the words of eternal life.

CHAPTER VII.

'Tis a deep joy, beyond the flickering clouds,
To see the far off heavens dappled with worlds,
So peacefully serene in glory.—But
Higher still, from earthen cares, and fears, and woes,
Within the blessed sanctuary veiled
By the heaven of heavens itself, repose
The thoughts, the hopes, the joys of new-born souls.

FROM this period, whatever time we spent together was exclusively occupied about these realities; what had made them her own; what the object of her love, and origin of her joy. I had no hesitation in speaking to her of death, and the unchangeable conditions beyond it; for whatever might be her hopes of recovery, the probability of dying excited no emotion, but such as tranquillized and made happy, instead of agitating or distressing her mind. She had not, indeed, attained those elevations of thought and feeling, for which she was afterward so singularly remarkable; but, certainly, she was so persuaded of her safety, that neither life nor death could intermeddle with her blessedness. Although her constitutional diffidence still modified the expression of her feelings regarding her state and prospects; as every successive interview disclosed to me more and more of her mind, I had no doubt of her fitness, while she herself seemed to have none of her willingness, to die.

The following extract from a letter to her sister, written early in November, shows, whatever might be the result of her disease, the obligations by which she felt her spirit to be constrained, whether in this, or in the world to come.

" I cannot, my beloved sister, give you a very favourable account of my health. I am much weaker since my return from Greenock, and easily exhausted. I hope, however, that you will not grieve yourself about me; I have very little pain, and if my cough was removed I might soon get well again. Our God is still very kind to me. O let us exalt his exalted name, let us dread to disoblige him.—O, I think Christians should be doubly careful to watch and pray, that they may be preserved from temptation. I know, my dearest sister, you pray much for me. O pray perpetually that I may be quite devoted to God, that I may glorify him in all things, that I may be entirely weaned from the things of time. I ardently desire to live more indifferent to them than I have ever yet done. I hope, by the kind permission of our merciful heavenly Father, we shall soon enjoy the sweet privilege of conversing of these delightful things in a verbal manner, and chant together the triumphs of redeeming love. O my sister, how changed our condition ! formerly heirs of wrath in common with all unbelievers, now expectants of fulness of joy and pleasures for evermore ! O Saviour, thou hast indeed triumphed gloriously. O Mary, when I endeavour to review those seasons of dark perplexity which we have witnessed, those hours of unutterable agony which we have passed; when the sight of each other's countenance was a terror to us, because *there* we saw depicted much of that misery which reigned within our tortured hearts: O when I contrast this with the state of feeling we now enjoy, I am immersed in wonder and gratitude ? O Jesus, cause me to prove the sincerity of these emotions, by a life singularly devoted to thy service.

" You must not, my dear Mary, come home, (God willing !) without seeing my dear, dear Mrs. ——. You are bound to inquire for her, because she is one of Christ's dear followers, and so part of yourself; and besides, I am aware you will give many thanks unto our God, for having permitted you an interview with this dear happy saint. O, how I love her!—how fondly I love her in our Prince of Peace.—A —— spoke of coming over when you came; she is a sweet girl; O that God would make her his own. I thought she had some faint views of her lost situation, when I last saw her.

" I have only written the last page of this letter and feel quite exhausted. Adieu, grace, grace be with you, my dearest sister,

'ISABELLA CAMPBELL."

For several weeks, her weakness, as well as her pain, so increased, her disease approaching one of those crises which periodically subjected her to such intense bodily suffering,* that her mother felt it necessary to send for Mary; who immediately left Falkirk, to witness, as she anticipated, the departure of her beloved sister. What occurred upon her arrival, she has thus detailed, and which I transcribe from her notes.

"When I entered Isabella's apartment, she welcomed me with a sweet smile, and holding out her hand, said, ' O dear, come and bless God, because I have seen you, before being called home. I am going even to my Father's house. It is true, I am unacquainted with disembodied spirits; but Jesus reigns there in his holy human nature: this Jesus is my trust, what have I then to fear ?' I remarked, she was weak.—' O yes,' she said, ' my body is fast decaying. I am weak, but it is only in the outer man. My soul is nicely fed, even as with marrow and fat.' When she had uttered these words, she shut her eyes, and clasping her hands together, exclaimed, 'Thou art a holy, holy, holy God, I adore thee; thou art a kind, kind Father and Redeemer, I reverence and love thee. O preserve this spirit, which thou hast redeemed, until the day of Christ Jesus. O Jehovah, my God, I commit it unto thee.' After this she lay for some time quite silent, seemingly lost in admiration. I approached her and said, What are you seeing ? Gazing sweetly upon me, she said, ' O my love, I was just by the aid of the Spirit viewing the glorious harmony of the glorious plan. Truly it is divinely finished !—it hath pleased the Father, and well may it please me.'

" She suffered much during the night from pain and weakness, but manifested great contentment, and would often say, 'The conflict will soon be over, I have not far to journey now. Jesus by his Spirit shall lead me on. O Mary, Jesus is a Divine Saviour. He is God; this is my joy and confidence.' Next morning when

*Her disease was not the ordinary form of tubercular consumption, but consisted in the successive formation of large ulcers on the lungs—which in Isabella's case periodically matured in about six or eight weeks. The intervals of comparative ease she enjoyed, occurred after the discharge: and then she sometimes seemed so convalescent as to afford to herself and others the prospect of recovery.

I asked how she was, she said, 'I am very weak, but very well; but O I am vexed at my ingratitude. Any thing is easily borne but sin; yea, bodily suffering is nothing, when compared with anguish of spirit on account of sin. O Lord, cleanse me, cleanse me, cleanse me. I wish my dear, dear Mr. —— would come to-day. I have a great deal to tell him. I am sure it would animate him to hear what the Lord is doing for my soul; and O I wish to make him happy, for my affection for him is great; but I am going to solicit blessings in the name of Jesus: will you retire for a little and watch for dear Mr. ——'s coming, for I have a strange desire to see him to-day.' "

Whenever her heart felt with peculiar liveliness the great goodness of her heavenly Father, she laboured, as with intense desire, to make it known to such as could sympathize with her feelings; her natural manner was then exchanged for an open, ingenuous, and confidential air. Anxious she seemed, as it were, to make her very soul visible, that she might be the helper of their joy. It was the overwhelming love of the Father that possessed her,—and that love, firing her with desire for his glory, made her tell of all she knew and felt, that others, seeing what he had done for her soul, might join in her hymn of thankfulness.

"A few nights after this, when sitting by her bed, she said to me: 'My dear sister, are you willing to part with me? Do you think you could rejoice at my exit from earth?' I said, I hoped God would prepare me for the trying event. 'O,' she said, 'that will not do, you should be able now to say Thy will be done. Go and pray to God, to enable you to follow my soaring spirit with songs; you know our will should be lost in his. Something is wrong, when the Christian cannot rejoice in all the dear dispensations of his Father's providence.'"

This sentiment was not uttered by an individual in the season of health and enjoyment, when it is easy to think correctly, and speak wisely regarding what is becoming in the object of God's afflictive dispensations. We then see, without difficulty, what ought to be; but when the visitation comes, alas! how seldom is the feeling experienced that ought to be cherished,—that feeling expressed by David when he says, " I esteem all thy precepts, concerning all things, to be right." Upon the present occasion, however, Isabella was herself the sufferer ; and in the counsel she give to her sister, she only declared what she habitually realized. In this matter she exercised a most godly jealousy over her feelings. She was not satisfied as to the entireness of her resignation to the divine will, unless consciously thankful for every pang that thrilled through her frame.*

The epithet she uses, "dear dispensations," is sufficiently decisive of her state of mind, which was not occasional but habitual; not at seasons of feverish excitement, but at all times, whatever changes occurred in her feelings, never, so far as I could judge, from my own observation, as well as the report of others, did she receive what befell her but with grateful joy. Indeed, to the examination of them all, she ever carried a sense of obligation beyond the expression of all language ; and the conscious reception of the unspeakable gift gave, in her estimation, a dignity and a holiness to even the least of the mercies of God, as she expressed herself upon one occasion, so beautifully illustrative of such a frame of mind, " I shall never be able to tell any person the sweetness I enjoy in the least of God's gifts, because I see the same love that gave his Son, inscribed upon them all."

It is obvious, that the deep persuasion of her having received the greater gift enabled her to receive, in the right

* Her expressions and feelings often reminded me of the memorable declaration of John Chalmers—a deeply interesting youth, who died a few years ago in a different part of the parish, after a long season of varied and excruciating suffering:—"Do you know, Sir, that every pang that pierces through this corrupted body of mine, gives me just a new glimpse of God's goodness."

spirit, whatever God bestowed. To think that you are thankful for any thing, so long as your hearts are not moved with gratitude for that *one thing needful*, without which nothing at all could have been enjoyed, would argue total ignorance of the spirit, and design of Scripture; which the first promise to the last, directly or indirectly, declares that by one thing all others consist, and are conveyed to man. Whosoever, therefore, presumes to give glory to God in the enjoyment of his mercies, and yet knows nothing of the enjoyment of the unspeakable gift, knows not what he is saying or doing. He sees not any mercy in the way God wills it to be seen, and he has not acknowledged by his gratitude, that which renders possible gratitude for the rest.

Her views of the love of God to sinners, were uniformly accompanied with the conviction of especial love to herself. Indeed it was this, that enabled her to have any just conceptions at all, of the nature of divine love, to any. She contrasted often, the unutterable agonies of her state of darkness with the light and peace she now enjoyed, as you see in her letter to Mary; and her heart melted away with ineffable raptures of thankfulness: her joy was full; but yet, never was it separated from a sense of her own guilt and vileness. I remember, indeed, distinctly, the reply, which, about this time, or soon after these recorded conversations with her sister, she gave to the question, "What showed her most her own sin?" "My assurance of the love of God. That shows me in every sinful thought such impious and godless ingratitude, and then I feel most melted into grief, for its continuance." "What," said I, "does not the contemplation of God's love give you perfect peace?" "My greatest peace," said she, "arises from the contemplation of the divine holiness." "How so?" continued I. "Because," she replied, "I see then most clearly the all-sufficiency of Christ, for so holy a being could not accept any thing less than a perfect sacrifice. O yes, it must have been a covenant ordered in all things and sure for those he loves."—The solemnity, with which she expressed this sentiment, I very well remember; followed, as it was, on her part, as well as my own, by a silence best fitted for cherishing the thoughts to which it naturally gave rise. The word she expressed to her sister regarding the gospel scheme, " the glorious harmony of the glorious plan, truly it is divinely finished!" were in perfect accordance with such a sentiment : for that is a divinely finished plan indeed, by which the love of God shows man his sinfulness, the holiness of God shows him his security: so that throughout all ages, even when time shall be no more; when love shall have triumphed in the perfected redemption of a lost world; within the gates of the Heavenly Zion, the same words will suit, which, at the dedication of the house of David, burst from the lips of the worshippers, —" Sing unto the Lord, O ye Saints, and give thanks at the remembrance of his holiness." It must be so. Whosoever finds in the contemplation of God's love, rest, and peace, and joy only, had well carefully scrutinize his feelings, lest they be excited by erroneous views of the Eternal Majesty ; representing him as actuated by a mere tender affection, melting into compassion, and stretching forth his hand only at the impulse of pity, that guilty men may cease to fear, and take to themselves rest; as if his eye looked not on their guiltiness. The Eternal is not a being of mere emotion, but of unchangeable and untainted righteousness, and there is a law which his whole universe knows, " the pure in heart alone can see God,"—and the eye must behold him glorious in holiness, to measure in any way the depths of his love.

Isabella's views were most consistent upon this fundamental principle, as may be seen, from the confidence which the knowledge and belief of Christ's divinity gave

11*

to her hopes of salvation. Upon the doctrine of his divinity—the mystery of godliness, her soul stood, as it were, beholding the holiness of God. The pardon of sin, she felt, might manifest love, but the way it was thus pardoned, could alone guarantee the removal of it from her soul, which she felt to be the only desirable salvation. In the shedding of the blood of the Son of God; in this sacrifice of himself, did holiness seem so gloriously manifested, that the continuance of inward sinfulness, which she deplored, never made her fear; since she saw its entire and final destruction predicted in the death of the Holy One Incarnate. These views she felt, however, were not to be occasionally, but permanently present. Her confidence, indeed, was the meekest and humblest and wisest you can possibly imagine. In proportion to its strength and consolation, were her views of her sinful condition vivid and melting; and her obligation to be jealous and watchful more binding. "I am a wonder to myself," said she upon one occasion. "O sin, when wilt thou cease to distress this poor heart? Thou and Satan have been busy to-day, in endeavouring to draw me away from Jesus, but he hath helped me; therefore will I praise him, and not be silent. O what great need have Christians to watch and pray, that they enter not into temptation; seeing that their adversary the devil goeth about continually seeking whom he may devour, and they cannot resist him but by looking to Jesus. O my God, strengthen thou me, and I shall be strong."

In the time of her darkness and agony, she had often been assailed by temptations, which, regarding as of Satanic contrivance and suggestion, led her to feel as if the great enemy of souls were in her very presence.—At such moments, when engaged in her labours of devotion, in her garden, or elsewhere, she has sometimes, through a certain preternatural fear, looked round, as if suspicious of

the visible appearance of the cruel adversary. When without knowledge or communion with God, it may be easily
imagined how such a fancy, originating in painful excitement, would increase her disquietude and agitation of spirit.

Although now, she had very different conceptions of the
power of the tempter, and the nature and object of his
temptations ; these still, from their vividness of power, assumed the aspect of a personal agency. "O," said she,
upon one occasion, to a Christian friend, "I have had a
sore conflict with the Prince of Darkness since I saw you ;
he attacked me the other night with fearful violence. O
what a vile fiend he is ; I was so tortured with his vile
suggestions, that I could not lie one minute in the same
position. I tossed till near morning, without being able
to do any thing more, than implore the Lord to rebuke
him, and endeavour to keep looking to Jesus. Our God
did at last rebuke him, by bringing to my recollection these
sweet words, 'There hath no temptation taken you, but
such as is common to man ; but God is faithful, who will
not suffer you to be tempted above that ye are able, but
will with the temptation also make a way to escape, that
ye may be able to bear it.' Yes, this was the weapon, the
powerful weapon that put him to flight, and made my soul
return to its quiet rest. O my soul, bless the Lord."

Upon another occasion, I remember, she expressed herself to me in a similar manner. " Long, long I struggled
in the agony of my soul. Get thee behind me, Satan, I
cried, but in vain. I found out at once, however, the error and the remedy ; for when the passage, 'Greater is
he that is in you than he that is in the world,' was brought
home to me, I prevailed, and found peace. God's power
was manifested in me all the while, although I knew it
not, thinking I had been struggling alone."

She was in the habit of most minutely inspecting and
watching, how her faith was bearing upon her thoughts and

feelings. She thus knew well what manner of spirit she was of; and what were the workings and devices of sin's deceitfulness within her. Undisturbed by outward cares; and not at this period, as afterward, in the habit of seeing many people, she was placed in the most favourable circumstances for acquiring useful knowledge of herself, and checking the very first beginnings of any sinful thought or desire. She already, as it were, occupied the highest vantage ground for this exercise. She watched, and resisted, and strove to extirpate appearances of evil: not that she might attain to a holy condition, or secure the favour of him who is of purer eyes than to behold iniquity, and whom the pure in heart alone can see ; but as it became one, already persuaded of her holy condition, and of the love of God and her Saviour. In the realization of what she did not doubt, consisted the continuance of the holiness she loved. The strength, or variety of temptations excited no suspicion of her safety ; while they never permitted her vigilance to sleep, always vividly portraying the perils of carelessness : fiery darts she often felt them to be, trying her soul's constancy ; but in the shield of faith quenched, each successful result of a struggle made her more confident, while taught wisdom and obedience by the things she had suffered in her way to victory. In all emergencies she went to him, who himself was more than a conqueror ; and who had been in all things tempted as she was, for the very purpose of knowing how, with greater tenderness, to give her succour.

Her looking to him, and realizing in him the promises, secured her triumph. When suggestions were forced into her mind with such power and vividness, as to induce a belief in the direct personal agency of the tempter ; her conscious union with him who had triumphed over the principalities and powers of darkness, making a show of them openly, excluded all fear, distrust, or suspicion from

her mental sufferings; although these often were very severe. Living in deep solitude, where there was little outward variety, her experience included striking contrasts of mental feeling: how different, for example, the experience of another night, from that which has been already recorded. When I asked her, one morning, how she had slept, she replied, that she had not slept at all: upon expressing my regret, " O but," said she, " I had thoughts far sweeter than sleep."—Often, indeed, it was so with her, and deeply would she enter into these scriptures. " In the night his song shall be with me, and my prayer unto the God of my life. Let the saints be joyful in glory; let them sing aloud upon their beds." With her, such feelings were not the result of excitement, or without a rational origin; for at this time when her sufferings were not greatly oppressive, she was constantly, as her eyes were able, pondering on the Bible; and no day passed away without securing from that exhaustless storehouse, refreshments for night's silent watches. Her progress in knowledge of the Divine mind, as unfolded in the blessed word, was singularly rapid. From the distance I could not see her frequently, but when possible, once a week I visited her; anxious, while impressed with the conviction of her speedy departure, to lose no opportunity Providence might afford, of beholding so memorable a manifestation of divine grace. Sometimes, I went on Saturday, finding in her conversation one of the most pleasing preparations for the holy duties of the Sabbath: occasionally, after the conclusion of the service, delighting to witness, in her sequestered chamber, an example of that beauty of holiness which, in the solemn assembly, I had been urging you to seek after and attain. Her Bible was, as I have said, continually with her; and that, we always read together, in less or greater portions; with the offering up of prayers, and the singing of some hymn or spiritual song.

The observations, which she made as I read, were often very interesting; and repeatedly I was thus induced to prolong this part of our exercise beyond my original intention.

Upon one occasion, for example, I commenced the 119th Psalm, purposing to read only a few of its parts; but the interest deepening as I proceeded, we could not pause till we reached its conclusion. I have no distinct remembrance of the greater part, but only a few of her observations, which I assert, in illustration of her manner, as we read the Scriptures together. Thus, at the verse, "Thy statutes shall be my song in the house of my pilgrimage," "O yes," she observed, "if not, he would not now have been able to sing of them. Whatever God says, may well make melody in our hearts." "I will speak of the testimonies also, before Kings, and will not be ashamed," made her eye kindle as with fervent sympathy, and raising herself upon her elbow, she exclaimed, "O what a glorious boldness—even before kings he says he would not be ashamed:" and when I read, "And I will delight myself in thy commandments, which I have loved;"—"Ay," said she, "there it is, his love was strong, and therefore he was bold. His delight in them took away fear." "I know, O Lord, that thy judgments are right, and that thou in faithfulness has afflicted me." "In faithfulness? O how true I feel that to be; without affliction, how could his promises of love be fulfilled. My sufferings have made my cup run over."—"I beheld transgressors, and was grieved, because they kept not thy word." "Yes, that must have been great sorrow to him, when he himself saw such wonders of love in it. I can feel that, in some degree: it is a sore affliction to see the word despised."—"Let my soul live, and it shall praise thee." "He might have added, and it shall have its true blessedness, for how else could he be happy?"

Similar observations and comments might be multiplied

to a great extent. The remembrance of one seemed to
kindle up, and make visible many others ; all expressive of
the common sympathy which she seemed to share with the
the holy writers, and the mind of God, unfolded in the
Scriptures.

While her attainment, in this matter, was very remarkable, and while obviously a pupil of the divine Spirit ; she
laid claim to no sudden, miraculous illumination, for she
was strictly a student of the holy Scriptures. Her mind
was never satisfied, without comprehending the meaning
of any passage, which had attracted her attention ; while
in the counsel, already recorded, which she gave to her
sister, to seek in the interpretation of scriptural mysteries the
Spirit's guidance, she never meant to exclude the necessity
of that diligent search of the revealed word, with which the
God of truth has, at all times, associated advancement in
the knowledge and consolations of the gospel. What she
could not herself comprehend, she was in the habit of requesting her Christian visiters, if they could, to explain ;
often in this manner introducing the subject ; " What do
you think of such a passage ? I don't fully understand it.
I think perhaps it means this, but am not satisfied about
it." And if, at any time, she received what she believed, or
felt to be the true meaning, she experienced a very sensible delight. She did not regard it as the discovery of another's ingenuity ; but gave God the glory, for having imparted to another light, which, primarily, he had not seen fit to
vouchsafe to herself ; but which, as one of his mercies in a
different form, was given her, through a brother, or sister's
instrumentality to enjoy. Thus did she, in every accession,
by whatever means, to her knowledge of the Scriptures, re-
verently give glory to the graciousness of the Father of
lights. Not only did she ascribe all she possessed to him,
although exercising a continual diligence ; but she was in
the habit also, of acknowledging in every feeling or per-

sonal application of the word, the metings out of his sovereign love.

As an instance of this, when longing very much one day to
see a friend whom she dearly loved, and yet not knowing
how the desire could be gratified, the words "Delight thyself in the Lord, and he shall give thee the desires of thine
heart," were frequently present to her thoughts. Very un-
expectedly her friend having visited her, she exclaimed,
"Well, it is wonderful that we should have been permitted,
once more, to meet in the wilderness :—yet I was satisfied
with that assurance, that if it was for his own glory, it would
be so ; I should have the desire of my heart." Her friend
observed, that the passage she alluded to, had been much
on her mind also, and that she saw, howsoever things were
ordered, it would be true in regard to believers,—that, if
the object of their desire was for their own good they would
have it ; if not they would still have their chief desire gratified ; namely, that God's will might be done. Upon this
she seemed greatly delighted, and rejoined, "That's quite
true, it was more than I got ;" meaning that she had not,
in the same way, been able to represent to herself the gratification of her desire, even in the disappointment of her
hope.

When any other thus saw more clearly the import of
any passage, or could apply it to states of mind or conditions of life more comprehensively : she recognised, with
the utmost simplicity and contentment of spirit, their common Father distributing, in various measures, his perfect
gifts of life and comfort. But more especially, she had a
great delight in examining Scriptures with her sister, whose
society she now enjoyed : who never failed, their tastes
and habits being the same, in so blessed a field, to join in
her labours and her sympathies. They were indeed pu-
pils of the same Master, and students of the same school.
As iron sharpeneth iron, so did their intercourse, by the

power of God, sharpen their spiritual discernment. If they confessed to each other, in obedience to the precept, their faults and infirmities, they interchanged also their joyful secret ; and what the one knew, soon became the possession of the other.—Thus, rapid as the progress of Isabella's knowledge would naturally have been, even although so solitary, her sister's society hastened its advancement.

The following extract from Mary's notes illustrates their manner when together ;—showing also how filled Isabella's soul was with the word, and how she pondered upon what she read.

" One day while sitting beside me, she said to me, 'Well, dear, what new wonders have you discovered in God's law to-day ? I have been reading that soon my sun shall go no more down. O what glorious news! I have been meditating upon this passage for some hours past, and so great has been my joy that I forgot I was unwell. What a field of glories is the Bible! but it is only in the light of God's Spirit we can behold them. In thy light we shall see light clearly.' "

Two letters now lie before me, written in February, 1826, from which I insert the folling copious extracts ; as they give an accurate picture of the mode of thinking and feeling, which Isabella and her sister exhibited, at this time, in conversation with such Christian friends as visited them.

"I have just arrived from Fernicarry, where last night I was storm-stayed. I left this, not intending to visit Isabella, having seen her so recently ;—but learning from her sister, that she was considerably worse, I felt a little anxious, and went ; when I found the intelligence was but too true. There has been, (can you help being sorry, although so assured of her translation to glory ?) a return of violent pain and sickness. Having heard from Mary of my intention to see her, before leaving the neighbourhood, she had avoided during the day every thing like effort; anxious to be able to share in the conversation. I found her therefore rather lively, although feeble and suffering much ; while she was in such

12

a delightful frame, that I could not but feel it as selfish and cruel, even to desire to detain her from heaven.

"The evening, as you know, became so tempestuous, that to return home was utterly impracticable—I was thus literally storm-stayed under the same roof with this dear child of the family of Christ. For some hours, I remained with her in her small apartment, which she calls her little sanctuary; and I confess to you, it often seemed to me, as if a glory shone in it, but seldom, if ever seen in the palaces of this world's princes. Many a time, during the evening, I rejoiced in spirit; feeling as if the storm to me was a blessing. We had a long discourse together, regarding religious joy—as contrasted with those dark experiences which believers of a melancholic temperament are apt to regard as the most decisive tokens of a work of grace in the soul. I read a great many passages from the Psalms, the Prophets, and the Apostles, descriptive of joy in believing; and we did indeed make melody in our hearts to the God of our salvation. Isabella seemed already to have her heavenly harp in her hand; while her face looked, so to speak, as she reclined in pain and weakness, all the beatitudes of eternity. What an exquisite delicacy there seems to be in her perception of what is fit and beautiful; and yet, this is not to be wondered at, her own soul being so beautiful through the comeliness which God has put upon her.

"When alluding, for example, to a religious friend who seldom smiled, I happened to remark, that, as well as by other reasons, such solemnity of aspect might be induced by the traditionary report of our Saviour never having been seen to smile. 'I do not think that could be correct,' replied one of those children of the Bible, 'for does not the evangelist describe him as rejoicing in spirit, and a smile must have been at that moment as natural to his holy countenance, as tears were to his eyes when he was weeping over Jerusalem.' 'And would not he smile,' said Isabella, 'when he took the little children in his arms to bless them?'

"The thought is delicate and beautiful, and do you not rejoice in spirit, my dear Sir, when you think of the fine moral perception that dictated such a criticism? A divinity does indeed seem to stir within them, teaching what they could not have acquired by conference with flesh and blood: so investing these sisters with a very rare capacity for all the finer proprieties of thought and feeling. I cannot help remarking as a peculiar circumstance, that in the first book I opened on my return, my eye caught the following passage, so beautifully accordant with Isabella's feeling, that I must transcribe it, to share with you the pleasure I had in its perusal:—

"'Thy embracing Christ, preached to thee in the gospel, will be as welcome news to heaven, I can tell thee, as the tidings of Christ and salvation through him can be to thee. There is joy in heaven at the conversion of a sinner. Heaven soon rings with this. The angels that sang Christ into the world, will not want a song, when he is received into thy heart : for he came into the world for this end. The highest created throne that God can sit on is the soul of a believer. No wonder then, that Christ calls his friends to join with him, at the soul's return to him, and reception of him. What joy there is in heaven, upon this occasion, we may collect from the joy it drew from Christ on earth. It was some great and good news that could bring then a smile from Christ, and tune his soul into a joyful note, who was a man of sorrows, and came into the world to be so ; yet when his disciples returned with news of some victorious success of their labours,—in that hour Jesus rejoiced in spirit, and said, " I thank thee, O Father." Of all the hours in his life, that is the hour, wherein Christ would express his joy; which, with the care of the Spirit to record this passage in the history of Christ's life, shows that Christ had an especial design in that expression of his joy at that time; and what could it be, but to let us know, how much his heart was set upon the work of saving souls ; and that when he should be gone to Heaven, if we meant to send him any joyful news thither, it should be of the prosperous and victorious success which the gospel hath over our hearts. This, this which could make him rejoice in the midst of his sorrows here on earth, must needs be more joyous to him in heaven, now when he hath no bitterness from his own sufferings, which are healed, past, and gone, to mingle with the joy of this news ; and if the kind reception of the gospel be such joyful news to him, you may easily conceive, how distressful the rejection of it is to him. As he rejoiced in spirit to hear the gospel prevail, so he cannot but be angry when it meets with a repulse from the unbelieving world.' "

"I have had another delightful evening with our two friends ; full indeed of lively and well-sustained conversation, upon a great variety of topics connected with the religion of the Bible. We were rather discursive; but uniformly was I constrained to admire the clear and comprehensive views, which these simple and holy maidens have formed, upon subjects of eternal interest to us all. I called them, I believe, in a former letter, children of the Bible,' meaning that their religious views and feelings seemed to be fresh from that fountain—unmixed and unpolluted—from that blessed fountain of truth and holiness;—their thoughts also being but little cast in the mould of human systems, and seldom expressed in the common idiom of theology. But you cannot imagine, till you have some additional conversations with them, how truly, by way of distinction, they merit the title. Their passion for the Bible is excessive; and every principle they have fixed, has been constructed from it with such wisdom and caution, as would astonish the most evangelical of Theologians. They do not attempt to move, you would suppose, either in thought or feeling, without that infallible counsellor; and they do enjoy a very precious freedom from the entanglements of all human authority. Mary was, at times, eloquent, as she contrasted the religion of which she had read in the Bible, with what was exhibited among many of the Christians of the present day. 'I cannot but believe,' said she, 'that the primitive Christians, those to whom the apostles addressed themselves, must have been very different from those I have often witnessed; at least infinitely surpassed them in meekness and simplicity of spirit.' The ostentation often exhibited by individuals, among classes or at meetings of professors, even those who seem to have within them the good seed, was to her a most melancholy kind of mystery, which often deeply affected her; want of charity also, in the judgments of good people, she often lamented.

" ' It is an awful thing,' she continued, with one of those solemn looks which gave to her words sometimes so powerful an expression; ' it is an awful thing to judge others, or to act as if we had passed the last sentence upon them. What would the world become if all Christians were to act so, entirely to separate themselves from the unrenewed; would it not be abandoning those whom we have no reason for believing God has left for ever ?'

" Neither of them was blind to the peril, to which Christain people were exposed, when without sufficient decision they entered the society of the unregenerate; but this only seemed to impose the greater necessity on all who, from their station or peculiar duties, are called upon to mingle much with the world, to be frequent and fervent in prayer for guidance and support. When I was sweeping the floor a few days ago, said Mary, 'I was thinking of this very thing, and the words of David came with great clearness to my mind. It was a great boldness in him to say, 'When thou hast enlarged my heart I shall speak thy word to Kings, and shall not be moved.' 'O it was grand,' said the sweet Isabella; 'he was then afraid of no one, however high and mighty, for he would speak of God's testimonies to Kings and not be ashamed. Now is not that first what we ought to do in the world? I am very sure that what reconciles me to the idea of living, is the belief, that he has something for me to do; I wish I may not be ashamed.' ' Never dream, my dear,' said I, 'that you will find the world a bed of roses. There is a fierce fight of afflic-tion before you, although your body should become as strong as my own; and be assured, that, although feeling as if absolutely free from all grosser and more obvious temptations, Satan will not fail to practise upon your mind. Remember, if possible, he would follow the saints of God even into the third heaven itself, in his cunning and desperate malignity; but go to the Bible—that was the only weapon your Saviour used in the wilderness, and you know the result.' 'O yes, the Bible; if I read at any time other books, they only increase my relish for it.' ' Stange,' said Mary, ' that Christians, when they meet, should talk about any other book.' ' Precious Bible, thou art mine—Holy Bible, book di-vine,' said Isabella, quoting from a hymn she had learned among the children, with an expression, as if the concentrated loveli-ness of the graces which the Bible enjoins and creates, breathed from her mind. ' O, would people but study the Bible; but even Christians destroy the temple of truth; often they leave standing only what suits their tastes. Now, this I cannot get over: we both wonder why it should be so. For example, positive precepts are disregarded: the Saviour requires us to ask to our feasts those that cannot ask us a again. Nothing in the statutes is clearer; but I never hear of the wealthy and opulent Christians asking the poor. O, I feel as if I would have an exquisite delight in sitting among a company of beggars, benefiting by the adoption of this blessed rule. The world is changed, they say; but the world likes none of Christ's rules more than this; reject one, reject all.' Is is not necesary to continue. The paramount authority and influ-ence of the Bible in their mind were very apparent; as also when speaking about young converts, or believers with disquieted minds, applying for directions to ministers and other Christians. I then asked them, if they did not regard it as very perilous to trust any one, to take the opinions or feelings of any mortal, for

12*

a guide or example ? At once they coincided upon this great principle, that no authority is valid but the Bible; and that all counsellors are deceitful, who would not direct the soul, in every emergency, to the Book of God itself. Rules drawn from the Bible, by implication or construction, that are not literally found there, they hold as very dangerous, and liable to deceive. As an illustration of this, one of them mentioned what had occurred to herself. A minister, whom she had heard preach in Falkirk, having laid down a certain test, by which believers were to try themselves; said she to herself, with a trembling heart, ' if that is true, I am gone ; but if not in the Bible I shall be very loth to let go my hold.' She searched to see, but it was not to be found in that infallible record ; and she added, 'I did not lose my peace.' "

From these extracts, in other respects interesting as illustrative of her feelings, it is manifest, how reverentially Isabella regarded the authority of the Bible. What, however, in her mind, gave dignity and importance to every jot or tittle of the record, was this unwavering faith, that divine wisdom in constructing it, had selected the best possible form for the manifestation of the glory of God, in Christ loving sinners ; and her gratitude for what she had received, drew forth such love and reverence towards the blessed Jesus, as led her habitually to ponder upon, and honour whatever fell from his own lips, or was taught by his Prophets and Apostles.

Hence her discriminating knowledge of the meaning of Scripture, which is thus alluded to in a letter written about this time, to a friend.

"In conversation, you would find, she has not merely a command of Scripture, but often she strikes out new light from passages, that commentators never dreamed of ; just as if the intenseness of her feelings guided her far inward ; and she thus beheld what ordinary Christians see but dimly or know nothing of, till the final removal of the veil. From what I have observed in her, there is no question, but that her power of divining the word, in so remarkable a manner, has arisen from the predominance, which the glory and the grace of Christ have occupied in all her meditations. No general idea of his character has satisfied her mind; she has so familiarized him to her soul, that in all her thoughts he is an ever attendant reality. That light of lights leaves no darkness or obscurity in what she looks upon: and thus, the perfection of her spiritual discernment is the result of her intense admiration and love of Jesus; while the reflection of his glory, in the word, by a natural re-action, still more vehemently draws out towards his person all her affections.

"You know that, constitutionally, she is gentle spirited, of a meek temper, with, at the same time, strong affections; stronger than generally belong to such classes of character. For a long period now, the general tenor of her religious experience has followed, a good deal, the analogy of her original frame : a glowing vitality of love to the Redeemer, with a sweet and blissful quietude of soul, arising from the assurance of reciprocal attachment, and a conviction of the unity of their interests, with a secret habitual prophesying of her heart, that they have one eternal home in the house of their common Father ; but occasionally, there are raptures which she feels, were they to continue for any time, would render existence here impossible. Such unutterable joys in the contemplation of the Saviour, and the heavenly condition, that her frail humanity could not endure, and live in this place of strangers."

In this manner, she often expressed herself, so decisive of such a state of mind and feeling. "The name of Jesus is a powerful name ; when understood, it purifies the heart. The natural man sees no excellence in it ; but I say, there is a world of attractions in our Lord Jesus. It is by gazing upon his beauty that we are sanctified. O Lord, keep mine eyes always upon him : I cannot be happy when looking at any thing else."—From the contemplation of Christ's glory and love, as she derived peculiar blessedness, so, it would appear, she often felt as if the cunning and power of her spiritual enemies were put forth to prevent it. One day she seemed very uneasy ; when asked the cause of it, she replied,—"O that vile enemy of souls has been torturing me all this day with his fiery

darts. Fiery! O what a correct name for them, for I have
felt their pain during the past night. He could not endure
to see me feasting so sweetly upon Jesus; and when he
could not succeed in turning my eyes aside, he must needs
harass me with vile suggestions, in order to mar my joy in
the Lord. Indeed I can account in no other way, for every
kind of blasphemous suggestion, than that, by presenting them, he means to start and terrify the Christian,
and so divert his thoughts from the object of worship; for
there are seasons, when, by the mighty influences of the
Holy Spirit, the mind is kept so fixed upon Jesus, that other
ordinary temptations would prove insufficient to make it
wander. How thankful do I feel, that the period is not far
off, when he shall grieve this poor heart no more. Yes,
blessed be God! who giveth us the victory, through our
Lord Jesus Christ. Return unto thy rest, O my soul."

Her joy in thus looking upon Jesus, so envied by the
great enemy of her soul, very obviously arose from two
causes: sometimes from the contemplation of his glorious
excellencies in themselves as altogether lovely; at other
times, of his character as the Redeemer of her soul. I say
nothing, regarding the question, when it becomes possible,
without any reference whatever to the work he hath done
for us, joyfully to meditate on his perfections; but doubtless,
Isabella's mind was capable of either exercise. At one time
she thus expressed herself: " He, the man, who was God's
fellow, is the Mediator of the new and better covenant. It
is a substantial covenant, ordered in all things and most
sure. All is done; he is not in the grave. O no. He is
exalted at his Father's right hand making intercession for
us. Our prayers are heard; yes, and answered too, because they ascend through him. Let us sing loudly unto
him; for he hath borne our griefs: he hath suffered, the just
for the unjust, in order to bring us to God. Our glorious,
powerful Intercessor! thanks be unto God for his unspeak-

able gift! O to see more of his excellencies, and be filled with more ardent affectionate gratitude towards him!"

Upon another occasion she exclaimed to a friend, " I have been so quite overwhelmed with the love of Jesus, since I last saw you, that I was made to cry, O Lord, hold thine hand, or increase my capaciousness. O, I was made to mourn sweetly under the influence of this love ; much deeper mourning, than I had ever experienced at the sight of Sinai's thunders. In this delightful frame I fell asleep, and awoke in the same joyous feeling. Eternally praised be our God, for such rich manifestations of himself and the glories of the heavenly world. Come and extol the Lord with me ; let us exalt his name together." She thus lived in the contemplation of the glory and goodness of God manifested in her Saviour. It was the habit of her soul; she had no other joy :—it was her meat and.drink ; her daily food, the manna given her by her Father. It might seem as if, according to the ordinary way in which God metes out his blessings, a long period had preceded such elevations of soul :—but rapidly she attained to a great height in the divine life ; and thence she went on her heavenly way, above the clouds and darkness that so often obscure the truth in the minds of more aged believers.

An old man, who had long been a follower of Jesus, thus very fitly describes her condition :—" I was particularly struck, every time I saw her, with her progress in holiness :—her rapid assimilation to the image of her Redeemer ; her great, her increasing knowledge in the Scriptures, and her facility in communicating what she thought of Jesus ; her strong views of the horrid nature of sin ; her striking humility, and her fine penetration in discovering the hypocrite and self-righteous professor. Many who have known the truth for twenty years might have sat at her feet and learned." It is very true what the old man said ; from what she spoke, and what she did, the most ex-

perienced of professing believers might have learned wisdom and understanding. They might have learned, above
all, how necessary to secure such blessed attainments, is
the living in the contemplation of the excellent and holy
loveliness of Jesus, and in the exercise of continual prayer.
She had him before her at all times, when awake ; also
when asleep, for then her heart was awake ; and she ceased
not to pray for a portion of his Spirit to herself and others.
We have seen how she looked at her Saviour ; and it is
known to many, and expressions of her own remain, to
attest how she prayed. In all time of her necessity,
she was ever found of one spirit with the apostle, when
thus exhorting the Hebrews:—" Let us therefore come
boldly unto the throne of grace, that we may obtain mercy,
and find grace to help, in time of need." But she did not
merely feel the obligation to pray, which desire of deliverance from any evil imposes ; her delight was in devotion,
and her thoughts were all prayerful. The beautiful description of prayer in Montgomery's Hymn, which we often
read together, excited her liveliest sympathies. In the
lines,

> " Prayer is the Christian's vital breath,
>   The Christian's native air ;
> His watchword at the gates of death—
>   He enters heaven by prayer ;"

she seemed to feel a pecular interest, so vividly portraying,
as they did, what her spirit habitually knew, how essential
prayer is to the very continuance of a believer's life. For
often she would thus express herself:—" Prayer is the
channel, through which food is to be conveyed, for the
nourishing and strengthening of the soul ; the pipe, by
which we draw water from the wells of salvation :" and
upon one occasion, with great emphasis and pathos, she
exclaimed : " O, I love to pray ! were this great privilege

denied, I should soon pine and die." Her prayers were,
obviously, not wrung from her in moments of necessity, as
if reluctantly making known her feelings to God ; but with
sweet filial confidence, poured out into the bosom of her
tender Father. Not only did she thus feel, in her solitary
devotion : when worshipping with others, her joy often
was unspeakable. For example, one night, after she had
parted from a friend, she said to her sister, " O, I am particularly happy. I thought, during prayer, that my soul
would have burst its frail prison and fled up to Jesus.
When shall I evermore behold his dazzling loveliness ! O
when shall I dwell in a peaceful habitation ! I long much
for rest from sin." But in prayer she was not selfish. Her
soul, with deep earnestness and sympathy, thought of the
necessities of others ; and while she wrestled vehemently
for the deliverance of all men from misery, by the exten-
sion of the Redeemer's kingdom ; she was in the habit of
fixing for especial prayer upon certain districts of country,
classes of people, families, and individuals. For the people
of this parish, she often set apart seasons of earnest supplication, in the manner and spirit of various examples in holy
Scripture. For *you*, whom she had so often met in the
solemn assemblies, and within the gates of Zion, she plead-
ed with great zeal of devotion. Like Daniel, solicitous
about the fate of his Hebrew countrymen, who set his face
unto the Lord, to seek by prayer and supplication with fasting and sackcloth and ashes : or like Nehemiah mourning
amid the desolations of Jerusalem, she often afflicted her
soul, praying for your religious prosperity. On one occasion worthy to be had in everlasting remembrance, when
she and another met for the specific object of entreating
the Lord God and Father of your Saviour Jesus Christ
that the truth of the gospel might have free course and be
glorified in her native parish ; that you might indeed be
a holy and believing people ; she was so deeply affected,

so agonized in spirit, when she thought how few among you made the message of the gospel and the things of eternity your only, or greatest and chief interest, that she could not utter a word, and wept bitterly.

When she heard of families or individuals being placed in peculiar emergencies, she would then more especially supplicate for them the Divine grace and blessing; whether they were of those who seemed to receive and honour, or those whom she feared still rejected and despised the truth. With regard to one lady who occasionally visited her, in whom, for various reasons, she was very deeply interested, she thus expressed herself: "I intend setting apart some hours every week for praying for Mrs. ——; she is evidently deceiving her own soul. May the Lord discover to her the danger she is in."

For her kindred according to the flesh, after apostolic example and precept, the desires of her heart went forth in prayer with peculiar vehemence. When speaking, one day, of the indifference of some of them to the things of God, she looked pensive for a little, then turning her eyes towards heaven, she said, " Well, believing prayer will do much for them. The Hearer of prayer hath said it will. O then let us be importunate in soliciting blessings for them; seeing we have an Advocate with the Father, even the man Christ Jesus." In prayer she not only had great joy; but in her desire to pray for particular persons or objects, she ever recognised the suggestion and influence of the Holy Spirit. She attached no importance or efficacy whatever to her supplications, but as they were expressive of the mind of the Spirit. For example, what she expressed in reference to one individual, with whom, during this season, she became acquainted, upon this point sufficiently indicates her feeling. "I cannot," said she to her sister, "I cannot tell you how much I am indebted to our friend for bringing Mr. —— here; for I have had such unutterable pleasure in

praying for him; he has scarcely been half an hour out
of my waking thoughts for several days past; every time
I attempt praying for him, the Holy Ghost enlarges my
heart, and bids me ask yet greater things than these. O
that the great head of the church would magnify his glory,
by making him do and suffer much for his name's sake.

"I have prayed," at another time, she said, "or rather
I have been taught to pray more for Mr.——, than for any
other person in the world. I believe God will enable him
to make proof of his ministry, by giving abundant testimony to the word of his grace, which, he hath now by his
spirit taught him, to declare in all simplicity and faithfulness."

Her prayers were not formal, lifeless effusions ; but her
very soul seemed to go out in communion with God. Of
her own condition, she entertained no suspicion. She felt
the blessedness of being born again, and living like a new
creature ; and never in any believer did love more ardently
glow than that she felt for her fellow sinners.—She longed
even unto agony for the conversion of others. The love,
that thus possessed her, gave life and energy to her intercessions. They assumed a greater tenderness and pathos
when put forth for any one, whom she especially loved with
a natural affection, and yet ignorant of the truth which
saves. Often in the midst even of her greatest sufferings,
her spirit had them in most vivid remembrance.

While thus feeling and praying for others, she never for
a moment dreamed that, in mere human agency, there existed any power of prevailing with God ; but having received
the spirit of the Lord, she could not but yield to that spirit
helping her to supplicate for things agreeable to the divine
will. She knew that God willed, that all men should come
to the knowledge of the truth ; and she seemed ever to
feel, that her prayers were a necessary recognition of his
will ; and that the more vehemently she poured them forth

13

for the salvation of any one, with greater submission and homage of soul did she in reality say, " Thy will be done."

As her knowledge and views of the truth became clearer and more extensive, her love for those, whom she regarded as believers, became more ardent and devoted; but this was no exclusive or sectarian love, for souls ready to perish, excited, as she thus advanced in the comprehension of the mystery of God's love, a more deep and tender interest in her mind.

Want of charity among professing Christians she often lamented ; leading them to exaggerate the importance of minor differences, so as to prevent the interchange of many of the blessed kindnesses of the divine life.   But still more did she condemn, as contrary to the love of Christ, the conduct of those who, after professing to know the truth, abandoned the society of such as were yet in error and darkness.   " How could they in this manner show their love to them ; while it was obvious, that true Christians," as she expressed herself, " should have only regret and pity for others, howsoever far away, through error and guilt, if they would always remember, that they themselves were once like them ? " It is a great sin," said she, " for people to avoid the society of the profane and hypocrite, if anxious to do them good.   We know not who are to be the reprobate, and by doing so, we may lose the great blessedness of being the instruments of their salvation." " The precept of the Apostle, enjoining the coming out of the world, could only mean a continual jealousy, lest we should comply with any of its practices positively sinful."

In accordance with such views and feelings, while cordially, and as if they had been old friends, she received any stranger whom she had good reason to believe the truth had made free ; she spoke with great kindliness and tenderness to those who approached her who seemed to be still ignorant of what she loved.

Although Fernicarry is a remote and sequestered situation, Isabella now not unfrequently enjoyed religious society. It being known in the neighbourhood, and at a distance, with what faith and patience she endured great suffering, that brought her to the brink of the grave; how she possessed her soul in such holy and divine tranquillity; how her sole desire seemed to be to glorify her Father in life or death, to speak of the love of Jesus while in the house of her pilgrimage; she was visited, from time to time, by various individuals who could rejoice in her joy, and speak with her concerning the things of the kingdom to which she was travelling. None of these ever went away from her bedside, without feeling that it was good for them to have been there. Some of them kept accurate notes of their conversation, and from one of these documents it gives me pleasure to insert the following interesting extract :

" She was at the time suffering much; but her language was not that of complaint, but of joy; it was the language of pious and unaffected resignation to the will of her Heavenly Father, who had afflicted her in love. 'Happy, perfectly happy,' was her usual reply to the inquiries made as to the state of her mind. 'Christ is with me ; he is precious, yes, he is precious to my soul.' Gratitude and joy, when visited by her Christian friends, were, as you are well aware, a conspicuous feature in Isabella's character. As I entered the room, she looked up, smiling, and said, ' I am glad you have come to see me. I hope the Lord will make me grateful for the visits I receive from my Christian friends, and enable me to improve by them.' These expressions of her grateful feelings were uttered with the utmost simplicity of manner. When sitting at her bedside, on this occasion, I said to her that her present appearance forcibly reminded me of the language of the inspired writer: ' For all flesh is grass; the grass withereth, and the flower thereof falleth away.' ' O yes,' she meekly replied, 'my situation affords an illustration of the truth of that text. The frail body is indeed just like the flower of the field ; it must fall to decay; but it is of no value in itself; it is dust, mere corruptible matter, a body of sin; it is the soul, the never-dying soul that is precious beyond all calculation.—O, Sir, when the soul is well, then all is well; then there is peace and joy: and when this is the case with a poor sinner, the death of the frail body is an object of desire and not of dread. Being reconciled unto God by the death of his Son, the believer does not fear temporal death as an enemy; for then the soul, being completely freed from sin and all its consequences, shall immediately pass away into glory, and be ever with the Lord.'

"Isabella, observing me lift a small hymn-book, asked me to read to her some of the hymns which she pointed out. I did so. She was pleased and edified, and it was evident the feelings of her soul were in fullest accordance with the sentiments expressed in the hymns that were read. It was remarked at the time, that how useful soever such and other compositions might be, they were not to be compared, for a moment, with the holy Scriptures, which convey to us that knowledge, by which the sinner who believes, is made wise unto salvation. 'Very true,' said Isabella, 'very true; the Bible is the only pure and unfailing source of support and consolation to the soul.' After reading the hymns in the volume alluded to, I rose to withdraw, saying, that I was afraid she had been engaged too much in conversation. 'O no, Sir, not at all; I am not so weak, don't leave me yet, for I am quite able to speak to you.' So anxious was she to speak of, and dwell upon the love, and grace, and glory of him whom her soul loved. I took my seat again, and from my notes I find the following conversation to have taken place.

'You will no doubt, Isabella, be able to point to the source whence you derive that joy which possesses and animates your soul in your present circumstances.' 'From my Saviour's love,' was her prompt reply.—'By faith,' it was observed, 'the believing sinner enjoys a captivating view of the Redeemer's character and worth.' Then in her own meek and unassuming character she replied, 'Yes, yes, my Saviour is indeed lovely. He is the chief among ten thousand. He is altogether lovely, and fairer than the sons of men.' I felt an anxiety to elicit as fully as possible her views of the scheme of human redemption, and therefore asked, 'What is the sole ground of your hope, Isabella, in view of entering the eternal world?' She replied, in an humble but firm tone of voice, 'My hope, my sole hope for eternity is in the justifying righteousness of my Saviour; I can have no hope in or from myself. I am altogether vile; all my best doings are polluted with sin: and O, how then can such a creature as I am, have any hope at all, save in the death of the Lord Jesus; in him I believe; in him I confide and rejoice as the only Saviour.'

" Some time after this I took up the Bible, and began to read in the 103d Psalm. This was a favourite with Isabella. The views which it gives of the divine mercy and compassion, filled her soul with adoring wonder. While I was reading, she listened with much attention and feeling. When I had done, she exclaimed, in a solemn and impressive tone, ' O how delightful! O what cause have I to adopt the language you have been reading, to call upon my soul and all that is within me to bless and magnify the name of my God, who hath forgiven all mine iniquities, who crowneth me with loving kindness and tender mercies. How beautiful, and also how true, the language of the Psalmist, when he says, " as a father pitieth his children, so the Lord pitieth them that fear him?" ' " Seeing her in a state of mind so delightful and heavenly, and so manifestly dead to this world and all its enjoyments, I asked her, ' Have you any desire, Isabella, to be restored to health, and to mingle once more with the society of men in this world?' She lay silent for a little, as in deep thought; and then with a look strongly expressive of the ardent and heavenly aspirings of her soul, she expressed herself in nearly the following language; ' No, O no, Sir, I have no desire, none whatever, to be restored to health. I have seen enough of the vanities of this world. Yes, I know that it is full of dangerous allurements. No, I have no wish to mingle with the society of this world any more. I am now dead to the world, and O, how pleasing, how delightful the thought! heaven is my home, and should I then desire to be longer absent from my Father's house, and from the company of the Redeemed?'

' Very true, Isabella,' yet Paul, you know, when he also longed to be absent from the body, and to be present with the Lord in heaven; he was at the same time willing, even desirous, to continue in this world a little longer.' ' O yes, that is indeed true,' said our dear friend, ' but it was that he might serve his divine Master, and promote his glory in the world, by seeking to advance the holiness, peace, and comfort of his disciples: but I desire to bow in cheerful submission to the divine will. If God should see meet to abate my trouble, and raise me up again to the enjoyment of health, I trust he will give me grace to be faithful and to keep

13*

me humble. And should this yet be the case, I will endeavour to devote my whole soul—all that I have, to the service and glory of my dear Redeemer. O what a blessed, what a glorious thing, it is, Mr. A., to be employed in any way in the service of the Lord Jesus Christ.'

" You need not be informed what deep and lively interest she felt at all times in the eternal welfare of her fellow-men. How deeply it affected her benevolent spirit, when she reflected on the carelessness and open irreligion of the great bulk of professing Christians in this land. The conversation happening to turn on this subject, she spoke with much feeling in the following manner; ' O how few, how very few, there are who care any thing at all about Jesus. The people are blind ; they don't think what they are about. O no, they don't feel their need of the gospel; they see no beauty in the Saviour why they should desire him. He appears to them as a root out of a dry ground.'

" Nothing afforded to Isabella's mind more delight than to listen to conversations illustrative of the divine mercy and compassion to our race. A remark was made by some one present, which led to a conversation on the probability that all who die in infancy are saved. Isabella listened with much interest and delight, taking also an active part in the discussion herself. Several texts of scripture were quoted, as distinctly favouring the idea, the force of which, as bearing upon the subject, she at once discovered and acknowledged. ' What a delightful thought,' she exclaimed, when we were about to drop the subject; ' well is it not a most pleasing and delightful thought. From what has been said on the subject, from the passages of scripture that have been mentioned, I really think there can be little room for any one to doubt, that all who die in infancy are saved.'

Isabella was always much delighted when she had an opportunity of joining with her christian friends in the praises of God. It was now getting late ; the family were called into the room to attend evening worship. While we were engaged in singing a hymn of praise, she seemed exceedingly happy and elevated in her mind. The 15th chapter of St. John was read. ' I am the true vine, and my Father is the husbandman.' After rising from our knees, she raised her hand from her pillow and stretching it out, said, ' T[...] thank you, Sir, for your importunity on my behalf,' I sa[...] 'I hope, Isabella, you will have a good night.' ' O yes, I shall have that. My heavenly Father is always near.'

I rose to withdraw, and bid her good night. In a subdued tone she said, " The Lord be with you and bless you—with me all is well. Come soon again and see me.'

Circumstances having led her friend to speak of the malice and vigilance of the god of this world, he adds that Isabella thus expressed herself :—

" ' I ought to guard continually against his deceitful insinuations. Our adversary the devil goeth about as a roaring lion, seeking whom he may devour; and who can stand against him in their own power ? None. I feel that I cannot ; that I can do nothing in my own strength to resist him : that my help cometh from the Lord who made heaven and earth. I look to him—in Him I trust : I rejoice in the all-sufficiency of his power to protect and save me.'

" Here I took occasion to ask Isabella, particularly, as to what had been the prevailing state of her mind since my last visit ? She replied, ' I have, upon the whole, been very comfortable and happy in my mind. I have indeed been very graciously dealt with : Jesus is precious. Feeling my own vileness and guilt, I look to the Lamb of God which taketh away the sins of the world. This gives peace. In myself I see nothing but sin and unworthiness; but in Jesus I behold an almighty Saviour. His character is perfect ; his love to the guilty and the lost is unbounded : and it is this, Sir, even the manifestation of his love, that gives me peace and comfort, and joy in the view of eternity. Yes, I do love him supremely ! O how can it be otherwise, when I think on what he hath done for my soul. He loved me and gave himself for me; when wandering in the paths of sin, he sought me out. He found me and brought me back to his own fold. Yes, he has blotted out all mine iniquities as a cloud, and my transgressions as a thick cloud, and has given me a good hope through grace. All this he has done for my soul. *I have peace in believing.* I am enabled to rejoice in tribulation."

The extracts you have read are from the letters of a highly valued friend, not of the Established Church ; but whom Isabella loved in the bonds of the gospel.

The comprehensiveness of her charity has been already alluded to ; and no language is too strong to express how

completely set free it was from all its ordinary entanglements. This did not arise, as it may sometimes do in
others, from extensive and varied intercourse with the
Christian world : with her it existed previous to her enjoying many opportunities of conversing with professors of a
different persuasion from her own. How seldom do rigid
Presbyterians, for example, cordially meet a conscientious
Episcopalian; and how frequently do devout Churchmen
look with suspicion on a pious dissenter. But Isabella
seemed to know none of those distinctions which such de-
signations imply : from her bosom flowed too mighty a
stream of love to be checked in its progress into other
hearts by any such barriers : finding out, under whatever
exterior, and gladly coalescing with those thoughts, and
feelings, and sympathies, that are common to the family of
God, in any communion ; ever remembering the words, so
often forgotten by the conflicting and distracted church :
"There is one body and one spirit, even as ye are called
in one hope of your calling : one Lord, one faith, one bap-
tism, one God and Father, who is above all, and through
all, and in you all."

When she had good reason for believing, that any one
had tasted of the heavenly gift, and been illuminated by
the Holy Ghost, she gave glory to God; and her heart did
not stay nor linger long, but made haste to obey the blessed
commandment,—"seeing ye have purified your souls, by
obeying the truth through the spirit unto unfeigned love of
the brethren, see that ye love one another with a pure
heart fervently ; being born again, not of corruptible seed,
but of incorruptible, by the word of God, that liveth and
abideth for ever."

While her heart was thus opened and enlarged, delighting to hold intercourse with professing Christians, of whatever persuasion, in whom the love of the truth prevailed ;
in reading also the writings of holy men, she was actuated

by a similar spirit. She cared not first to ascertain, whether this work was written by an Arminian, or that by a Calvinist; but rejoiced to discover, or trace in either, whatever savoured of the spirit of Christ, or harmonized with any truth which had edified or consoled her mind, while searching for eternal life in the Scriptures. As an instance of this, when reading, one day, a beautiful hymn of Wesley's, she exclaimed, "Dear, dear Wesley, he is now an inhabitant of heaven. I love him much; yes, I feel happy in the mention of his name; but I differ widely from him in some points. I firmly believe that all, for whom Christ died, shall believe in his name, and be brought to glory; and consequently he only died for a portion of our race; neither does his intercessory prayer extend but to a portion of our race."*

* I am aware, that not a few will object to the language of this passage, and, while I rank myself among that number, I would say that no class of Christians ought of right to be deprived of the testimony which some individuals among them give of deep and fervent piety, notwithstanding the peculiarity of their opinions. The *idea*, that was in the mind of Isabella Campbell, was obviously correct, and would be so considered, I presume, by all who believe the doctrine of the Atonement. The idea was, that the righteousness of Christ is imputed only to those, whom God has chosen; and this is held in common by those who use the phraseology that Christ died for all men, and by those who say that he died only for the elect. The benefits of his death, viz. pardon and justification extend only to the true disciples of Christ, to the sheep of his fold, to the lambs of his flock.

It is a matter to be deeply regretted, that so much misapprehension should prevail upon this subject; and that the Church has been driven into such a state of warfare, when the practical, the spiritual idea is the same among both parties. There may have mingled with the feelings of both, views of truth that were not precisely scriptural; and the joyous and peace-giving meditations, on the Atonement, may have been associated with such erroneous views; until the tares could not be removed without endangering the wheat. But the foundation resteth sure. The one party carries the analogy of a debt too far, perhaps within the boundary of error; the other speak of the universality of the Atonement, and of the nature of imputation, in such a way as seems to some to impugn the justice of God as an independent attribute. But look at each party in the service of prayer, or upon a death bed, and note the actual posture of their mind. I speak not of possible deceivers, or

She was persuaded of Wesley's love of truth; rejoiced in sympathy with his zeal, in preaching the gospel of her Saviour; and although in doctrinal views they did not entirely coincide, the multitudes whom, beyond all question,

of occasional exceptions. There is Mrs. Graham and Isabella Campbell, for example, in the one case; and Mrs. Huntington and Dr. Payson in the other. And did these individuals have *essentially* different views of the nature of the Atonement? Surely not. Trace the history of their thoughts and feelings, not their expressions look at their conceptions of Jesus, as their Saviour, and it will be perceived that the same *idea* is embraced by each of them, as the foundation of their peace. But the notion of an Atonement that embraces all men, is rejected by the one party. In rejecting this phrase, what is it, that is rejected, or what is intended to be rejected? Why, that all men are literally forgiven, and general amnesty proclaimed in virtue of which, no condemnation remains. But in doing this they reject not the thing held and believed, by those who speak of a general Atonement, but *their own interpretation of that language.* But this interpretation is not admitted as true, by those who speak of a general Atonement. When those who teach a general atonement say, that the *imputation* of Christ's righteousness is not universal, they have precisely the same foundation for self-appropriating Christ and the benefits of his death, as the other class. Their practical, spiritual feelings spring from the same source, and are compassed round about by the same limitations. A friend at my elbow suggests, as the only difference between the parties, the meaning of the little word—*for.* Settle that, and the controversy is ended. One says, Christ died for (instead of the elect;) the other, he died for (the benefit of, because of) all. He died for, or because, all were dead. Ask one, who believes in general Atonement, who Christ died for, (*i. e.* in the stead of) and he will answer for the chosen of God alone, or as he may prefer to express it, his death is effectual, its benefits transferrible only to the chosen of God—those, who repent and believe.

The one class of Christians, I know, insist, that their view leads more directly to that assurance, which banishes fear and darkness, and fills the soul with unspeakable delight. But it does not appear in looking at the principles involved in both, that the one has any pre-eminence over the other, in this respect. The foundation of Assurance is the finished work of Christ, the possession of it, results from resting without fear or doubt upon Him; not from drawing inferences from treasured attainments in the soul; and the finished work of Christ is the foundation, is at the bottom of both systems—it is the *idea* couched under both forms of expression—it is the supporting, sustaining, consoling thought in both.

Those, who hold to the phraseology of limited Atonement, likewise insist that the Saviour is more appropriated to the individual, in the act of

he and his followers awakened to serious meditation on
their spiritual conditon, afforded just so many arguments
for loving and revering his name and memory. Whitefield, however, was still more attractive to her soul than
he. She had read his journal, and a volume of his ser-

Faith, by which they rest on Him, than can be by other Christians. And
the religious history of individuals, who have been instructed in this form of
the *idea* of the Atonement, do usually speak of their interest in the Saviour
in a more appropriating manner, and with a deeper sense of personal union
to him, than the other class. Indeed those, who hold to a general Atonement,
have too generally, from the fear, that strong assertions of believing would
be taken for Faith, and, that the personal and appropriating manner in
which Christ as *our* Saviour, was contemplated, would give occasion for the
exercise of selfishness, have directed their attention too exclusively to
other sources of evidence to learn whether they are children of God.—We
have spoken too much comparatively of Regeneration, its nature, and effects,
and too little of the necessity and evidence of a personal union to Christ,
by which we might live in Him, and find the strength, which is adequate
to our spiritual necessities. But this arises not from essentially different
principles, concerning the Atonement, but from an improper application of
them to the wants of human nature. One of the two most prominent and
jealous advocates for unquestioning Assurance, at the present day, uses the
phraseology of limited Atonement in the most exceptionable form; going
so far as to object in the most determined manner to saying that sinners
received, or could receive Christ, as their Saviour—that they are so incorporate with Christ, as their head, in the Atonement, that no act objective or
subjective can be predicated of them. To believe in Christ is to suppose
yourself incorporate with him, which is done by assenting to the testimony
of God respecting Christ as true. The other repudiates this phraseology
with abhorrence, and deprecates its influence, as most disastrous, on the
success of the gospel; and holds the doctrine of general Atonement in
perhaps as exceptionable phraseology, going so far as to say, that, from the
fact of an Atonement, all men are " pardoned"—that the belief of this pardon, or rather the belief of the circumstances and moral meaning of this
pardon, as stated in the Bible, secures, of necessity a holy life, an unquestioning, purifying FAITH. Pardon, however is not used as synonymous with
salvation, nor is it necessarily connected with salvation, according to Mr.
Erskine.

These men in prayer and in deep devotional feeling are very similar.
Both of them apparently living much in communion with God; both earnest students of the Bible; both deeply and anxiously alive to the progress
of personal, spiritual religion; both dwell much, in their public exhibitions
of the truth, upon the same point, the necessity of receiving, at once, the

mons; treasured up many of his striking sayings; and
when she thought of the religious deadness of the great
mass of the people, he, more frequently than any other
arose to her mind, as the exemplar of such an Apostle,
as was most likely to rouse from their slumbers the souls,

testimony of the Bible concerning Christ; both advocate Revivals of Religion, and the conversation of both is eminently calculated to promote
them; and both regard their peculiar forms of presenting the truth as very
necessary to obtain the purpose of the gospel. Suppose Dr. Malan, at Geneva, should commence a public attack on Mr. Erskine of Scotland, the two
gentlemen above alluded to, and Mr. Erskine should reply, and there should
come in our waters a shoal of Vindications, and Strictures, and Reviews, and
Replications, and Rejoinders, and Postscripts, and the citing of authorities
of what Calvin, and Grotius, and Luther, and Knox, and Fenelon taught.
Suppose this, what would become of the souls of the poor people that
weekly flock to L'Eglise du Temoignage, of Dr. Malan, without the walls
of Geneva, and who are edified by reading his simple and affecting tracts;
and what too would become of the poor cottagers of Lithlalin, and the light
giving Christian circle of which Mr. Erskine is the radiating centre?
Would not these places, sanctified as they now are, by prayer and spiritual Religion, become the arena of intellectual and metaphysical gla-
diatorship? Let every one answer such questions, on his knees, in his closet, when he feels as did Brainard, who said " *I could not help crying to
God* for those poor Indians; and after I went to bed, my heart continued
to go out to God for them, till I dropped asleep;" and he will believe, that
something beside magnifying our differences, is the business of the Disciples
of Christ; even the study of that *idea*, or principle, which is common to both,
and common to all, because it is the life-giving, and life-supporting power of
all spiritual Religion.

  When I think of Jesus Christ as my Saviour, my soul is filled with delight,
not because he is *exclusively mine*, or exclusively the Saviour of the chosen
of God; but, because he filleth all my soul, gratifieth all my pure desires, and
swelleth my bosom with holy, immortal rapture. Some think of Jesus
mainly, as their purchaser, and rejoice in Him because He has bought them;
not with me, there is none of the feeling of bondage from being brought
under a weight of obligation. This view of the Saviour gives only the feeling of freedom, delightful freedom. But freedom is not what my soul desires
as a negative, as something past and accomplished; freedom permits Jesus
to dwell with me, and my soul, to receive Him and dwell in Him, and live
upon Him, and here in the *reciprocal dwelling*, is the great satisfaction—the
immortal rapture, the holy blessedness—the unreproaching, and the unsin-
ning foretaste of all that Eternity can bestow. My soul contemplates the
Saviour, in different forms—sometimes, as head over all things to the

whose pollution and misery she deplored. In his way of preaching, also, she seemed to discover still more heart and fervour, and his picturings of gospel freedom and blessedness, still more of simplicity and beauty. In the following extract of a letter from one of her friends, you see what effect the perusal of his writings sometimes produced upon her feelings.

" She spoke much that day of Whitefield, and desired Mary to let me see his picture in a volume of Sermons. She told us of her having once seen a letter, addressed to him by the little children, who had been impressed by his preaching, which seemed to have given her great delight. She then, as if from surveying his character and doings, observed with considerable emotion, ' He was a highly honoured servant: does it not rejoice your heart to think of the bright, bright crown, which now adorns his head ?' Then, again referring to the children, she continued, ' And with what unspeakable joy would these dear Lambs welcome his arrival in the realms of glory, and how often will he rejoice in them while he exclaims, " Behold I and the children whom thou hast given me !" He had very exalted views of the character of Jesus and his love to sinners. Often, in reading his sermons, such perceptions of the Saviour's beauty have been granted, that I have been constrained to lay aside the book, and begin to praise the Lord.' "

Church, which is his body. How safe then I feel, in his Almighty arms ! How safe too the poor and despised Church appears ; and as His, partakes of His spirit, as the ground of its *unity*, and not its *forms* ; how single, how glorious, it seems without spot or wrinkle or any such thing—the beauty of the whole earth, the glorious and everliving manifestation of His love, of His character, of Himself. Sometimes, I look at Jesus, as the author and finisher of the scheme of reconciliation, the friend of sinners, the compassionate Redeemer of man, because he is man—sinful man. I can weep with Him over the ruins of the world, and, as He stands upon the hill of salvation, I can love, and admire, and adore that infinite compassion, that said unto Jerusalem, as representing a sinful world; ' Thou that killest the prophets, and stonest them that are sent unto thee ! How often would I have gathered you together, as a hen gathereth her chickens under her wings, but ye would not ! O, that thou, in this thy day, understood the things that belong to thy peace ! '

May God grant, that none of the readers of this book may be unmoved by this merciful pity, and this infinite love.

AMERICAN EDITOR.

14

There is something very delightful in the contemplation of such a spirit as Isbella's christianity displayed; " with long suffering and meekness, ever endeavouring to keep the unity of the spirit in the bond of peace:".—The great and holy Baxter somewhere, in one of his folios, exclaims in nearly the following words, " I have often wept in secret, and sighed for the time when those, who name the name of Christ, will be as anxious to discover wherein they agree, as for nearly 1700 years they have been anxious to discover wherein they differed."

Beyond all doubt Isabella was one of those who had discovered the great secret, and experienced the blessedness of such a spirit; for each uncharitable judgment that tended to disunite the family of believers, seemed to her like the tearing asunder, with profane and sacrilegious hands, the seamless garment of the Saviour she rejoiced to love—a marring of that untainted beauty which her soul lived in looking on. She mourned, as we have seen, over any one whom the truth had not set free from harsh judging, or from whose heart it had not cast out that old leaven which anciently prompted the question, can any thing good come out of Galilee? filling the void with a capacity of glad and willing sympathy, with those feelings which occupied the Saviour's bosom, when with such generous and liberal joy, so to speak, he thus judged of a poor Syrophenician widow, " I have not found so great faith, no, not in Israel."

This spirit was associated in her mind with an exquisite delicacy of feeling; and indeed, what can give such delicacy to any mind, as the habitual contemplation of the infinite love and tenderness of the Saviour, so comprehensive of human frailty and misery.

She never, to her most intimate friends, not even to her sister, would communicate what she saw wrong in the conduct of others, unless she had previously represented it to themselves. If made sensible of their error, she conceived it equally sinful to reveal what she had observed, or the result of their intercourse. If she failed in convincing them, she would then make known the error she deplored to her confidential friends, but only for the purpose of requesting their prayers ; for she scrupulously avoided the mention of any name. To use her own words :—" I have long been taught to respect that precept, ' moreover, if thy brother shall trespass against thee, go and tell him his fault between thee and him alone : if he shall hear thee, thou hast gained thy brother.' " Were such feelings universal, how and when would the errors and frailties of our brethren be thought of ?—only with deep sorrow, and at the throne of heavenly mercy. Where would censoriousness be found ? neither in the heart, nor upon the lips of professing christians, banished for ever beyond the limit of the visible church.

From what you have read, you may form a pretty accurate notion of the state of Isabella's mind, during the first year of her divine life. The peace of God beautifully ruled in her heart ; and the love God shed abroad in it, assimilated to itself the habitual current of her thoughts and feelings. Mindful of the Apostle's precept, " Be ye followers of God, as dear children, and walk in love, as Christ also hath loved us ;" she went onward in the path of Christian perfection, diligently seeking to prove what was acceptable in the Lord. To her peace there seems to have been no interruption, from the time she had received the word in much affliction with joy of the Holy Ghost. Her afflictions, even her temptations, but seemed to minister new occasions for the exercise of her faith, rooted and grounded in the knowledge of the love of God. Howsoever clear her perceptions of her sinfulness were, they inspired no doubt of her safety ; but only the more promptly impelled her to seek the all availing remedy ; persuaded, as she never ceased to be, that her diminished power or enjoyment,

ever attendant upon present sin, arose not from what is
called desertion, but to use her own words, " her eyes having turned away from beholding."

During the summer, many professing to know the truth
visited her; with these I have often conversed regarding
her religious character and attainments, all of whom seem
to have been astonished at the singular union of graces, her
spirit, and conversation, and demeanour displayed. There
was about her christianity so much of wisdom and discretion, combined with such warmth of zeal; faithfulness,
with delicacy and tenderness; firmness, with meekness; so
much confidence toward God, with such self-abasement and
broken-heartedness; such anxiety to kindle up in all grateful wonder at the love of God, while she herself was astonished at their deadness; yet catching so readily the most
transient expression, that would intimate a feeling of sympathy, howsoever faint, with the passion that engrossed her
soul. None, however, of those who saw her about this
time expressed themselves more beautifully than ———; and
certainly none more affectingly, when you consider that
he is now among the spirits of the just made perfect. Although then himself in perfect health, even before Isabella's
departure he was translated into their blessed habitations.

" I cannot describe what I felt upon first beholding her lovely
countenance, beaming with celestial fire. It bespoke the inward
serenity and settled composure she enjoyed, from the merits of her
crucified Redeemer. It told me who reigned triumphant in her
soul; that although her outward frame might sicken and decay from
time to time, yet the soul was growing up mightily to him who is
head over all things: that although death and the grave should
join league together to gain possession of her, their feeble efforts
would be in vain; for Jesus had ransomed her from the power of
the grave, and redeemed her soul from destruction; had planted
his adorable image there, and there he remained in perfect tranquillity; weaning his dear-bought Isabella from the vanities of a
sinful and a dying world. O for such complacency, when I draw
near the confines of the Eternal world, to aid me in all my ways,

and to evidence the new creation within my too-easily irritated heart."

The visits of these friends she esteemed valuable privileges, for which she gave glory to God ; but the one among this class of privileges which she esteemed most valuable of all, was the occasional society of a venerable divine, who, with his family occupied, for a considerable time apartments in her mother's house contiguous to the little chamber where, she used to say, she first saw the truth, and learned how to enjoy communion with God. She often spoke to me of the delight she had in her interviews with Dr. S. From his extensive experience of the manifestations of religious feeling among the sick and dying, through all gradations of strength in believing, he was well fitted to form a just estimate of the kind and degree of Isabella's faith and piety. To him she unfolded the history of her mind, her progress through the dark valley of spiritual death, to the light and glory of eternal life, which beamed upon her from the hill of Calvary. He tried her by the Scriptures, by his own knowledge of the powers of the incorruptible word, by the tokens which indicate those to whom there is no condemnation, having passed from death to life, and he found her not wanting in all things approving herself a believer that needed not be ashamed, showing forth the love and grace of God in whatever pertained to life and godliness.

I am happy in being able to insert in his own words, the estimate of which I have spoken, and which he had such excellent means of forming.

" You ask me to ' give you the result of my intercorse with Isabella Campbell, and my opinion of her christianity.' Had you made this request two years ago, when the impressions of that intercourse so pleasing, so edifying to me, were fresh, I could have better gratified your wishes, and done more justice to the eminent work of grace in her heart. Now, l can venture to trace only some
14*

remarkable steps in the progress of her being translated into the Kingdom of God's dear Son; but what I have since meditated on, and spoken of with admiration and gratitude, for the benefit of myself and others, I think I can describe almost in her own simple expressive language.

"During a residence of three months in her mother's house I, enjoyed favourable opportunities of conversing with her. Every interview increased my wonder at, not the elements, but, the completeness and polish of christian character, in one so young in years and even in christian profession. The propriety of her sentiments and language, her quick discernment of the glory of God in every occurrence, the readiness with which her soul received the impression of that glory, whether humbling or encouraging her, and the thoroughly sweet, lowly and greteful temper of her mind, filled me with astonishment; but the Scriptures laid open the mystery, reminding me that ' the testimony of the Lord is sure, making wise the simple—the secret of the Lord is with them that fear him, and he will show them his covenant—and all they, with open face beholding the glory of the Lord, as in a glass, are changed into the same image, from glory to glory, even as by the Spirit of the Lord.'

" One day I had been conversing with her on the state of her mind, in communicating which she looked and breathed unspeakable humility, faith, love, tenderness of heart, heavenly mindedness, with patience and resignation, in a manner that laid me low before God, and filled my eyes with tears of adoring thankfulness in her behalf. In her, every grace seemed to exist in its proper place, and to exert itself in its proper season; and if there were one that predominated more than another, it was an enlightened and fervent love of God her Saviour—all her salvation, all her desire,—which prevaded and cemented, which animated and beautified the whole. The sight of one so young and lovely, laid on the bed of languishing and of death, in her own apprehension, blest with the temper of a child of God, wonderfully mature in grace, and meet for the inheritance of the saints in light, naturally led me to inquire into the origin of this uncommon work of the Holy Spirit. Without hesitation, I may say, a more concise, and distinct, and satisfactory answer I never received to any similar inquiry.

" ' About two years ago,' said she, ' being deeply affected with the death of a dear relative, I became more thoughtful and more engaged in reading my Bible One day I read these words: ' This is the accepted time, this is the day of salvation ; to-day, if ye will hear my voice.' They pierced me to the heart. Many a day, said I, have I read these words, but none of them all has been to me a day of salvation. O, is the accepted time clean gone for ever! Or, may not I, this day be made sensible of my miserable state, begin to hear the Lord's voice? From this time, I began to read my Bible, that I might know the will of God revealed for the salvation of sinners, and to spend much of my nights in weeping and prayer, when I could do it without being observed. As I came to see my life, and then my heart, in the light of God's word, my anxiety and my terrors increased—and increased to such degree, that, at length, I felt within me a hell of torment, and a hell of pollution.' Here I asked, if she ever consulted any one: ' No,' said she, ' I thought my situation so uncommon, so dreadful, that I had not courage to mention it to any one.' I then asked, did she never recal what she had learnt of the person and offices of the Lord Jesus Christ, freely offered to every sinner who hears the gospel. ' All I had learnt of this subject, was to me at this time as if I had never heard it,' was her answer. This led me to observe, that the hell of torment drove her neither into despair, like Judas, nor into the world for amusement, like Saul; while the loathsome hell of pollution constrained her to persevere in seeking salvation, from both her misery and her vileness, in the way God might point out to her in the use of the scriptures and prayer. To me this seems to draw an obvious line of distinction, between the convictions of sin and misery produced by the word and spirit of God, and those produced by the word and the natural conscience.

"She returned to her narrative, saying : ' When this awful state of mind had continued some months, I read, " the bruised reed he will not break, the smoking flax he will not quench." Surely, I am a bruised reed, surely I am smoking flax, then there is hope. that he will not break me, that he will not quench me. From that time, I went on reading and praying, in a continued struggle between hope and fear ; but without my former terrors, and without being at any time wholly deprived of hope. From this I learnt, that, on the testimony of God in the Scriptures, she belived the Lord Jesus Christ, the promised Messias, to be the appointed Saviour of sinners, mighty and able to save, but she doubted whether his mercy extended to such a sinner as herself. And I could not but admire the grace of her heavenly Teacher, in directing her attention to a passage, persuasively illustrating the tender mercies of the omnipotent Saviour—in enabling her to understand the character of the objects of his compassion ; and to apprehend the resemblance of them to her own state of helpless distress about her salvation, from sin as well as misery, by Jesus Christ; and to draw from it the just and refreshing inference of hope towards the Lord. What followed impressed on my mind that saying of the inspired Psalmist, beautifully illustrated in Isabella's experience, ' the eye of the Lord is upon them that fear him, upon them that hope in his mercy.'

" She resumed: ' At the distance of several months more, in the course of my reading, I met with these to me ever-memorable words of my gracious Lord, " Come unto me, all ye that labour and are heavy laden, and I will give you rest." They came home to my heart with power. The Lord made them spirit and life in me. I came to him, and found the rest he promised. And blessed be his name, he hath never taken it from me; though in his sovereignty he calls me, daily and hourly, to mourn over the painful conflict of the spirit against the remains of an evil heart of unbelief and enmity to my God.'

" Long have I admired the answer to ' What is effectual calling?' in our excellent Shorter Catechism, as a short and striking delineation of conversion; and I am not sure that I have ever witnessed a living instance of the great and important change, which more accurately corresponds to that scriptural representation of it, than this of Isabella Campbell. And if her coming to Christ remarkably corresponds to the answer of that question, assuredly her after experience no less accurately corresponds to the answer to, ' What are the benefits that accompany or flow from justification, adoption, and sanctification ?' consisting in, ' Assurance of God's love, peace of conscience, joy in the Holy Ghost; increase, of grace, and preseverance therein unto the end.'

" In conversion, God is sovereign, is tied down to no one method; and his procedure is various. In the conversion of Isabella Campbell, he asserts his prerogative. It not only bears undeniable evidence of being the work of God, but of being his own work in a peculiar manner—a work begun, carried on, and finished, by his word and spirit, in the use of prayer, without the aid of man.

" The Divine Architect founded this house deep in the rock of salvation, reared it with more than usual speed, at once solid and graced with the ornaments of a spiritual building, that should delight and benefit admiring spectators, and should remain unshaken, uninjured, when the rains descended, and the floods came, and the winds blew, that afterwards beat on it, with continued and increasing violence."

The Hymn.

Our earthly ties are weak,
  Whereon we dare not rest,
For time destroys, and death will break
  The sweetest and the best ;
Yet there's a tie which must remain,
Which time and death assault in vain.

The kindred links of life are bright,
  Yet not so bright as those
In which Christ's favour'd friends unite,
  And each on each repose.
And O ! how sweet, where in each mind
A throb to echo their's they find.

Tho' lovely many an earthly flower,
  Its beauty fades and flies,
But they, unchanging, form a bower
  To bloom in Paradise ;
Sprung from the same immortal vine,
In him they live, and round him twine.

And their's is not an earthly love,
  By nature's fondness nurs'd ;
As they love him who reigns above,
  Because he lov'd them first,
So they all minor ties disown,—
The sweetest for his sake alone.

The Scripture.

A NEW Commandment I give unto you, that ye love one another; as I have loved you, that ye also love one another.

If there be any consolation in Christ, if any comfort of love, if any fellowship of the spirit, fulfil ye my joy, that ye be like minded, having the same love.

Be ye followers of God, as dear children; and walk in love, as Christ also hath loved us.

Let all them that put their trust in thee rejoice: let them ever shout for joy because thou defendest them: let them also that love thy name be joyful in thee. The Lord thy God—he will save, he will rest in his love, he will joy over thee with singing.

They that feared the Lord, spake often one to another; and they shall be mine, saith the Lord of hosts, in that day when I make up my jewels.

And the ransomed of the Lord shall return and come to Zion with songs and everlasting joy upon their head; they shall obtain joy and gladness, and sorrow and sighing shall flee away.

CHAPTER VIII.

THE joy of freedom prompts the sorer grief,
That sin should linger in my ransomed soul.
No stranger intermeddles with such thoughts:
But those who meet on Calvary's hill are friends.
Come then my chosen:—I have seen thee there;
The secrets of my soul before thee lie
Be helper of my joy,—be sharer of my grief.

THE life of a young woman, confined to her chamber by
disease, is seldom varied by new or unexpected incidents.
It generally is a routine, from day to day, of suffering and
of sympathy ; of the manifestations of approaching death,
and the multiplying anxieties of affectionate and tender-
hearted relatives and friends.   For many months, Isabella
had been in her solitude, as we have described, with no
prospect of any occurrence in the relationships of life to
give to her history, independent of its religious character,
any thing like romantic interest.   It so happened, however
that during her illness she contracted a friendship, memorable for strength and tenderness of affection, with an individual of her own sex, whom she had never seen. About the time
she first embraced the truth, she had frequently heard of a
young lady, of her own age, residing at a considerable distance, whose eyes God had opened to see the vanities of a
world lying in wickedness ; and into whose heart God had
put the power of renouncing them all, for the labours and
enjoyments of a religious life.   A keen desire was excited
in Isabella's mind to see her.   Their difference of station
almost precluded the probability of their having any intercourse ; and yet she yearned for it with a feeling she used

to describe as intensely vehement. Her extreme diffidence and reserve of manner, upon one occasion, prevented the accomplishment of her wishes. She had gone with
a message to the residence of the young lady ; but had not
sufficient courage to request an interview. Upon coming
away, she walked round the house with one of the servants, if possible to obtain a glimpse of her through the
window of her room—but in vain. She returned home
greatly disappointed ; while she eagerly availed herself
of every opportunity of hearing of her and her movements.
From the circumstance of two daughters of a contiguous
cottager being servants in the young lady's family, these
opportunities she frequently enjoyed, and concluding from
all she heard that Miss —— delighted in the same objects,
and was engaged in the same great pursuit with herself, her
love for her increased, and she only the more vehemently
longed to see her. Of this however, every day diminished
the probability and the hope. She was now confined by a
disease, from which she was persuaded she would never
recover ; and the young lady herself was siezed by a malady which subjected her to excruciating sufferings, and
rendered her incapable of moving from her pillow. The
very hopelessness of an interview only excited a deeper interest ; and when she learned, how, amid her tribulation,
God glorified himself by Miss ——'s faith and patience,
her love and sympathy flowed out more tenderly towards
her. By this time also Miss —— had heard of Isabella, of
her singular piety and holiness, and of her meek resignation
to the will of God, from various quarters, and a strong desire arose in her bosom also, to see, and hold communion
with so remarkable an instance of the grace of God. To
her, however, as well as to Isabella, such an event seemed
as if utterly hopeless, before they should meet in their Father's house. Isabella, gradually decaying, already incapable (as Miss —— understood) of travel, every day less

able to move from her bed, and herself affected with an
agonizing and what might possibly prove an incurable malady; the possibility of meeting ceased to be contemplated
although the joy and blessedness of such an event, if it
could have been, was often pictured in her mind. Every
detail of their mutual suffering and patience, of faith and
peace, of hope and love, only knit more closely their hearts
to each other; although neither, at this time, knew of the
anxieties and feelings of the other. At last, however, an
intercourse did begin; as if the holy love that actuated
their hearts could no longer delay its expression, but break
forth and flow into each other's bosoms. Isabella, as you
know, was in a lowly condition; and was also at an incon-
venient distance for procuring what comforts her delicate
health might require. Miss —— was aware of this; and
she naturally felt it her peculiar privilege to assist in pro-
moting the bodily comfort of her already beloved friend.
You may easily conceive what joy she had, when her messenger returned with the following letter:—

"MY VERY DEAR MISS—

"I desire to return you my heartfelt thanks for your
great kindness. It was indeed a seasonable supply to my necessities; and will I doubt not be remembered at the great day of rewards, among those kinds of graces concerning which our blessed
Saviour speaks, when he says, ' In as much as ye did it unto one
of the least of these my brethren, ye did it unto me.' I would
sincerely sympathize with you in your great sufferings. I have
heard more than once, that you suffer intense pain; yet I trust
that you receive grace to profit withal, and are rejoicing in hope
through the mighty power of the Holy Ghost. I often feel refreshed, when I think that it is given us in behalf of Christ, not
only to believe on his name, but to suffer for his sake; and all who
will get in through the gate to the New Jerusalem, must suffer in
some way or other.—O that we were more frequently importu-
ning grace to glorify our God and Father, even in the fires. I
must inform you, in answer to your kind inquiries after my health
that this poor clay tabernacle is daily *impairing*. I have been

15

much worse for a fortnight past :—my cough and difficulty in
bre thing are at a'l times very great, and I have not the most
distant hope of ever regaining my lost strength ; yet, my dear
Miss ———, although this is the case, I will say of the Lord, he is
my rock and strength, my shield and buckler; and I shall not
through his grace be moved even at the greatest convulsions of
nature.—He only is my sure defence and refuge in all my distresses:—yes, blessed be the Lord God, his salvation is precious
to my soul, and I shall ever have cause to praise him, for his distinguishing love in saving me, the chief of sinners, from the wrath
to come. I shall be glad to hear again, how you are; and I trust,
that if we meet not here, we shall soon, even at furthest, meet on
the shores of boundless glory. Wishing you much of the presence of your God and Saviour—1 remain, with much Christian
affection, yours,   I. C."

This was the first direct intercourse between these two
young believers—amid their great sufferings comforting
each other with the consolations of God ; and although
friends not according to the flesh, helpers according to the
spirit of each other's joy. Soon afterwards, when visiting
Isabella, with a very happy expression of countenance,
and holding a small note in her hand, she asked me if I
knew whose it was ? It proved to be the note, to which the
letter you have read was a reply. I do not now recollect
particularly our conversation, but the impression remains
of the obvious joy wherewith her heart was filled. Her
sister, however, has very particularly recorded what she
said when the note was received : "O, what shall I render
unto the Lord for all his benefits ? I will sing praise to him
so long as I have any being. O come, and exalt the Lord
with me ; let us exalt his name together. To-day, I
have heard from one of the beloved friends of Emmanuel,
whom I have never seen, and may never see in this world.
Blessed be the God and Father of our Lord Jesus Christ,
who, according to his abundant mercy, hath begotten us to
a lively hope, by the resurrection of Christ from the dead.
May she sing loudly, that new song which God hath put

into her mouth, that many may see, and fear, and rely upon the Lord. Like myself she is very delicate, and may soon be called away from earth. O how cheering to think, that we may soon have a glorious meeting before the throne of our Father." They were now, as it were, at home with each other ; assured of each other's love they continued to correspond from time to time, after the manner of a most confidential friendship.

Miss ——, when she received Isabella's letter, was enduring great bodily agony. For some time afterwards, although the letter gave her great joy, she was not able to express her feelings to Isabella ; but as soon as she could, she sent her the following note :—

"I cannot tell how your note has gratified me, and how much I have rejoiced in your present peaceful foretaste of Eternal Glory.—Such hopes do shed a ray, a cheering ray, across the valley of the shadow of death ; and it cannot be a night of darkness to those who are looking, in faith, beyond the narrow bounds of time, to the dawn of everlasting day.—The Lord has indeed done great things for you, whereof I am glad: and I would again offer my affectionate wishes for your continued joy and peace in beliving. I am very desirous again to hear how you are ;—but fear writing is too great an exertion for you. With regard to myself, I know you will pray for the sanctification of all that is sent ; that Jesus may sit by, as a Purifier: and that his grace may be glorified in all his dealings with me. Believe me most affectionately yours."

Isabella did not long delay replying to Miss —— in the following words :—

"MY DEAR MISS ——,

"I feel thankful for all your kind inquiries after my decaying health, and would have answered your affectionate note sooner ; but I have been much weaker for a week past, and now although my cough is somewhat easier, my weakness is, I think, fast increasing : yet, blessed be our God, I enjoy a peace which more, far more, than compensates all my sufferings. I am grieved to

bear that your complaint is in nowise removed, yet I trust your
soul is flourishing, and bearing much fruit, to the Glory of God.
I sincerely pray that you may experience, yet more abundantly,
the purifying influence of his grace upon your heart, leading you
to glorify him in all things. Perhaps neither you nor I may have
many days to spend in this sinful world; may the Lord threfore
enable us to be faithful to those who are still living without God,
and without hope in the world. O that we may have grace to
tell them affectionately of the love of Jesus. My dear Miss ——,
may we never be ashamed of the gospel of Christ, but may it be
our daily boast: and may we be willing to be counted fools, that
Christ may be glorified in us and by us.

" Yours, in Christ,
"I. C."

Soon afterward, Miss ——— had written to Isabella,
with some fruits of the season.—To the basket, when returned, was appended a slip of paper with the following
words—" In returning my gratitude for the fruit, I pray
my God, whom giving doth not impoverish, nor withhold-
ing enrich, to bless you an hundred fold."—Her sense of
gratitude was intensely keen. She felt every attention,
howsoever slight, very deeply; not only drawing out her
kindness towards those who bestowed it, but most devout
thankfulness to God, whom she never ceased to see in
every thing she enjoyed. Her feelings upon the present
occasion were expressed more at large in the folowing
letter :—

" MY DEAR MISS ——,

"I feel grateful to my God, my rock, my all, for having
again, in his adorable providence, put it in my power to tell you
how much I love you. I hope I have been taught of God to love
you; and to be kindly affectionate towards you for the truth's
sake. I enjoyed much comfort while perusing your very affectionate note; and cease not to give thanks to the God and Father of
our Lord Jesus Christ, who hath delivered you from the power of
darkness, and hath translated you into the kingdom of his dear
Son: and now, although you do feel the immense load under which
the heirs of immortality groan while in the body, our dear Re-

deemer has provided a noble remedy. O yes! he has a crown for every soul. My prayer for you is, that you may never be destitute of the witness of the spirit, witnessing with your spirit that you are born of God. I must again, my dearest Miss ———, return you my unfeigned thanks for your dear brother's visit. My mother being out, I felt desirous to see him; yet after I went where he was, I became so agitated at the sight of a stranger, that I could scarcely utter my thanks for his kindness: but I would take it kind if you would inform him, I felt grateful, very grateful, and that I have not forgotten him to my heavenly Father. It was surely great kindness in him to come on such a message. Although I myself am full of disease, yet for the sake of the gospel I could wish, nay rejoice, to hear of your recovery: this I regret to learn is not the case; but ah! why should I regret it—does not your Father know what is best for you? My cough and breathing have not been so bad these few days past, yet my strength is very weakness: but why should I complain; the storms of life shall soon, very soon be past, and we are assured no wind shall blow, nor trouble rage, on the peaceful shore of Emmanuel's happy land. Adieu, my dearest Miss ———. I am yours, in the best of bonds,

" ISABELLA CAMPBELL."

The lady, to whom these letters were written, was now removed more than twenty miles farther from Isabella; but their interest in each other was not diminished but deepened, and from time to time they corresponded as formerly. In one of her letters, Miss ——— had thus expressed herself, after alluding to various incidents, in which she knew Isabella would be deeply interested:—

"What, O what shall I say of the Author of all these marvellous works; well did the Psalmist say, all my springs are in thee!—Yes, for he is made of God unto the sinner, wisdom, and righteousness, and sanctification, and redemption; and well did the Apostle resolve to know nothing, and to glory in nothing, save Jesus Christ, and him crucified. We may forget, and rejoice to think that very shortly all that is ours shall be destroyed; but how can we forget Jesus, our light, our life, our ransom, our righteousness, our everlasting portion. Blessed be God, he never forgets us. Let his faithfulness make us faithful, let the steady beam

15*

of grace, that emanates from his reconciled countenance, attract, revive, and quicken our souls, and eclipse every other object.— Let the waters which flow from this smitten rock, that follows his people through the wilderness, go down sweetly, causing those that are asleep to speak, and refreshing their oppressed souls, by anticipating the day when every breath shall be praise. We cannot, as we would, sing the praises of Jesus or the songs of Zion in this strange land; because it is his presence that fills each heart with joy, tunes every mouth to sing, and when the soul is taken away it will be true:

> " By day, by night, the sacred courts
> With glad hosannahs ring."

Isabella, in reply, thus expressed herself in the following letter:—

" MY BELOVED SISTER IN JESUS,

" I would bless and adore our reconciled Father, that he hath again, in his adorable providence, permitted me to converse with you on that sweet and soul-refreshing theme, the love of Jesus.— O may he now shed abroad his love more abundantly in my soul, and enable me to praise and extol his all-glorious name, even for the truth and kindness of his love.—O it surely becomes us, who have tasted somewhat of its power and sweetness, to be loud in its praise. With what admiration did the holy Paul speak of it, when he broke out in the following glorious language:—O the height, and depth, and breadth, and length of the love of God, which passeth knowledge. Yes, truly it passeth knowledge; the more we think of it, the more are we over-whelmed with its gloriousness. O my beloved sister, what a great and glorious Saviour is our Saviour! how completely has he finished the mighty work, which, from affection to our poor souls, he undertook to perform.—How graciously has he magnified that pure law, which we rebels had so basely violated; and not only so, but he has brought in an everlasting righteousness, even a righteousness wherewith God hath declared himself well pleased, and for this cause God hath highly exalted him, and given him a name that is above every name, and O is he not worthy; is he not deserving of all this! Yes, he is worthy; worthy to receive the combined adoration of men and of angels. He, who is the root and the offspring of David, and the bright and the morning star, is indeed worthy to receive all glory, and honour and blessing, and dominion, and

praise. Were my strength adequate I could continue to talk of
this altogether lovely, this inconceivably fair and glorious Jesus;
but although I had the tongue of an angel, yea of ten thousand
angels, I could not praise him enough. Yet, sweet thought! the
time is not far distant, when I shall have nothing to do but to
praise him. O how different now!—often, when I would do good,
evil is present with me;—but then I shall be completely purified
from all this vile dross. I tire much for this—I long to be completely conformed to the image of Jesus—to be holy, even as he is
holy—to be meet for the society of the redeemed.

"I sincerely hope and trust that you, my beloved friend, are
enjoying much of the presence of your covenant God ; that being
justified freely by his grace, you are receiving much of its purifying influence, to finish the work of sanctification in your soul. O,
what cause for gratitude, that he, who is our best beloved, has engraven you on the palms of his hands, and hath given you, on behalf of Christ to believe on his name, and for this cause hath he
cast all your sins into the depths of the sea. Never more shall
they be imputed unto you. No, the hills may remove, and the
mountains depart, but his wonderful loving kindness shall never
depart from you, because he who is true and faithful, hath spoken
it. Well does it therefore become us, unhesitatingly to believe
and rejoice in such rich promises, and to trust in the Lord at all
times, for in the Lord Jehovah is everlasting strength.

"How would it have cheered me, on my pilgrimage-road, to
have seen one whom I have been taught by the spirit so much to
love, had our kind Father permitted your visit to ——; but I
would not at all repine. No, good is the will of the Lord, let mine
at all times be swallowed up in his; and although we should never
have the pleasure of saluting each other in this weary and parched land, we shall meet—yes I do not cherish a doubt that we
shall, O glorious consideration, around the throne of the Eternal,
and be for ever employed in adoring that blessed Saviour, whom
now not having seen we love. And should my tired spirit be first
freed from this bondage of corruption, O, with what glowing ardour shall I, my dear Sister, welcome yours; and if the joy in
Heaven, at the arrival of a redeemed spirit, be at all similar to
that experienced at his conversion—how unutterable will be my
joy at the arrival of yours! O how pure then will be our gar-
ments, even linen clean and white, and with what unspeakable delight shall we cast our crowns before him, and shout aloud his

praise, without the least intermission. Yea, we shall sing a song which the angels themselves cannot sing with self application, viz. 'He was slain for us.'

"Your very affectionate note, which I only received last night, appears to have been written some time ago, and I cannot tell you how grateful I feel for it, that amid your own sufferings you should thus kindly have remembered me. My joy was not small to hear of a poor sinner even seeming to inquire the way to Zion. O may the Lord, by his good spirit, lead her unto Jesus, and may she take to herself no rest nor enjoyment until she has the evidence in her own soul, that she indeed be arrayed in the robe of her Redeemer's righteousness, and created anew in Christ Jesus unto good works. She has not been, neither will be forgotten by me at a throne of mercy : and O my dear friend, may you be enabled to show that you are not ashamed of the Gospel of Christ, but rather that you count all things you possess but loss, for the excellency of this grand, this humbling knowledge; and should you ever again favour the least of Christ's children with a note, I shall be happy to hear of your convinced friend.

"I am surely much indebted to you for the soul refreshing sentence you have sent me from Dr. Love's sermon on Dr. Balfour's death. O it was a sweet morsel to my poor soul, and the more so, because I myself have for a few weeks past, been enjoying similar feelings, having lately lost one of my most dear and best beloved Christian friends.—The trial has been very great to me in this weak state : I had just been delighting myself, that in a few days we should meet, and have the pleasure of exalting the Lord together; but ah! how little did I think, that at that very moment he was skillfuly tuning his golden harp to Emmanuel's praise, and unceasingly singing that song which on earth we so much loved, ' Worthy is the Lamb.' Never, in this vale of tears, did I behold one on whom the lost image was so thoroughly reinstated.—He was truly a tall cedar in the house of our God; a shock of corn fully ripe—but why should I mourn? My beloved brother is now rejoicing, happy as his soul can wish.—O for more grace to imitate him as he imitated Jesus.

"I must now express my unfeigned gratitude to you, and those ladies who have so liberally ministered to my necessities.—You will, I dare say, have the kindness to tell them that I earnestly pray they may want for no good thing; but above all, that they may rejoice in the light of God's countenance, and be glad in his salvation. How liberally is that great and gracious promise fulfilled in my daily experience, ' Seek ye first the Kingdom of God, and his righteousness, and all things shall be added unto you.

" I was glad to hear that you were pretty well when you wrote: I hope you still continue to gain strength. Perhaps your Father has much work for you yet, to perform in this sinful world. My cough has been easier for some weeks past, but the hectic fever that comes on in the afternoon consumes my strength greatly. Yet my tranquillity of soul is so great, that I will not dare to say any thing more about the fast decaying casket.

" And now, my beloved friend, farewell. That the Lord, even our Father, strengthen, uphold, and comfort you, is the sincere prayer of your very affectionate friend, in the faith of the glorious gospel, "I. C."

An event to which she alluded in her letter a little previous to this time occurred, which placed Isabella in circumstances that powerfully called forth her christian sympathy. She would have felt deeply the departure of any dear friend, but now she had to sympathize with a sister's peculiar sorrow : but although real mourners, it was a godly sorrow. They both felt they delivered in blessed hope the friend God had taken away ; for not even a transient fear darkened the sepulchre where his holy dust reposed. Suddenly the intelligence came; he had fevered, died, and was buried, while they thought he was still in the land of the living, and yet to hold sweet communion with them, rejoicing to meditate together on the wonderful things of God. The undreaded bereavement was final and complete ; and only the remembrance of his holy society, now, not the enjoyment of it, remained as an element of their earthly felicity. But the soul could glory in tribulation that would thus think and feel ; for the evening she heard of his death, she exclaimed, " Holy Father, it is well, I had expected to have got my harp before him ; but his work was first finished. O I know not whether to weep or rejoice. It is not sad intelligence at all, to hear that a pilgrim has arrived, not only in safety, but in triumph, at

the end of his journey. Eternally lauded be that matchless, endless love that hath guided him safe to Zion; so
that I have not one request to make for him, for he is now
dwelling amid the ravishing and endless glories of the
land of love and delighted spirits. Little did I imagine,
when we last met, that our next meeting would be before
the Throne. Thou art now what thou so much and so
constantly when on earth longed to be, even holy as our
God is holy. Adieu; soon, soon shall this shattered frame
crumble into dust, and I be permitted to strike my golden
harp along with thee; soon shall we meet, never more to
sever, never more to turn aside from gazing upon Him,
who hath loved us, and washed us from our sins in his own
blood."

The sorrow of Isabella, you cannot fail to see, was not
the sorrow of the world, which if drawn forth by the grave
of those they love, only worketh death, making death more
terrible, and increasing the grave's desolate gloom.

The world cannot understand Isabella's sorrow, which
as it flowed, opened up, so to speak, fountains of most
blessed hope and joy, losing entirely whatever it might naturally possess of pain or bitterness. That holy mother in
Israel, however, with whom I have often spoken concerning
Isabella, can, as well as all believers of the same school,
well understand how joy may be in the heart, although full
of natural sorrow. While the dead body of her son, who
had fallen asleep in the faith of the gospel, was deposited
in the grave, although weeping she was seen to smile.
Why? ask the world, who know not how faith can triumph
over, without destroying, the tenderness of nature; because
as she expressed herself, " I felt since I was chief mourner
it was my peculiar privilege to be joyful." The tears, which
mingled with the dust that covered what had been so en-
deared to her motherly tenderness, were sufficiently expressive of nature's travail and suffering; the smile could

not but be from the soul, at that moment inspired by a power higher than that of nature, productive of a joy unspeakable and full of glory.

Another subject, to which she alludes in the letter, and to which she turns with peculiar fondness, in the person and the character of the Lord Christ. Her love and admiration of the Saviour, I have already noticed; but there was an obvious increase in her affection as she familiarized her mind to the contemplation of his excellency, in his various relations to his redeemed people. Whenever a believing visiter spoke with more than ordinary affection of the Saviour, while her soul yielded to a joyful sympathy, her heart easily kindled even into a stronger love than that which she felt towards other brethren. A new tie seemed to be created between them, since the beloved of her soul excited emotions similar to those which she herself was ever feeling. "Dear, dear Saint," said she, after the departure of a believing sister, "how much she has refreshed my soul, by her warm expressions of attachment to Jesus, and her deep consciousness of the evil nature of sin. Yes, she has viewed it in the light of the cross, and there she has seen its vileness.— My soul is tenderly attached to hers—blessed be the dear uniting love which has so cemented us in Christ; we shall see new cause for loving each other through eternity. O may I have grace to appreciate properly the acquaintance of this dear blood-bought soul; to thee, O thou adorable Saviour, I owe all this." The joy which she felt upon meeting with any who could enter fully into her feelings drew forth her gratitude, and caused her to pray only the more vehemently that she might rightly value the blessing; while she saw the especial kindness of the Saviour, in allowing her the blessedness of singing, with another of his redeemed children, the praise of his excellent glory and beauty. "To thee, to thee,

O thou adorable Saviour, I owe all this," she repeated, adding:

> "O to grace how great a debtor,
>   Daily I'm constrained to be,
> Let that grace, Lord, like a fetter,
>   Bind my wand'ring heart to thee."

The continual presence of her Saviour, realized in all her ordinary movements, induced her to think of the various conditions of his sorrowful pilgrimage, when he had emptied himself of his glory ; that she and all his redeemed might be made rich through his poverty. This often gave a peculiar tenderness to her feeling, while his humanity was more especially present to her mind. One night, for example, when her sister was giving her a little wine, she burst into tears, and said, "Ah Jesus, when on earth, was an hungered, and knew not where to lay his blessed head, while I, a vile ungrateful creature, even a sinful worm, am daily loaded with his benefits. Surely this is the depth of compassionate condescension? Bless, bless the Lord, O my soul." The more she studied his character, the more desirous, obviously, she was, to be conformed to him in all things. From the contemplation of his jealous compassion for miserable souls, she felt more deeply her own insensibility, while her soul was all on fire with love to those for whom he died. "O! I wonder," on one occasion, exclaimed she, "how I can be cold and unconcerned, so backward and unfaithful, when I see souls perishing around me. O for more of the spirit of our divine Master, to make me jealous for the immortal welfare of souls." She became, in consequence of such feeling, more and more faithful in the intercourse with all who approached her, fearful of the sin of uttering any of those smooth and deceitful things the ancient Jews desired of their prophets, and loving only to speak like him who is the truth.

As an example of this, to a relation to whom she had often spoken of the Saviour, faithfully warning her to flee from the wrath to come, who had visited her one night when she was very weak and struggling for breath, she thus expressed herself, as appears from her sister's notes :—

"O, eternity stares me in the face: were you in my situation, could you view it with as much composure, could you greet joyfully the approach of death? Ah, I fear you could not. Why, why, do you linger in the city of destruction? believe me your state is awful. Often have I requested, yea, craved you to be reconciled to God; to come and close with Christ, to take him as he is freely offered to you, without money and without price: I find you have not yet done it. I would now again pray you to come; O come! why will you not come? he will take you now, if you will come. The value of your never dying soul, I see at this moment in the light of eternity. Again I say come, but, if you *will* not come, it is not harsh in me, O no, I must tell you the pains of hell shall be your everlasting portion."

To another who had made a profession of religion, but of whose sincerity she had some painful suspicions; from her having heard of her apparently finding satisfaction in objects and pursuits, incapable of yielding any to those who had once known the enjoyment of communion with God, she used these faithful and memorable words :—

"You have either been deceiving me or Satan has deceived you. If you have not known the satisfaction of which you spoke, you have been deceiving me; and if you really did find enjoyment, as you said, Satan has deceived you, and led you to suppose those to be gracious affections which are merely the excitements of natural feeling. Your coming to see me is just a part of that religious profession by which you are so fearfully dishonouring God. You cannot serve both Christ and Belial; and we cannot have such sweet counsel together as we might so long as ye halt between two opinions, and delay casting yourself at the foot of the cross, where a guilty sinner alone can find peace and safety. Had I not said these things to you I could not have died in peace."

16

This inconsistency between profession and practice occasioned grief beyond all expression. One day Mary entered her room, and found her weeping. Upon asking
the cause of her sorrow, she replied :—

"O dear, I am mourning over the abominations which abound.
My soul is pained within me at the inconsistency of many professing characters, but Christians they cannot be ; it is true they
cannot, because God himself has said it. We cannot love God
and mammon ; how then can we account for the earthly mindedness, the want of brotherly love, and the spirit of calumny and
revenge, manifested by many who profess the Christian name.
We must try them by the word of God ; we shall find they are
Christians only in name. O that they would act in their true
character; then would not the way of truth be evil spoken of, nor
the religion of Jesus judged of by the conduct of those who have
never come under its renovating powers.—It has often been urged,
that we have instances of the inconsistent walk of several of the
scripture saints. Ah, we indeed have ; by turning aside from the
great source of happiness, they began to seek it where it did not
exist, and thus fell into sin, but were theirs such lives of inconsistency ? O no ; may the mighty one of Israel shine forth gloriously,
and dissipate the awful covering that the enemy of souls hath cast
over thousands in the land."

While she thus mourned over the prevalence of unbelief and ungodliness, and religious inconsistency, she rejoiced exceedingly when she either saw or heard of any
instance of faith and holiness, and devotedness of the heart,
to the cause of Christ and God. Any holy zeal, especially
among the ministers of religion, she hailed with peculiar
gladness. Of one individual, from whom she occasionally
received visits, she thus expressed her conviction and feeling :—

"Well, I cannot tell you how gratefully happy I feel to-day ;
it is really animating to witness that dear man's progress in the
knowledge of Jesus. His conversation to-day was most deeply
experimental, and warmed my cold heart. For many months I
have watched his advances in holiness, and admired his growing

conformity to Emmanuel : now he has left me far, far behind, and is making wonderful approaches towards perfection ; he is ever mounting upwards, as on eagle's wings, going on from strength unwearied. O my Father and my God, enable me to praise and extol thy name, for the mighty workings of thy spirit in this thy dear servant ; glorify thyself yet more abundantly in him, and by him."

In the emulations of the world, what is found but envy and jealousy,—some form or other of selfishness ? Where is there in any mind a pure and unmingled joy, upon dis-covering a glory that excelleth its own? In minds pos-sessed of the light and love of Heaven it is far otherwise; the joy of complacency, the joy of gratitude, springs from the contemplation of all excellency, however superior to their own: for they see in it only an emanation of the glory of *Him* they adore and love, to them the chief among ten thousand, *beaming with an altogether perfect love-liness.* In such a manner did Isabella feel : whenever she witnessed any remarkable growth of grace, or any attain-ment in the divine life more rapid than her own, she glad-ly gave God glory, and beheld therein blessed fruit of the Saviour's travail of soul, sympathizing with the satisfaction that springs up in his bosom. For example, after a dear friend had prayed with her, she said, "I was going to en-deavour to celebrate the praise of our God for what he has done in him since we last met ; but I believe I had better lie still and wonder, for I am lost in grateful aston-ishment, and feel that though Gabriel were to descend to assist me, our united praise would be far too feeble for such rich manifestations of his transforming love. O ye glorious hosts, praise ye the Lord."

When she heard of any who were remarkable for their piety or devotion, she would long to have intercourse with them; and sometimes, even frequently, her desire was gra-tified. In one instance she felt peculiarly thankful ; for the gratification was connected with the promotion of an object which so engrossed her heart—the glory of her Redeemer by the faithful preaching of the word. A young clergyman of the church of England, of whose zeal and devotedness she had often heard among the contiguous mountains, she longed vehemently to see—God one day gave her the desire of her heart. He came to her residence, to witness like others so singular a piety, and not only conversed with her, but collected the neighbouring cottagers, and from a station within her hearing, addressed them on the great things of the Kingdom.— "My wish is now granted," said she, to a friend, "I have not only seen the man after whom I so much longed, but I have heard him proclaim a full Christ to empty sinners. Oh! all this goodness is insupportable—what, what shall I say of it? I shall indeed remember this day with adoring gratitude. Have you ever heard such a God-glorifying discourse? I cannot tell you what I feel—I am quite satiated with, the good things of Heaven. Surely the angels have been rejoicing with peculiar joy this memorable day. One thing is sure, his word shall, yea has not returned unto him void. O! our souls praise our God. Praise his powerful name."

During this service she seems to have been unusually refreshed and blessed. At its commencement she was very weak, so much so that when Mr. —— gave out the psalm, she asked a friend sitting by her in her apartment, "May I sing?" "Yes," replied her friend, "If you can, sing and praise your God." While singing she appeared quite absorbed. When the psalm was ended, she said, "O! I am afraid that the view of so much glory will soon wear me out, and prevent me from listening at all to the sermon. O Lord, remember I am in the body; thou knowest I am dust." Her joy during the whole of the sermon was so excessive, that she found it necessary to employ herself principally in prayer, that the Lord would preserve her from crying aloud and disturbing the people. With her hands sometimes clasped together, and sometimes having a hold of her friend's, she would look upward and say ; "O, our God shall be glorified. He is glorified in our hearts to-day. What nourishing truths do I hear ; what great and glorious things are now spoken of Emmanuel. O my Father, what compassion, what love to thy poor ungrateful child, that thou shouldst permit me to hear the gospel once again, before I go hence and am seen no more."

To this individual she seems to have had a particular affection, regarding him as a faithful and devoted minister of Christ. Upon one occasion she urged her sister and a friend to go and hear him preach, although at the distance of ten or twelve miles. "I am sure," said she, "you ought to go and see our dear Mr.———, ere he leaves this land. Were it my Father's will, how gladly would I go and talk with him of the great mystery of godliness. How I love this servant of Jesus. How I admire Christ in him : seldom have I seen one who exhibits so much of his image. Never shall I forget ; no, I shall follow him in spirit, though I cannot in person, to distant lands, and often please myself with the thought, that we are holding communion at the throne of our Father. Yes, I shall labour along with him while he travels from place to place, preaching the gospel of the kingdom. I shall wrestle with God in prayer, that he would strengthen him with all might in the inner man."

The emotion which she seems to have experienced during the singing of the Psalm, was similar to what she felt often during that part of religious worship. We never parted without singing a hymn. It was not, however, the melody that in her excited emotion, although she had an exquisite taste for the simple, sacred tunes of our country : for in the reading of passages of scripture, I have seen her as much moved as in singing verses of hymns. It was the truth seen in both which excited her; the view which they contained of God's glory gave her the joy.—Whatev-

16*

er rapture was felt at these seasons, was obviously drawn forth by nothing connected with the world of sense ; it was rather the unavoidable expression of some great and bless- ed thought with which her mind was filled. So far from such a state of mind or feeling depending on circumstaces, or intercourse with others, in the solitude of her chamber such views would fill her soul, that, as she expressed her- self, " I saw often so much of the height and depth, and length, and breath of the love of God in Christ Jesus, that I could find no relief except in weeping ; and those tears were sweet which flowed before the cross of Christ. At other times, such a flood of glory rushed in upon me, that had it continued, I felt this frail body could not have endu- red, I must have died."

Rapturous as such expressions are, and though at first sight they seem the result of feverish excitement ; all who approached Isabella, or knew any thing of her mind, could not but conclude they described real feelings, and had an- other source than mere elevation of spirits. For such states of mind occurred at all stages of her disease, at any time of the day or night, and without any obvious connection with her acuteness of suffering, graduating, so to speak, throughout all degrees of intensity. Besides, when so im- pressed, she never lost the perfect command of her mind; for example, her resorting to prayer during the service al- luded to, for the purpose of tranquillizing emotions excited by the contemplation of the glory of God in Christ, is de- cisive of her peculiar wisdom and propriety.

She was indeed a singular model of calmness, peace, and solemnity of manner, during the whole period of her illness ; so that although affected with a malady which subjects its victims to facility of excitement, it seemed to have had little or no power over her mental feelings. The great source, with her, of excitement, was obviously spirit- ual and divine. When weakest and most depressed, the praise of her God and Saviour would kindle her soul to a holy enthusiasm ; when strongest and most elevated, the same means would mingle awe with her most fervent and passionate thoughts and feelings.

Not unfrequently, indeed, I have applied to her manner an expression in our psalms, and said, that there was a "grave sweet melody" in it, which I had never witnessed in the world before. Often I have found her much exhausted, little able, or apparently inclined to speak, occupied with her own thoughts, but not many sentences were necessary to effect a change upon her entire aspect. Thought after thought seemed to breathe life through her frame. She would become more fluent and eloquent, and at last would converse, her voice strengthening as she proceeded, and with great energy of manner, upon the glorious things which were never absent from her waking, and as has been already remarked, not even from her moments of deepest repose. After sitting for hours by her bedside, although exhausted myself, I have left her more vigorous than I found her, so wonderfully did the exhilarating thoughts of Jesus nerve and brace her bodily frame, while her mind, occupied upon the noblest objects, seemed as if triumphing over the infirmities of her body and retarding its decay.

For a long period her disease continued, as you know ; and of this I am persuaded, had it not been that she was so occupied she must have at a far early period sunk into the grave. Indeed she herself had no other conviction. Upon hearing, on one occasion, that an unbelieving friend, who had no sympathy with a soul exclusively occupied about the realities of eternity, had observed that it was her con- constantly thinking about religion that made her so ill; with a look of rapture, she replied, "The Lord grant him such joy as he has given me ; I am weak just because I am a sinner, why should it be thought that religion is the cause of my illness ? Are not many ill who never think of reli-

gion ; are not many ill who blaspheme God, because of
their pain? Were it not for the blessed religion of Jesus, I
should be the most miserable of creatures, hastening on to
the blackness of darkness for ever. The person who says
that religion will make one dull, knows nothing about it;
he has never yet tasted the sweetness of holding converse
with the Father, through the blessed Spirit. I would say
unto all who think me dull, my soul doth magnify the Lord,
and my spirit doth rejoice in God my Saviour. I would say
unto them, dull and dreary was my life until I knew Christ,
but finding him, I have found what makes me happy
now, and shall make me happy throughout eternity. O that
men would but learn what true happiness is !"

That such should be the effect is most natural : in the
most dreadful operations, how often do professional men calculate upon a favourable result, from the tranquillity of the
mind, from its self-possession, or the diverting of its attention from the bodily suffering. The great agonies Isabella
periodically endured, and which induced her repeatedly to
feel and to believe as if in the very crisis of death, had her
thoughts been unable to fix themselves, dispersed, desolate,
agitated, amid the unreal and shadowy whole of visible and
temporary interests : her body, dissolving, relaxed, distracted through all its fibres, without some strong energy sustaining and preserving the coherence of its parts, it must
have crumbled to its original dust ; but in Isabella's greatest agony, there was a deep, undisturbed, blessed repose of
thought ; each pang that seemed to threaten instant death
was met and counteracted, as it were, by a joy springing
from the glory beyond the grave. The dew of her Father's
love was ever dropping upon the fiery darts of her excruciating suffering. How little the world knows of this, and
yet how true, that the severest pangs may ever find a rich
compensation in the experience of the tenderness of God,
who afflicteth not willingly, nor grieveth the children of

men. As truly as one like unto the Son of God, was seen walking with the three children in the midst of the fiery furnace on the plain of Dura, (and often that record was brought to her remembrance with great power,) did Isabella realize in the time of her greatest extremity the presence of him whom her soul loved. How foolish, how very foolish is the wisdom of the world in the chambers of disease! Religious conversation is scrupulously avoided, lest apprehension and disquietude invade the mind of the patient, and thus diminish the probability of recovery; whereas, for want of fixed principle and certain prospects, the mind having no strength to endure, and thus without any counteractive, the body yields to its own tendencies to corruption and decay. Isabella's experience of the power of religion sustaining her amid suffering, you know; and when she heard of any afflicted like herself, she was anxious to ascertain whether they had the consolations which so sustained and comforted her mind, and when possible, to use whatever means might induce them to lay hold of what she had found so effectual. As a proof of this, she engaged in a correspondence with a young woman then resident in the parish, a native of Ayrshire, whom she had not seen, but in whom, since affected with a similar malady, she felt a peculiar interest.

The last of her letters, addressed to this young woman after her return home, is preserved, and which I believe did not reach its destination till she had been gathered to her fathers. It gave Isabella great joy, however, when I told her that from her brother's account of her last days, she seemed to have died in the knowledge of the peace of God.

"MY DEAR AFFLICTED FRIEND,

" Hearing, from our dear friend, Mr. ———, that your health is still on the decline, and that little if any hope is entertained of your recovery, an intense desire for the happiness of your immortal soul has again induced me, notwithstanding my weakness, to write you a few lines; and before proceeding farther, I would ask have you yet experienced any of the blessedness of that man whose sins are forgiven, and whose iniquities are pardoned; has Christ yet been formed in your soul the hope of glory ; has his blood purged your conscience from dead works to serve the living God ; and do you feel his spirit witnessing with your spirit, that you are indeed one of his peculiar people—that being justified freely by his rich grace, you have peace with God through our Lord Jesus Christ ? Do you long to be holy even as God is holy, and look forward with joy to the period when you shall be entirely freed from sin in all its direful influence ? If this, my dear friend, is your blessed and delightful experience, I would rejoice in your joy, and give glory to God on your behalf. But if, on the contrary, you have realized no such feelings, you have much reason to fear, however correct your views of the truth may be, that you have never yet cordially embraced the blessed gospel ; for the scripture clearly shows that confidence toward God and delight in the hope of glory, are immediately connected with being justified by faith: see Rom. v. 1 and 2. Many indeed content themselves with the belief that they may be justified, and that God is able to save them, if he pleases ; but this is not sufficient. It may indeed yield a relief from despair, but cannot fulfil that peace and serenity of soul, which a knowledge of our being already justified does. The Apostle, when writing to the saints and faithful in Christ Jesus, supposes them to be susceptible in a greater or less degree of this joy, just in proportion to the strength of their faith. Rest not then, I sincerely entreat of you, my dear friend, unless you have ample evidence of the new creation in your soul. Many maintain that we may be believers, and yet ignorant of it; and there is great reason to fear, that Satan often makes use of this as a powerful argument to prevent men from examining themselves, suggesting that a knowledge of our justification is unattainable in this life. But ever blessed be God, the sacred volume is very explicit on this head : see the whole of the second chapter of the Epistle to the Ephesians : see also Eph. v. 8.—2 Cor. vi. 6 and 13; Col. i. 13. and 21, and first epistle of Peter, first chapter; from which you will see, that believers are exhorted to holiness, from a recollection of the immense price at which they are purchased. But I must draw near a conclusion, as I feel my strength almost gone, and I would do so by again imploring you to cast yourself entirely on Jesus. He, he alone is the only sure refuge from the awful blast of the Divine displeasure. He is willing to receive you, yea, he is inviting you to come; he is saying whosoever will let him come and take of the water of life freely. The Lord hath sworn that he hath no pleasure in the destruction of sinners; no, he would rather they would come to him, and live: cease not then to cry mightily to him, to enable you to lay hold of the Saviour. Faith is his own gift, and my soul rejoices that it is: O may he grant unto you that faith, which will uphold you in the last conflict, and cause you to triumph over death, hell, and the grave. Adieu, my dear friend: my sincere prayer for you is, that you may be saved.

"Believe me, your true friend,

"ISABELLA CAMPBELL."

In such a way, in the secluded abode of Fernicarry, lived and felt, the holy Isabella. Of what she had received, and for which her soul was continually framing hymns of joyful gratitude, she was anxious, in the enlargement of her loving heart, that all should partake. She could not go out and in among you, to tell of all she knew, and all she wished you to know, but she kept not silent to any that approached her; and frequently individuals who were seriously impressed and in quest of religious counsel, visited her, whom under the influence of such a spirit she delighted to address. She was very faithful, while her great discretion and tenderness peculiarly fitted her for such a duty. Her very appearance tended to give effect to her sayings. One young woman, for example, thus exclaimed on her return: "O how gentle and kind she is; what a cough she has, and what she suffers, yet she is as meek and patient as a lamb!" And another, in the notes new lying before me, thus expresses herself: "When I saw her, I was so much struck with her appearance, that I wept for some time: I thought there was nothing so heavenly to be seen on earth."

The following is an extract from the account of a third, which I insert as illustrative of Isabella's intercourse with these young people:—

"At my first visit we did not enter into particulars; she, however, dwelt much upon the love of Jesus, his faithfulness to his promises, and on God being fully satisfied with his atonement, and his being well pleased with believers in him. Upon this subject she dwelt with a confidence that astonished me at the time, particularly as she expressed her assurance of being herself in covenant with God in Christ. She also spoke with peculiar energy and delight of some christians, whom she heard had died rejoicing in the Lord. I often observed her raise her eyes, as if engaged in prayer and communion with her heavenly Father. Indeed should she not have spoken one word to us, yet the expression of her countenance, at such times, was enough to have convinced even those who never thought of these things, that there is a reality in religion. Her cautious prudence also, in entering into conversation on these things, struck me very forcibly. When I visited her again, I was left alone in the room with her, having felt a strong desire to unbosom myself to her, on the subject of personal and experimental religion. I gladly embraced the opportunity of revealing my whole soul to her. I began by giving her an account of the deep and painful exercises of mind, through which I had passed. Her sweet countenance immediately assumed a rather clouded expression, and she said with much emphasis, 'You have been shaken to the very foundation, and it is of the Lord's mercy that you have remained unto this day. I myself,' said she, 'have been assailed with many temptations, but I knew that he would with the temptation make a way to escape.' 'You had,' I observed, 'the advantage of me, for I did not know at the time it was an enemy that did it.' 'Yes,' she replied, 'I knew it was an enemy that did it. I had been tried with many temptations; but there was one which my soul dreaded above all others; and with that one he tried me with double severity.' She then asked, how I came to think on these things. I told her how I was religiously educated; after which she spoke of the sad delusion that some were under, supposing that, since they had had a religious education, all was well with them. 'The case of such,' said she, 'pains me very much, as it is impossible to come at them. There is another class, that is a great burden upon my spirit; I mean those who think themselves religious, and are not; my soul trembles for the consequences, if they should continue in this state, until they appear before the judgment seat. When such persons come to me,' she added, 'I feel my whole frame shaking with agony for them;

and blessed be God, that he has in many instances enabled me to be faithful to them.' Talking of the struggles of inward corruption, she said:—' I cannot think that all is well where that is not felt. In passing through a church-yard, all is still and quiet, because all is dead; but when passing through a town, all is bustle and noise, because all is life: in like manner, where there is no spiritual life, all goes on without any struggle: but where there is most spiritual life, corruption is most felt!' We talked next about the holiness of God's character: her feelings she could not express on this subject, but closed her eyes and groaned.—At parting, she took a most affectionate leave of me. ' Now my dear,' she said, ' watch unto prayer, for the great enemy of souls is continually going about, seeking whom he may devour; and he well knows what is in us to answer his purpose.' "

When leaving her, says another of her young friends,—

" I frequently asked her what advice she had to give me; she in general said, ' Keep near the throne, cleave unto Jesus, and be not ashamed of his name; but confess him before the world; and in all things may you adorn his gospel, walking in much wisdom towards those that are without.'—If I happened to say, ' When shall we meet again?' her usual answer was, ' Perhaps we shall never meet on earth again, but what does that signify—we shall meet around the Throne of the Eternal.' "

These extracts are sufficient to give you some idea of the kind of intercourse carried on in Isabella's " little sanctuary." She was indeed well fitted to speak of heavenly and eternal things to her young friends; she had been so long lying on the very verge, so to speak, of this transitory and polluted world, peacefully and intently gazing on the untainted purity and loveliness beyond it. In the figurative, but expressive language of a Highland cottager, to whom she was much attached, and who delighted to hold communion with Isabella; " She carried her frail body far on her road to Heaven. She even ascended with it to Mount Pisgah; and from that height she enjoyed many a sweet view of the promised land." Indeed her

17

whole mind seemed so absorbed in these contemplations, that when occasionally I cherished hopes of her recovery, it always seemed to me that she was fitter to die than to live. Under this impression, I said to her one day; "Well, Isabella, were you in reality to recover, what would you do, or how would you feel." "O I think I would weary; but no," she suddenly checked herself, "I could never weary in telling of all that my Saviour has done for me; and in entreating others to behold and see the beauty in him which I see, that they might desire him as their portion."

We had frequent conversations regarding the jealousy with which believers ought to watch their longings to depart. That there is often sin in such feelings, is unquestionable; while they may also be employed by the enemy of souls, as engines for insinuating his most cunning temptations. These longings are thus sometimes the nursery of murmurings, allowed often to arise, even fondly cherished; as if, when on the borders of the promised land, Satan could no longer assume the garb of an angel of light. Sometimes I thought Isabella had yielded too readily to these longings, as if she had forgotten a lesson often taught her; that if Christ left Heaven to die for sinners, the desire in a believer's mind to remain, to promote the objects for which he died, although amid peril and suffering and sinfulness, cannot but be more acceptable to him, than a desire to depart and join in the choirs of the redeemed, that have reached the Heavenly Zion with everlasting joy upon their heads. At last, her mind seemed generally affected in the way described in the following reply from her sister to one of those questions I put, for the purpose of procuring the most accurate information possible, of the state of her feelings when I myself was no longer permitted to enjoy her society. Her chief desire for heaven, arose from the wish of being conformed to the will of God,

and therefore she was satisfied to remain, because that was
his will ; or in what she herself said to one of her friends :
"When most filled with God and Heaven, and longing most
to be with my God and Saviour, then I am most content to
remain." Her life was indeed a progressive conformity to
this will.   While her persuasion of safety remained ever
present to her mind, this arose from no perception of any
excellence in herself; its origin or continuance was not co-
existent with any imaginary perfection or attainment in holiness; belief in Jesus as her Saviour she ever regarded as
the spring or principle of holy living; but neither in her own,
nor in any other case did she imagine this effected an in-
stantaneous conformity to the mind of Jesus, whose meat and
whose drink it was to do his Father's will.   " His law," to
use her own words, " is not written in the hearts of believers all at once, but as it comes with power by the Holy
Ghost ; and as his law is written in the heart, the image of
Jesus more and more appears."—So it was with herself;
and her progressive conformity to that blessed and glorious
image is affectingly described in the following extract from
a letter of Mrs. ——'s who saw her about this time, to
whom, as has been recorded, at an early period of her life
of faith, she unfolded the state of her mind.

"Her strength of body was much reduced, but the inward man
greatly strengthened since I had parted from her. Her first words
to me were, ' How much have I longed after a meeting with you,
that I might tell you how unspeakably precious Jesus is to my
soul.' It was remarked, ' My beloved is mine, and I am his;'
when she replied, ' That has been a precious portion to me of late,
and indeed the whole of the song. I cannot tell you what I have
enjoyed, while meditating upon it, for it has been for some time
my favourite passage of scripture.   His love is better than wine;
his name is as ointment poured forth ;' and she went on, mentioning passages of divine inspiration, with a life and appropriateness
of which only they who were privileged to hear her, can form
any idea.—She said, ' Daily am I discovering more and more of

the desperate wickedness of my heart; but this only serves to
make Jesus more inexpressibly precious to my soul. The change
which he has wrought in my heart by his own spirit, is so great, I
can have no doubt of its being the Lord's work.' She encouraged
us all to live near to him. She spoke to Mr. ——— about the
snares attending the business of this life, and warned him affectionately, pointing out the danger of being over much careful
about the perishing things of time.—' I felt your kindness to me
deeply; but what shall I tell you, or where shall I find words to
describe to you the wondrous kindness of Christ Jesus to my soul?
Although I were in a dungeon, and no earthly friend near me,
with such manifestations of his love, I would be happy beyond the
power of language to express.' Then, when speaking of her
restless and feverish nights, 'O but he gives songs in the night,'
said she; ' his word is made sweet unto my taste.'—She went on
talking of his goodness in giving her these desires of her heart,
and in sending those friends to see her in the flesh, whom her soul
loved for his name's sake.—We were about two, or at most, three
hours with her, which seemed only a few moments; one of those
highly privileged seasons, when foretastes of the heavenly country
are enjoyed; when the soul rises on wings of faith and love,—leaving objects of sense far behind; viewing the King in the beauties
of holiness, obtaining enrapturing glimpses of the land which is
purchased and preparing for all the redeemed : one of those seasons, when the soul is constrained to cry out, ' O how dreadful
is this place; it is none other than the house of God and the gate of
Heaven.' We were all dissolved in tears, not of sorrow, but of
the deepest gratitude and joy, for having been permitted to experience such manifestations of the power and reality of divine grace,
of his gracious remembrance of his own words to those who meet
together in his name, condescending to be in the midst of us, causing our hearts to burn within us, and breathing on us by his holy
spirit, and kindling in our souls devout and lively affections, and
ardent desires after more enlarged communion with him. Isabella's
lovely countenance beaming heavenly joy, conveyed to us some
faint emblem of that state of perfection when the body shall be
raised a spiritual body, a fit companion for the soul to bloom in
immortal youth and beauty.

" We left this Bethel place, expecting to behold this lovely
Saint, who so conspicuously reflected the image of her blessed
master, no more on earth ; but our hearts overflowed with thanks-

giving and praise to our Father in Heaven, who was so abundantly glorifying the riches of his grace in enabling Isabella to bring forth so much fruit to his glory. The impressions made upon our minds by this interview, were of that kind which are far too deep to be communicated in words; they were such as the world can neither give nor take away."

Some time afterwards, Mrs. ———— received a letter from Mary, containing the following interesting message :—

"Dearest Isabella bids me say to you, that her joy is truly equal to her capacities; that the inextinguishable flame within her is, she humbly hopes, becoming daily more strong, and she trusts the day is not far distant, when it shall entirely consume every particle of remaining iniquity, in that land of unsullied purity, where the highly favoured inhabitants uninterruptedly triumph with increasing ardour in their glorious Head."

In such a way, for about eighteen months subsequent to the time she attained to the knowledge of the truth as it is in Jesus, did her heavenly Father manifest himself to our dying friend; continuing to her such joy and peace in believing that her sins had been taken away by the expiatory blood of his eternal Son :—or to use her own expression in one of her messages to me, that they were all "cast by himself into the mighty depths of his gracious forgetfulness, " exciting within her an unceasing flow of love and gratitude.

The Hymn.

Come on, my partners in distress,
My comrades through the wilderness,
  Who still your sorrows feel ;
Awhile forget your griefs and fears,
And look beyond this vale of tears
  To that celestial hill.

Beyond the bounds of time and space,
Look forward to that heavenly place,
  The Saints' secure abode ;
On faith's strong eagle pinions rise,
And force your passage to the skies,
  And scale the mount of God.

Who suffer with our Master here,
We shall before his face appear,
  And by his side sit down ;
To patient faith the prize is sure ;
And all that to the end endure
  The cross, shall wear the crown.

Thrice blessed bliss—inspiring hope !
It lifts the fainting spirits up,
  And brings to life the dead ;
Our conflicts here shall soon be past,
And you and I ascend at last,
  Triumphant with our Head.

The Scripture.

Dm not our heart burn within us, while he talked with us by the way, and while he opened to us the Scripture?

A friend loveth at all times, and a brother is born for adversity.

Hast thou seen the doors of the shadow of death?

Yea, though I walk through the valley of the shadow of death, I will fear no evil.

We glory in tribulations; knowing that tribulation worketh patience, and patience experience, and experience hope; and hope maketh not ashamed, because the love of God is shed abroad in our hearts by the Holy Ghost.

For our light affliction, which is but for a moment, worketh for us a far more exceeding and eternal weight of glory.

CHAPTER IX.

WHAT our good Lord does for me! night and day
I find him with me, and he shows me still
Fresh wonders! What a thing is Jesus' love!
Soft is my heart as infant's flesh; yet able
Like adamant or steel, to stand the shock
Of death and hell, and cut its way thro' all.
There's something in me, moment after moment,
Spreading and rising like a tree of life:
I follow it, I scarce feel the ground I tread on—
I'm wholly Christ's!

THE summer and autumn of 1826 passed away; many
had seen Isabella, and many had listened to the words
which fell as the dew of heaven from her lips, for which
they must answer at the judgment seat of Christ. I myself feel, that to have seen so much in her, and to have
heard so much from her, of the glory and love of the Lord,
imposes a responsibility from which time cannot set me
free; but which, in so far as it has led me to lay this record before you, this faithful record, I am desirous to bless
God.

The stormy weather of the winter season prevented me
from visiting her frequently, but I was thus able perhaps,
when I did see her, more easily to mark her progress in
the life of God.

During the intervals of personal communion, I had,
either from her sister or directly from herself, intelligence
of her health and feelings. To show you how this intelligence was often conveyed, I insert the following note
from Mary :—

" I intended to have written yesterday about the state of our
dear Isabella, but was prevented by her painful suffering. The
spitting of blood has almost left her, but the pressure on the lungs
is very great ; so great that I almost tremble to hear her attempt
to speak even a single word. But the soul of our well-beloved
Isabella is without doubt in health. Jesus is her constant theme :
she appears to be holding uninterrupted communion with him. I
cannot tell you, now, any thing of her joyful feeling, but will write
to you soon more fully.—She desires you to rejoice in the Lord
always ; and bids me say, how much, how very much she has rejoiced on your behalf. She bids me tell you also, how fast she is
hastening to behold with unclouded eyes that Saviour who has
done so much for you both, and not only to see him, but to enjoy
him for ever. There she rejoices in hope of enjoying your company throughout endless ages :—' and tell him,' she now says,
' how much I long to enjoy his company for a little, even in this
gloomy vale.' "

As a specimen of Isabella's own communications, the
following has considerable interest :—

" MY WELL BELOVED FRIEND IN JESUS,

" I have detained —— I fear much too late; but hope you
will pardon me. Indeed we felt so happy, that we could scarcely
think to sever. I humbly trust the Lord has abundantly refreshed
our poor weary souls with a glimpse of his glory in the face of
Jesus. O my beloved friend, how sweet, how passing sweet, to
drink from that river which maketh glad the city of our God ! I
sincerely hope that you are drinking copiously of it ; and enjoying sweet fellowship and communion with your reconciled God
and Father through the blessed Spirit. May he ever be near you,
and fill all the cravings of your soul with himself ; and enable you
to sow, with much zeal and affection, the incorruptible seed, and
to wait with patience the increase. I was just thinking of you to-
day, and thinking how easy a matter it was with God to gladden
your soul, by bringing unto the obedience of the truth many of
the souls of your charge. O that for his own glory's sake he would
do this ! I shall weary much until I see you. I long greatly to
talk with you over again about Jesus, our dear compassionate
Saviour, and the inconceivable glory which shall be revealed.
Dearly beloved —— is, I think, in a most encouraging state ; the

spirit seems to be convincing her more and more of her unworthiness, and will, I feel assured, in his own due time apply unto her soul the healing balm of the blood of the Redeemer.

"Yours, in the truth, with much affection,

"ISABELLA CAMPBELL."

A few days afterwards I saw her, and remained with her for many hours. At this visit she alluded to, and more particularly described many passages of what may be called her spiritual history, with which in this record you are already acquainted. My impressions still are very vivid, of the rare union she displayed of confidence in God with profound self-abasement; of the absence of all doubt of her relationship, with broken heartedness and contrition of spirit. Never did assurance of faith sit more meekly on any believing soul, or the appropriation of Christ's salvation, with an ever present apprehension of the unmerited grace manifested by God in its bestowal, more beautifully harmonize. She had deeply studied the character of Jesus: in his person discovered a superlative beauty; and formed such just conceptions of his official character, as to see and feel at all times that his priestly sacrifice and intercession, however sufficient to justify and perpetuate her confidence, only imposed upon her the greater necessity of listening to his counsel as a prophet, and obeying his injunctions as a king. Through him she obviously was advancing, day by day, to clearer and higher views of God. She was lost in amazement, as she contemplated the glorious Godhead. It was not, however, the amazement of ignorance, but of knowledge; that knowledge which, originating amid a world of guilt and death an immortal life of holiness and felicity, enabled her to understand why the apostle exclaimed, "O the depth of the riches, both of the wisdom and knowledge of God; how unsearchable are his judgments, and his ways past finding out." "I am lost in a sea of wonders," she would say; and in her was indeed exemplified the great truth, that those only who know something of God, do truly acknowledge and apprehend the incomprehensibleness of his perfections ; that those who now know the love that passeth knowledge, manifest a capacity of being ultimately filled with all the fulness of God. Her most frequent expression regarding God was, " O his boundless, changeless love, manifested to a rebel universe in the gift of his dear Son." Although she held the doctrine of election, this never induced her to limit the freeness of the gospel. Her lowly conceptions of herself, her (if we may use the expression) unspeakable abasement of soul, seemed of necessity to keep ever present to her mind the idea of electing love : the habitual remembrance of her resistance to the truth, from the days of her early childhood till the attainment of peace, irresistibly convinced her, that, but for the interposition of God's love, she must have perished for ever. But in the gospel she had received, she saw what all ought and were called upon to embrace ; nor did she ever imagine that any of Adam's family should have it to say, either in this or in the world to come, " I am miserable, because my Creator would have it so ; I am in poverty, because the unspeakable gift was not given to me."

The idea, therefore, that some were and others not elected, never palliated in her mind the guilt of rejecting the Saviour ; in each unbeliever she saw the contraction of guilt as great as if the blood of the Lord had been shed especially for him. She knew as much of God as enabled her with holy reverence to think of his secret counsels ; and she saw so much of his manifested love, as to mourn continually in secret places, that any one of the same flesh and blood with herself should turn away from beholding it. She attempted not to reconcile the mystery of the guilt of unbelief, and the incapacity of believing : she saw love every where, and more especially on the hill of Calvary ; that was sufficient in her thoughts, to establish the guilt of a blind, a scornful, and unbelieving world.

Having herself seen the great sight of divine love, a light went with her through the whole scripture, directing her to whatever declaration or promise was suited to sustain or console her mind. " For this God is our God, for ever and ever : he will be our guide even to death. Can a woman forget her sucking child, that she should not have compassion on the fruit of her womb? yea she may forget, yet will not I forget thee ; yea, I have loved thee with an everlasting love, therefore with loving kindness have I drawn thee. The mountains may depart and the hills be removed, but the covenant of my peace shall not be removed." These more particularly seemed, that evening, as upon former occasions, to stir up in her soul the most lively conceptions of the immutable faithfulness of the love of Him, who having rescued her from such misery, still encompassed her with songs of deliverance, and girded her soul with such continual gladness. Then, she would fix upon various passages illustrative of his love ; of the way he caused the cup of his promises to run over, so attractive of their notice yet so scorned by men.—When quoting for example—" Seek ye first the kingdom of God, and his righteousness, and all these things shall be added unto you"—" How wonderful," said she, " as if his kingdom and his righteousness were not of themselves sufficient." How alluring to thoughtless men to say all other things should be given to them ; or as she exclaimed much about the same time, " How wonderful the goodness of the Lord ! In having Jesus, I am happy had I nothing but a bed of straw ; but he says all things shall be added unto you ; I think myself the most ungrateful creature upon earth, because my love is so cold." Then, as at all other times, she seemed entirely free of any thought or care for to-morrow. Some, by a strange inconsistency profess, if indeed they are worthy of belief, to depend on God

18

for raising their body from the dust ; when it is too evident,
they often mistrust his providence for a crust of bread to
preserve it in life. By such let her expressions, in connexion with the passage you have read, be held in everlasting remembrance, be woven, as it were, into their daily
thoughts and feelings : " I would not give up the sweetness
of relying from day to day on the bounty of Providence,
for the best worldly portion." O what a blessed poverty !
How truly, in possessing the kingdom of God, was it given
her all things richly to enjoy. Truly in her were realized
the declaration of heavenly wisdom, " I lead in the way
of righteousness, that I may cause those that love me to inherit substance, and I will fill their treasures." She was,
in the contemplation of God, already as it were, filled with
his fulness ; and divine contentment pervading her spirit,
her joy was indeed full. Her poverty and sufferings, seemed to have become in her mind high and holy privileges ;
because they enabled her with less uncertain sounds to
speak of what she saw in divine goodness, and what was
the origin of her mental blessedness. " If I had been in
possession of health, and freedom from want, people of the
world might say, I had the same to make me happy that
they had ; but amid weakness and suffering, when nothing
in this world had any power to relieve it, it becomes obvious that my increasing happiness is the enjoyment of God."
The following letter to her friend Miss ——, about this
time, (the last she wrote to her with her own hand,) is at
once expressive of this increasing happiness, and the delight she had in speaking of divine love :—

" MY DEAR FRIEND, WHOM I LOVE IN THE TRUTH,

"Grace, mercy, and peace, from God our Father, and from the
Lord Jesus Christ, be multiplied unto you God is my record,
how much I long after you, in the bowels of Jesus Christ ; and
although my bodily weakness has prevented me sooner returning
my heartfelt thanks for your kind remembrance of me, and more

especially for your two last letters, the which were in very deed
a refreshing to my poor soul: yet I trust I have not been forget-
ful of you, at those seasons when, for the sake of our dear Intercessor, I have been admitted into intimate communion with the
Father. O my beloved friend, how astonishing, that this infinitely
pure and holy Being should condescend to dwell with such creatures as we are ! Well, well might the angelic hosts desire to look
into this amazing mystery of love; and surely, it becomes us who
are the more immediate objects of it to begin our hallelujahs,
even in this militant state. Thrice welcome happy home, when
we shall have no evil hearts to mar our adorations; but when,
with glorious delight, we shall admire the unclouded beauties of
our dear adorable Emmanuel. Yes, dear, dear Saviour, thou art
all. How sweet to think that thou shalt be our theme for ever
and ever; O yes, nothing shall ever be able to separate us, unworthy though we be, from thy love. Grant, O grant us then
while here, more grace, to enable us to proclaim to all around,
to taste and see that thou art good, and that they alone are blessed who trust in thee. Because it is our compassionate Father's
pleasure, I will not, my dear friend, grieve at your weakness : he
is wise, and since he has given you eternal life in his Son, he
will cause all things else to work together for your good. I bless
him for what of his gracious presence he vouchsafes unto you;
and pray that, for Jesus' sake, you may enjoy still nearer fellowship with him ; and when you are so favoured, I hope you will not
forget me, who oftentimes groan, being burdened.

I think myself considerably weaker these some weeks past,
and would fain hope the time is not far distant when I shall join
my unworthy voice to those who are at this moment triumphantly
singing, ' Worthy is the Lamb.'—And now, my beloved friend,
farewell ; may you go on all the day in the light of your Father's
countenance. Commending you to Jesus, I remain,

Your affectionate friend in truth,

" ISABELLA CAMPBELL."

Soon now, however, my intercourse with Isabella was
to be interrupted by the providence of God. A few days
after the interview I have already recorded, I was visited
by the malady which so long prevented me from going
out and in among you as at other times. Her conversa-

tion and society I felt to be one of my greatest bereavements; while amid my sufferings, it was very pleasing to think of the way I had seen my dear young friend bear what the hand of our Father imposed upon her. I knew also, that although not able to express her sympathy in person, that was not wanting and unexpressed where it is most blessed to give and to receive,—at the foot-stool of our reconciling Father's throne. The following note from Mary was at the time, and is still to me, a pleasing token of her affectionate anxiety; while expressive of those loving and devout feelings so becoming in the intercourse in this valley of peril, and through disease, and death, to the city which hath foundations, whose builder and maker is God.

" Our beloved Isabella bids me say, that she would have written to inquire for you many days ago, had not her great weakness disabled her. She sympathises deeply with you in your affliction, and rejoices to know that Jesus sympathises in all the sufferings of his dear bought people ; and prays, that while in the furnace, you may behold the Son of Man walking beside you, and that your soul may drink deeply of the consolations of Zion. Before she heard of your being confined, she often said, how much I long to see him ; he has not been so long away for many months: and hearing of your serious indisposition, she much fears that she may never behold your face in this weary land ; but rejoices in the anticipation of meeting you before the throne, there to join your voices with the countless myriads of angelic and ransomed spirits, in celebrating the wonders of redeeming love ; to which blessed abode she is evidently very fast hastening. A little time since she was seized with a most alarming cramp in the stomach; and she as well as ourselves, imagined the important hour was at hand. Her Father has however averted it for the present. She cannot now stand for half a minute without assistance. I am sure were you to see her now, you would be much struck with her weakness. She earnestly solicits an interest in your prayers, that she may be ready whenever her Lord shall call. Should God spare her, she will send you a few of her messages next week."

The messages, which her sister alludes to and promises, were contained in the following letter :—

Saturday Evening, April 27.

" MY WELL BELOVED FRIEND,

" You cannot imagine with what emotions of joy I learnt to-day from our friend ——, that you were somewhat better. Indeed the intelligence was peculiarly soothing to my poor weary soul; because I had just heard a little while before, from ——'s servant, that you were suffering great pain.

" O ! my dear friend, how little do we know of the future ! At our last interview, neither of us, I dare say, thought that we should so soon have been deprived of the privilege of conversing together of the joys, the immortal pleasures of Emmanuel's happy land ; far less that it should remain doubtful, whether we shall ever meet again in this world of vanity, evil, and pain, behold each other, and be favoured with a renewed opportunity of talking of the great mystery of godliness—God manifest in the flesh. Alas! when I think, that I may never here behold your face in the flesh, I am made to weep for sorrow ; and to upbraid myself for the ill use, I fear I have not unfrequently made, of your dear visits. Yet notwithstanding my ingratitude, never, O never! I trust, shall I forget those sweet, those much to be remembered hours, which you have spent by my bedside, when Jesus, dear Jesus, was our principal theme.—How often have I, upon such occasions, felt the feeble spark of love within me gain additional strength, and my soul, as it were, drawn up nearer to him, whose presence alone can satisfy, delight, and animate the soul. And you, my beloved friend, I trust, also realized much of his favour and friendship.

" When I think of the many long walks, which you have often had by the side of the Gairloch on my account—frequently when the multitude were enjoying their refreshing repose; my obdurate heart is sometimes mollified by grief, and I am constrained to make the inquiry, ' What am I, that the Lord should have been so mindful of me.' And I can find no other answer than this, ' He loved me, even because he loved me.' O yes! nothing in me, nor about me, could possibly induce him to love me, for I was his decided enemy in my mind, and by wicked works. But eternal glory to his name, that me, vile worthless me, hath he reconciled. It gave me great delight, and has furnished me with another cause

18*

of gratitude, to learn the serene state of your soul, and the happy view your Father is enabling you to take of your present severe affliction. Truly you and I, and every saved sinner, are monuments of divine mercy; and it well becomes us to feel thankful that our sufferings are only temporal, and work out for us a far more exceeding, and eternal weight of glory.

The Lord, my dear friend, has not afflicted you for nought. O no! he will not unnecessarily grieve one of his dear children; but has a wise and important end to accomplish by all their trials. My fervent prayer for you is, that you may come out of the furnace much beautified; and receive the sanctified use of every pain you feel. O! that your soul may climb mightily those steeps which separate us from our real home, and at all times experience the witness within you, that ' all things are yours, whether life or death !' Often do my thoughts wander towards you ; and sometimes before I am aware, I conceive myself conversing with you, and was my strength equal to the desire I feel, I would soon be beside you in reality. I am a great deal weaker than when you saw me ; how true that ' all flesh is grass !' I suffer a good deal from exhaustion and pain. But I will say no more on this subject ; for what are my pains, what are my weaknesses, compared with my mercies? They are even very nothings, and ought to be forgot amidst my blessings. That gracious Saviour who has hitherto been the light of my countenance, is still at hand, supporting my aching spirit with fresh supplies of his bounty ; and causing my whole soul to rejoice. O! I cannot tell, neither do I think I shall ever be able to tell, so long as I sojourn here, what I feel of *his* love and care! I am sometimes almost overwhelmed with a sense of his glory and admirable adaptedness to my every want. At other times, I am led in thought to Mount Zion, and for a time suppose myself an inhabitant of that blessed place, until my wicked heart by some of its evil suggestions arouses me from my reverie, and reminds me that I have still much to get rid of, before I can get there. O! my dear friend, the amazing privilege of joining yon immaculate company that inhabit the new Jerusalem, in singing the praises of our dear conquering King ! O ! how glorious he at this moment is ! *He* who was once a man of sorrows, and acquainted with grief, is now a mighty Prince and Saviour, receiving the adorations of thousands, whom his efficacious blood hath washed from their sins. Let us then praise *him !* for angels who are without sin, and need not his blood to wash them, nor his grace and spirit to sanctify them, seem delighted with the employment. When you draw near to his footstool, remember me; tell him that I want to love him much more, and to be conformed more to his likeness. But I must stop, although I have much more to say. I shall be longing much for Mary's return, until I hear how you are bolding. Farewell! Commending you to the care of the Good Shepherd of Israel,

> " I remain, yours affectionately,
>> " In the faith of the Gospel,
>>> "ISABELLA CAMPBELL."

The state of her mind is sufficiently indicated by the letter you have read, as well as by the following, written about the same time to the friend whom she had never seen; but to whom it is very evident she was every day become more and more tenderly attached in the bonds of the gospel.

" MY DEAR FRIEND IN THE SAVIOUR,

" I cannot express the pleasure which the perusal of your dear note has afforded me ; I was just saying to Mary a short time before its arrival, how much I longed to hear from you, and the delight I often experience when contemplating what the Lord hath done for your soul. But O! my dear, dear friend, how limited while here, are our most enlarged conceptions, of what Christ has done for ourselves and others. It is only when we arrive on the heavenly shore, and view the awful gulf from which we have by distinguishing grace been snatched, that we shall be able to estimate aright the glorious privilege of being heirs of God and joint-heirs with Christ.—How invigorating the thought, that we shall one day be able to render unceasing adoration to him who hath loved us, and washed us from our sins in his blood, and look on the way by which he made us meet for such exalted services. O! my beloved friend, when I think of being permitted to follow the Lamb amid the glories of Mount Zion, and of being led by him to those fountains of living waters, and of being completely freed from all pain, and sorrow, and sighing, and our daily enemies sin and Satan, I am almost swallowed up with delight. O! the comfortable hope of purity, not to speak of any thing else, but happiness as well as holiness is promised to us; yes, my dear friend, such happiness as even the deeply experienced, and lofty soul of Paul, who had been in the Third Heavens, could not at all comprehend. O! how animating, that unworthy we shall one day be partakers of so much blessedness. Now, we must needs taste the painfulness of rebellion against the source of all excellence, but in that land of delights, holiness and happiness shall continually attend each other, and each contribute to the glory of its companion. There shall the Christian be eternally freed from all his imperfections; there shall he be permitted to eat plentifully of the hidden manna, and to gaze throughout unnumbered ages on the incomparable beauty of our adorable Emmanuel:—

> ' Millions of years our wondering souls
> Shall o'er his beauties rove,
> And endless ages will adore
> The glories of his love.'

"But my beloved friend, do we here know nothing of the heavenly joy? Yes, I am aware you can with sincerity say we do. Are there not seasons when the soul enjoys much sweet communion with the Father, and with Jesus through the blessed spirit? Are there not seasons when he is pleased to chase away the languor and frightful insensibility which so frequently affect our souls; and pour out upon us the spirit of grace and supplication, giving the soul a keen relish for divine things? And are there not seasons when the glorious sun of righteousness is pleased to look with beauteous effulgence through those mists which sometimes eclipse his admirable suitableness from the view of the soul, filling it with joy unspeakable and full of glory? But I must quit this dear exhaustless subject for the present. I am most happy to hear that your dear —— is now well; may the Lord by his spirit lead him unto Jesus, the only true refuge!—I felt much for you, when I heard of his serious indisposition. The last accounts we heard from the manse, our beloved friend was somewhat better. O! my friend, I cannot tell you how much his illness has affected me. What has he not been to me! Yea, all that I could desire, and more than I could expect a human friend to be.

Pray, my beloved friend, that he may lose much of what is his, and receive more of what is Christ's in the furnace; this I doubt not will be the case. The news of your recovery has greatly cheered me. O! I trust you will yet be spared to tell many of a

Saviour, and of their miserable condition without an interest in him. O! that you may at all times be enabled to glorify your Father who is in Heaven, by your walk and conversation; and may he open your lips and cause you to speak boldly for his name. I have been thinking lately of the way in which the Lord made you to think of me, and I have been filled with wonder and astonishment. Two or three years ago, when I used to hear and talk of you, I felt such an inward glow of affection and delight, and often wondered whether I should ever know more of you; wishing at the same time a wish that I might once behold your face in the flesh; and now that I look back on the sweet intercourse we have had, and the many pleasant thoughts I have enjoyed concerning you, I cannot help thinking that the Lord himself must have inspired me with the former desire. Were it not for my weakness, I should have written to you long ere this; but I am much weaker at present than when I last wrote. I was much reduced about a fortnight ago, by intense pain, so that I thought my time, even the happy time was come, when my soul should mount on high, and appear before the Lord in Zion. The Lord however has been pleased to restore me a little; and I only want not to be impatient, for his time is surely good. Mary joins me in christian affection to yourself and your beloved sister, while I remain in bonds which no man breaketh,

" Yours,

"ISABELLA CAMPBELL."

From both of these letters it is obvious how much heaven and its glory occupied her thoughts. The incomparable beauty, however, of the adorable Emmanuel, was that which gave to heaven in her mind all its attractions. The "comfortable hope of purity," as she beautifully expresses herself, "was ever drawing her soul to the future," howsoever lively her present joy, in believing that all was well; and the accomplishment of that hope she felt must be in the contemplation of the King in his beauty. Then, "we know we shall be like him, for we shall see him as he is," was habitually present to her mind: the prospect of that beatific vision of her Saviour, excited no

enthusiastic or irrational rapture, but gave to her unspeakable blessedness, in the assurance that she should be conformed to his image, being made like him in moral purity
and loveliness. As she grew in grace, experiencing the
sanctifying influence of the truth, the excellent glory of
him who is the truth, became more and more vividly present to her soul. He had made atonement for her sins,
he had instructed her in the things of the kingdom, he had
defended her from her spiritual enemies, he had raised
her from death, cherished her life, encompassed her with
all desirable blessing: her heart, therefore, full of gratitude, with passionate love continued gazing in constant
contemplation of all he was, and had done for her soul.
Language, she felt, could not express her emotions; and
latterly, they found vent by using the beautiful imagery of
the song of Solomon, to express their relationship, and her
feelings; her estimate of his excellency, and the feelings
which its contemplation awakened. Latterly she read and
studied much that portion of scripture. It might have
been supposed, that the fervour with which she speaks
had been excited by the language and sentiments of that
impassionate song. It is remarkable, however, that till
within a short period of the date of these letters, it had
not particularly attracted her attention. It is true that
the fancy of young converts has often been excited strongly by the mystical descriptions of this inspired song; and
transports have thrilled through the bosom when thinking
of the altogether-lovely rose of Sharon, that would have
been motionless and silent in the contemplation of the
severe holiness of the Saviour. But with Isabella it was
different: she had studied his character elsewhere, and,
labouring to express the glorious beauty seen, the exquisite
love felt, she found in the song what other language failed
to portray. From the song, in fine, she did not learn
what her Saviour was; but having attained already that

blessed knowledge, she shed the light of that knowledge
upon all the mysteries of that divine composition. Occasionally my young clerical friends visited her; and one
of them returned, declaring that he saw in that book what
he never saw before : that Isabella had a key which un-
locked all the chambers of its imagery.

The manner her attention was directed to this portion
of scripture, was remarkable and worthy of record. One
night, when she was very weak in body but comfortable in
mind, these words were brought to her remembrance, filling her with unspeakable joy. "His left hand is under
my head, and his right hand doth embrace me." She could
not recollect where they were to be found, but feeling dissatisfied till she saw them in the word of God, she got a
light, and soon discovered they were written in the song
of Solomon. She derived so much comfort and joy of
spirit from the realizing of the Saviour's presence with
which its discovery was accompanied, that she was led
irresistibly to study it over and over.

For many months indeed, and in her various states of
mind, it was her favourite book, ever finding in it something to·express or show forth the suitableness of the blessed Saviour to her condition. So impressed was she with the
great importance and value of the treasure it contained—
seeming to her an exhaustless treasury of spiritual comforts—that she felt dissatisfied when any believing friend
failed to see what she saw, or sympathise with the feelings
its perusal excited. Often, to her sister, whom she so tenderly loved, she could not conceal this feeling. Although
naturally, from her greater liveliness of fancy and acuter
sensibility, more likely to be passionately affected by the
composition of the song, at that time, she did not so fully
comprehend its meaning, and Isabella from the very greatness of her love to her, felt exceeding sorrowful that it was
so; because she could not but think she was deprived of a

source of most exquisite enjoyment. Finding in it what was so suited to express her views and feelings regarding the Saviour, it is easy to conceive, how, by a natural reaction, those views and feelings were affected by the study of the song. How her perceptions of Christ's glorious beauty became clear—how still more fervent love and attachment to his person possessed and pervaded her soul. Her great sufferings from time to time required peculiar soothing and consolation; and the distinct personality of the Saviour continually before her, enabled her to realize, more thoroughly those feelings and sympathies in him, by which, according to the record, he is touched with the feeling of our infirmities, and afflicted in all our afflictions. Some weeks subsequent to these letters, a crisis arrived when more peculiarly she needed the presence of her Saviour, preceded by feelings described in the following extract of a letter, which, at the time, had been sent to her beloved friend.

"Mr. ——, who is with me, had gone to see her on Friday, when he found her very weak indeed, and much exhausted. She revived before he left her, as indeed she always does when by any excitement of Christian communion, heaven, or the truths of heaven rise with greater brightness before her mind. On Saturday she had been livelier, but the nightly perspirations have returned; which, independent of other causes, must accelerate her decay. Without artificial means she now cannot sleep. A little opium, however, has the effect of soothing her pain and procuring occasional repose. These perspirations, the doctor says, indicate the formation of another abscess, which must diminish her strength already so greatly exhausted; but it is the will of God. No fear follows her to the grave: all is light, and hope, and joy. She has been long, as if blessedly gazing from the margin of life upon the glories of the other side of the stream, turned away entirely from what interests the perishing children of men, and far too frequently even those who seem to have a hope within them. But, from her correspondence you know her, and yet, I think, were you to enjoy her personal communion, your impressions of her singular

spirituality of feeling would be still deeper than they are. Her
very bodily frame seems to cease to be earthly, so possessed she is
with the greatness and glory of the truth. She seems, as it were,
all over soul, and that soul all breathing of heaven and divine
things. Is it yet possible, (for I was told such abscesses sometimes
wear themselves out, should the constitution endure, and termi-
nate in recovery,) is it possible that she may yet be preserved, as
a burning and a shining lustre in this dark world? In the valley
of the shadow of death she has indeed been long shining, with a
radiance seldom seen in the walks of the divine life: but in health
and vigour, in the sunshine of youthful activity, were she to meet
the eye of a professing world,—many I trust, who cannot approach
her now, might be constrained to glorify the grace of God, and
call her blessed. Often, I wish you could meet—often I have said
so to herself: and although you may see from her letters how she
loves you, you cannot know as I do how vehement her affection is.
I would, that not you merely, but that the whole Church might
see her, that in her they might glorify him she so adores and mag-
nifies in all her thoughts and feelings."

Often, as you know, Isabella had felt within reach of the
grave: not merely then, had she in her meditations, and
as from a distance seen, but experienced as it were all its
fears and hopes, all its sorrows and joys. She had found
indeed nothing terrible there. The Father had been ever
with her, and she had not ceased to know in whom she had
believed, or to feel that he was indeed faithful in whom she
had reposed her all for life or death, for judgment or eternity. Now, however, all around her were persuaded that
she had not long to survive—she herself had formed the
same judgment of her condition; and although in great
weakness and suffering, she dictated the two following letters to be delivered after her death. The first, expressive
of her faithfulness and anxiety for the spiritual welfare of
one of her kindred whom she had long loved; but who yet
was, as she dreaded, in the gall of bitterness and in the
bond of iniquity.

19

" My Dear ———

" Nothing but an earnest desire for the salvation of your immortal soul, could possibly prevail with me in this weak and enervated state to write to you; and in all likelihood, before this be put into your hands, this poor frail body shall have lost its immortal inhabitant, and these eyes shall be for ever shut on terrestrial objects. If my memory does not greatly deceive, I think that upon some former occasion, I endeavoured to represent to you, the absolute necessity of flying immediately to Jesus, the only refuge for the guilty. But as yet I have received no evidence that you have done so. O! the salvation of the soul is not a matter of moonlight. O no! it is impossible for you to conceive, or me to describe, the awful misery of your condition, so long as you remain a stranger to God and holiness. See what the Scripture saith on this head. St. John, iii, 36, ' He that believeth in the Son hath everlasting life, and he that believeth not the Son, shall not see life, but the wrath of God abideth on him.' ' Tribulation and anguish upon every soul of man that sinneth, on the Jew first, and also on the Gentile.' Now, my dear, we have all sinned, and are lying under the curse of a broken and violated law. Yes, though many do not think it, the best moral character that ever trod the world, and the man who is a pest to society, are alike the children of wrath. But God, who is rich in mercy, for his great love wherewith he hath loved a lost and sinful world, hath provided a glorious way by which he can pardon sinners, and yet be a holy and just God. Yes, the eternal word hath assumed our nature, and was made sin for us, he who knew no sin, that we might be the righteousness of God in him. And now the message to all is, ' Believe on the Lord Jesus Christ, and thou shalt be saved;' and I now declare this message to you, and I conjure you to believe it. Do not think that you believe already, or that you never doubted it. ' That which is born of the flesh is flesh,' and to say that you never doubted that Christ was your Saviour, is a sure proof that you doubt it still. O my dear friend ! be not deceived. If you believed the Gospel message, you must be influenced by it. But you may be ready to ask me, '' How can any be sure, whether they believe it or not ?' O! this is an awful delusion. I would just ask you, how are you sure, when you believe the witness of man ? You know well, that we cannot believe any report, without being fully convinced that we do so. Far less can we believe that God hath given us eternal life in his Son, without being conscious of it. O no! it is impossible. Faith, as you must know, is just belief. The only difference is in the thing believed. For instance, were one of your acquaintances, whom you had always regarded as a person of integrity, to come to you and say, 'O your brother got himself dangerously hurt,' you would not question his sincerity, but in all likelihood would fly to your brother's assistance. Now what evidence had you, for believing that what the individual told you was true? None other, but that you had always heard this person speak the truth. Well now, my dearest, can you suppose you would be thus influenced by believing the witness of man, and be nothing at all moved by believing the testimony of God who cannot lie? Can you believe that the Lord Jesus bled and groaned and died for you, and not be filled with the deepest contrition for sin?—And can you further believe that you have redemption through his blood, even the forgiveness of your iniquities, and not be filled with love, joy, and grateful astonishment? Ah no! My dear, as you love your own soul, do not think you are believing in Christ, when you are still his enemy in your mind. Can you be a follower of Jesus, and yet give no proof of it in your walk and conversation? Can you love the adorable Saviour, and yet look with contempt upon his dear followers, and count them fools, and the offscouring of all things? No! no! I speak to you as one who must shortly give an account to my God and Father. Do not think I am carrying the matter too far. Does not your own conscience bear witness to the truth of what I have said? Does not that faithful minister sometimes tell you that all is not right? And can you, O! can you thus sport on the brink of everlasting wo? Can you thus mock the God who made you, and make him a bell, by rejecting the testimony he hath given concerning his Son? Will you seek to fill up the designs of your soul with very vanities, and neglect to seek that grace, which alone can satisfy all its cravings? Believe me, my friend, the time is rapidly approaching, when, unless you repent, these very nothings with which you endeavour to occupy your time and thoughts, shall increase your misery and pierce your very vitals.—'Beware what earth calls happiness. Beware all joys, but joys that never can expire.' Fly then, O fly from what earth calls happiness. It may promise what it pleaseth, but it hath no solid happiness to bestow. All its joys are transitory, and very unsatisfactory, even while they remain. I speak from experience, and well, well I know I never enjoyed real happiness until I knew Jesus. Will you not then begin to seek after this happiness, this joy, that will admit of the closest investigation? Say not there is yet plenty of time for repentance. A few more setting suns, and your doom may be fixed, irreversibly fixed. 'Now then is the accepted time, now is the day of salvation. To-day, if you will hear his voice, harden not your heart.' Jesus now sits upon a throne of mercy, and invites you to come and take of the waters of life freely. Cast yourself, then at his adorable feet, and entreat him to make you what he would have you to be. May he, by his blessed spirit, thus enable you to surrender your all into his hands, and so you shall be safe. And now, my dear, adieu! and whatever use you may make of this letter, remember the day will dawn, and a terrible day it will be to many, when you and I shall meet around the Great White Throne. I then will have to give an account for having written, and you for the use you have made of this letter. Again, farewell! I am exceeding joyful in the prospect of death. O yes, leaning on Jesus, I could at this moment, with the utmost composure, launch my soul into the vast ocean of eternity.

'I long to see a smiling God
In everlasting light;
When I shall reach the blest abode,
And gain th' enraptur'd sight.

My towering thoughts disdain to roll
Amongst these earthly toys;
Jesus is dearer to my soul
Than life and its all joys.'

"I have left as a token of my affection for you, a copy of the Olney Hymns, the which, my dearly beloved sister, Mary, will deliver unto you.

"Your affectionate friend,
"ISABELLA CAMPBELL."

"P. S. Tell dear —— from me, to fly while it is called to-day, to the hope set before her in the gospel. "I. C."

The next was intended as the last service of her singular friendship—feeling, as it were, that she could not depart to heaven, without leaving her dear Miss ——, a memorial of her tender and devoted love.

"*April*, 1827.

"MY DEAR AND TENDERLY BELOVED SISTER IN THE
LORD JESUS,

"Before this shall be put into your hands, all that is mortal of
her, whom you have so often, and so affectionately called your
dearest Isabella, shall be mouldering beneath the clods of the valley, exposed to the devouring greed of the hungry reptile. And
the spirit which now dictates, shall be shouting with inconceivable triumph the praises of our Emmanuel, before the throne of
the most high God. Yes, my dear sister, while you are reading
this, my unincumbered spirit shall be swimming with infinite delight in the spacious and eternal ocean of God's fathomless and
unchanging love; wondering, and every moment seeing new cause
for wonder. And although to the unconcerned and mere formal
professor of the name of Jesus, this may, and I know will appear
strange and presumptuous language, yet believing him faithful,
who has promised me eternal life in his Son, I dare use no other,
I dare indulge no other prospect than that of being more than conqueror through him who hath thus loved us. For, sooner than
question for a moment my being justified freely by his grace,
would I question whether I had ever received a letter from my
beloved sister whom I now address. Being justified, then what
follows, but that I shall be sanctified and glorified. Yes, and I
believe the period is not far distant, when, respecting me, all this
shall be accomplished. Indeed many things combine to strengthen
the thought. The spirit seems desirous of a better lodging, and
the frail tottering cottage seems unable long to afford it shelter.
O no, I feel that it is fast, fast decaying, and must soon tumble
into dust. The enemy of souls, also, as if weary of the warfare,
as if quite worn out by opposing Omnipotence, seems almost re-
gardless of casting at me his fiery darts, and even the remaining
corruption of my nature, will, I believe, soon be annihilated,
through the communication of rich, free, purifying grace. Yes,
my much valued sister, worn though I be, I shall soon sing louder
than Gabriel, and a song too, which he never sung. Yes, I shall
soon compose part of the number who stand upon the sea of glass,
having the harps of God, who sing the song of Moses and the
Lamb. O yes! yes! I shall see that Lamb who was slain, even
our adorable Emmanuel, even him who is now the joy and rejoicing
of our hearts, even him whose glorious effulgence irradiates with

unfading lustre the length and breadth of the New Jerusalem. O
what unutterable delight must seize my astonished and unfettered
soul, when I behold the wondrous majesty of him, who in the garden of Gethsemane was sore amazed and very heavy. When
I see him, who condescended to assume our nature, and become
obedient unto death, even the shameful hated death of the cross,
crowned with glory and honour, the joy of his church on earth,
and of his church in heaven, reigning king in Zion; O! my dear,
dear friend, surely when I see him, I can never look from him.
But why do I talk thus? Where can I cast mine eyes around the
sacred place, where his glory doth not shine. Yes, I am persuaded there is not a single spirit among the thousands of redeemed,
but sees him, and that plainly too. O Jesus! Jesus! Jesus! thou
art all! We shall praise thee, and that eternally. O what a
theme! The creator of the ends of the earth in our nature, even
God our Redeemer! Wonder, O heavens! for the Lord hath done
it. Ah! my dearly beloved sister, how does my feeble imagination
falter, when I would attempt to pry into the profound subject!
Surely, surely, it is when we come into close contact with the great
and Almighty God, that we feel our own nothingness, our want
of knowing any thing as we ought. But seeing, my loved friend,
that I shall soon cease to talk in the language of mortals, I hasten
to say a few things unto you, which I wished. O! may the Lord
God give me grace to speak in much wisdom—to speak according
to his holy will in all things. O! I would speak as one who has
seen the perishable nature of all beneath the sun, who has found
them inadequate to satisfy the vast desires of an immortal spirit.
I would speak as a sinful and dependent creature, as one who has
seen the complete adaptedness of Jesus to her very need, who has
embraced him as all her salvation and all her desire; and lastly, as
one before whom eternity appears with awful importance. And
O my dear, dear friend in the Lord, I would first request of you
as my dying wish, to rejoice much in Jesus, in the Lord your
righteousness and strength. I know that you already rejoice. I
bless and adore our God always, in your behalf, making mention
of you always in my prayers. I thank him, that he hath given
you to see the simplicity that is in Christ, and caused your soul to
rejoice in the contemplation of his gloriously finished work, but
· I wish you to rejoice yet more and more. I wish great things for
you, but not greater than God is willing to bestow. I wish you
to be valiant in the cause of the Redeemer, that in the most try-

ing circumstances you may be able to say, I am not ashamed of
the Gospel of Christ, and to exhibit this by the whole tenour of
your life. O my friend, indulge, live much in prayer. It is a glorious privilege granted to sinful dust and ashes. O! that we should
prize it so little!

"When I think how little the professed friends of Jesus live in
prayer, I do not, cannot wonder at their inconsistencies. Can
you not, do you not say that prayer is a privilege? Have you not
at the throne of your Father, enjoyed seasons of unspeakable delight, moments which you would not exchange for this world, and
all that it contains. In holding communion with him, through the
blessed Spirit, has not your soul been feasted as with marrow and
fatness, and have you not longed to make your escape and be
gone? Let your life then be a life of prayer, and while others are
wearying themselves with the transient things of time, you shall be
walking as a stranger and pilgrim, seeing how you may please
your God and Father in all things. O see that you lose no opportunity of commending Jesus. It pains me now, that I have lost
so many. Endeavour to press the precious, the important truth,
that our God is love, upon all around. Pray for, and rejoice much
in the prosperity of Zion. Soon, my friend, the night cometh
when you can no longer work. My dear, dear friend and sister,
I use great liberty of speech in addressing you, for though I have
never seen your face in the flesh, I have received ample proofs
that you have been taught to love me, and I ask and believe my
Father will reward you for it. Yes, you have oft refreshed my
body and spirit. Often have your letters refreshed this poor soul,
and sent me to a throne of grace, when otherwise I would have
been cold and barren. And I bless our God and Father, that our
union shall not be dissolved when my spirit leaves the body. O
no! It shall exist, yea, exist for ever! O my sister, weak as I
am, I find it pleasant to review the singular manner, in which our
acquaintance commenced, and the soul-satisfying intercourse we
have since enjoyed. I do not know how it is, but I never felt to
any one I had never seen, the intensity of affection I do towards
you. O! my ever dear friend, I could wish to see you, I could
wish to clasp you in those feeble arms. I could wish to talk with
you of Jesus, and by the eye of faith to take a survey together of
the promised rest. But good is the will of the Lord, should it appear right unto him, that I should never behold your dear countenance in this weary land. If in heaven, the spirits of the just made

perfect are ever called to accompany the angels in going forth to
minister to the heirs of salvation, who knows (at least mortals do
not know) but my glorified spirit may, some time or other, hover
above thy bed, and see you, though unseen. And at all events,
although we should never see each other's faces till the resurrection of the just, our souls, long before that momentous day dawn,
shall mingle with yon untainted company who surround the throne.
I am not afraid, my well beloved sister, to leave you a sufferer in
this insalubrious clime, for I believe that as your sufferings abound,
your consolations will much more abound, that your Father will
mightily support and comfort you, and enable you to glorify him
in the fires. In the hands therefore of that God, to whom I myself
am going, I with much confidence leave you. Now may the God
of Peace, that brought again from the dead our Lord Jesus Christ,
that great shepherd of the sheep, through the blood of the everlasting covenant, make you perfect in every good work to do his
will, working in you that which is well-pleasing in his sight,
through Jesus Christ; to whom be glory for ever and ever. Amen.

" Tell your dear sister, that though I do not know her much, I
love her much for the sake of Jesus, and believe I shall know her
better in heaven. Till we meet there, my dear, dear sister, farewell.

" ISABELLA CAMPBELL."

Some time after having performed these duties, she was
seized as with the very agonies of death—she felt, at least,
as if the house of her tabernacle was at last giving way, to
afford to her spirit the joyful freedom from sin and corruption which she had long panted after.

In these circumstances she dictated the following letter
to myself:—

" May 27.

" MY WELL BELOVED FRIEND IN JESUS THE SAVIOUR,

" This will in all probability be the last letter you shall ever
receive from one who feels towards you no ordinary affection, and
whose soul has often been refreshed in your dear company. Solemnly impressed with the amazing-realities of the invisible world,
I find no time to say any thing more about this poor diseased body, than merely that it is fast decaying, and will soon be an unfit

habitation for this immortal spirit. Yes, my dearest friend, I am fast, very fast, hastening to Emmanuel's peaceful land.—There, no temptation shall ever prevail to separate me for a moment from our best beloved. There, throughout eternal ages, shall I gaze with uninterrupted delight on his matchless loveliness, and sing with unutterable fervour, the wonderful riches of redeeming love. Yes, my dear, my very dear friend, there shall be no want of communion then; no dark, no insensible, no ungrateful feeling is ever experienced by any of the favoured inhabitants of the new Jerusalem; happiness, even consummate happiness, in its highest signification, is enjoyed by them.

With what profound humility do they worship their God! Yes, my beloved friend, and our God, even our God. If those pure beings who know nothing of sin, veil their faces, as they proclaim his holiness; and if the heavens be not clean, in his sight, O, how glorious, how passing glorious must *He* himself be! and (humbling consideration,) how faint and imperfect our most exalted conceptions of his unheard of excellence, when we can approach him with so little reverence! Language fails me, my dear friend, when I would attempt to describe unto you, the extraordinary beauty, fulness, and adaptedness to my condition, which I see in Jesus. He is truly a plant of renown, a physician of infinite skill and value, and although he sees meet to allow my body to languish and die, I feel assured, that by the abundant communication of his grace and spirit, he will soon have effected a complete cure upon my once perishing soul. Be stirred up, O my soul, and all that is within me, to bless and magnify his holy name! World! thou couldst never have afforded one such pleasure as I find in Jesus, the dear refuge of my very soul. Ah! how vain! how unsatisfactory! how passing! are all things beneath the sun! Surely they are vanity and vexation of spirit. Yes, I have found them to be so. O that immortal minds should so demean themselves as to be pleased for a moment with any thing short of the friendship and communion of God. Man pretends to loath what is unworthy and mean, but when we think how far below the dignity of an intelligent being he is content to dwell, we shall find that he is really vile and mean. What an humbling object in his natural state, and yet how fair and lovely with Christ's comeliness!

The immense value of souls, is at present very clear before me. So much so, that I hate and abhor myself for my unfaithfulness to these poor creatures around me, whose conduct awfully demon-

strates whose servants they are.—Had we only such a message as
was given to the angels, to deliver unto the inhabitants of Sodom
and Gomorrah, to tell them of, we might well be filled with trembling, as we endeavoured to make it known; but then, when
there is such a glorious way of escape from the fire, and when
Christ is the way, the truth, and the life, why be silent? It is
cruel, it is awfully cruel to be silent. O my Father, and my God,
pardon, pardon for thy mercy's sake, my unnatural hatred to
souls!—But why should I occupy so much of my time in talking
of myself? it is Christ, Christ alone, I wish to extol; and have I
not much cause to extol him for what he hath done for you, my
dear friend in the gospel? Yes, I undoubtedly have; O how it
has refreshed my soul to hear of your faith and patience under
tribulations. I hope you have got such a meal, as shall make
you vigorous for a long while, and enable you to press on with
redoubled ardour to the mark, for the prize of the high calling,
that you may know more and more what is the hope of his
calling, and what the riches of the glory of his inheritance in
the saints, and what is the exceeding greatness of his power, to
us-ward who believe. I pray not only that your own soul may
grow in grace and prosper, but for the sake of your poor people,
do I earnestly pray, that you may be a scribe well instructed into
the mysteries of the kingdom, and be the messenger of peace to
many souls. The Lord enable you to be instant in and out of
season; this I am assured no gracious soul will ever regret. O
the many opportunities I have allowed to pass, without commending the blessed Jesus to sinners, wounds me at this moment very
keenly. But I must prepare to bid you adieu. And shall I never again, my most affectionate of earthly friends, be permitted to
behold you in this gloomy vale? O! shall I never be permitted to
talk with you in the language of mortality, of our Jesus, our Saviour, our all? Shall I never again ease my overburdened soul, by
acquainting you with my spiritual secrets? If not, surely even
amidst the glories of heaven, I shall still remember you my dearest
of friends; still remember those soul-satisfying seasons which you
have spent at my bedside, and adore the wisdom of our Father,
for all the measures he adopted to meeten my soul for the society
of angels.

" My sincere gratitude I return you, for having allowed dearly
beloved —— to come and see me. I rejoice greatly because of
her faith in Christ, and love to all the brethren. Providing I am

spared a few days, I should like to see her once again: she is a dear, dear soul, and will, I believe, be a useful member in the house of our God. She is making rapid progress in the path of peace. Now, my ever dear friend in everlasting bonds, farewell! Our God hath said, be faithful unto death, and I will give you a crown of life. We shall meet in glory.

" Your's throughout eternity,

" ISABELLA CAMPBELL."

These exertions were wonderful for one so weak : but her soul, she felt, was sustained by divine nourishment, which nature knew not of, as was indicated by even her most incidental expressions. For instance, when asked by her sister to take a little wine and cake, she said, looking at the bread :—

" O! it is sweet, but it is bitter when compared to Jesus the bread of life. I cannot eat much earthly bread now, but blessed be God, I feel inclined to take a little of the heavenly food."

Upon another occasion, when helping her to drink :—

" O it is refreshing, but I would rather have a little cold water : yet surely I am drinking water—yea water of life, which causes this barren soul to bud. It is watering within me the incorruptible seed of the word, which liveth and abideth for ever. Yes, the Lord will perfect that which concerneth me;—soon, soon shall I drink more abundantly of the water of life, that proceedeth from the throne of God and of the Lamb."

When so nourished and refreshed, and with these glorious anticipations, with a soul mightily active amid such weakness and infirmity, she could not but endite such compositions as you have read, whenever she felt the desire. Thought sprung up rapidly and vehemently in her soul, and without an effort did they flow out in dictation to her sister, after the manner she thus describes :—

" One evening she requested me to come and write a letter for her to a Christian friend. ' O,' she said, ' come as quickly as you can, for matter is rushing rapidly into my mind. I feel as if God meant to glorify himself by this letter; for new glories seem disclosing every moment to my view: and I feel his love a fire within me, making me eloquent in his praise. O I am lost, I am swimming in love; shout, O my soul, for great is the Holy One of Israel in the midst of thee.' "

At this season of extreme endurance her anxieties appear to have been peculiarly drawn forth for her unbelieving relatives; all who were still without that comfort and support which she felt to be so important in the hour of suffering and of death. Of this the following extracts from her sister's notes are striking memorials.

During another night she said, 'I am fast hastening to eternity. O how important does time now appear unto me. Let me spend every moment that now remains to the glory of him that hath justified, is sanctifying, and shall soon glorify me. I can speak to you all but F * * * *; dear F * * * *, poor young man! he is in a land of strangers—in a land of heathens; living, I fear, without God and without hope in the world. O I cannot tell you, what wrestling of spirit I have had of late on his behalf. Am I to hear of his having turned unto the Lord before I go hence and am seen no more, or is this joy reserved for heaven? O Lord, I cast him upon thy care: O Lord, save him. O do this thing, that thou mayst be glorified.' Then clasping her hands, and looking up, she said, 'I have faith that he shall be spared in the day of the Lord, as a man spareth his own son that serveth him.' Then looking at me, she said, 'O see that you cease not to press the love of God upon him, when I am gone; see that you forget not to inform him what a Father of mercies and God of all comfort he has been unto me in all my distresses, that he also may be encouraged to take his sister's God as his God for ever. Dear F * * * *! how my soul yearns after thee; ah! if he would but leave the vanities of time, and taste and see that God is good, and that they only who trust in him are blessed.' 'Poor F * * * *,' she said at another time, 'I am more occupied with him than with any of you. You all enjoy such privileges, but he is among those who know not God, and carried away by the things that are around, to forget God; what would I not give for an opportunity of talking to him! but why do I speak thus? Is not God ever present there as well as here, and can he not in one moment, by his spirit, cause him to feel the bitterness of having hewn out to himself broken cisterns, and lead him to the fountain of living water."

Again, while under the influence of similar feelings, she thus expressed herself :—

"I have great heaviness and continual sorrow of spirit for my kindred according to the flesh, because few of them know what it is to be born again, of the incorruptible seed of the word. O that I had them all around this bed, that I might tell them of the deep compassions of my God—of the necessity of tasting and seeing that he is good. They are sleeping upon the brink of everlasting destruction, and vainly conceiving themselves safe. They are just trusting in the same refuges of lies in which I myself once trusted, and by which I would have been plunged into hell, had not grace interposed. O that I could but tell them what it is to live without God and without hope in the world; could they but know the many sleepless hours and tears which their sins and indifference to the things of God have cost me. But why do I say *me !* Me, a worm! Could they know the tender anxiety with which Jesus entreats their return, they would surely cast down the weapons of their rebellion, saying, ' Lo we come unto thee, for thou art the Lord our God; O that he himself would grant unto them the hearing ear and the understanding heart.' "

To Mary, about whom she had not these anxieties, and in whose faith she had confidence, her heart from time to time went forth in most pleasing expressions of love ; and in prospect of separation from her, the following is a specimen of the kind of feeling with which she regarded her remaining behind her at a distance from their father's house. When in great agony, she said to her sister, as recorded in her notes :—

"I think ere to-morrow I shall be in heaven. I cannot say much unto you, my love, neither am I much disquieted about you—you are in safe keeping; you are in the hands of Emmanuel. O be faithful to the cause ; all that you have to do in the world is to glorify Jesus; see that you do it : and O remember that you can only serve him with his own strength; you know nothing, he must

20

teach you all things : be continually aware of this. I have prayed much for you ; I believe God will answer my prayers. It has often struck me that you are to suffer much for your adherence to him, that your path shall be strewed with prickly thorns. Dear love, you cannot be trusted with temporal tranquillity, you must be weaned from all beneath the sun. O ! obey my dying request, and live solely to Jesus." Clasping her hands at this moment, she looked upwards and said—' O ! holy Father, I give her in charge to thee.' Being seized immediately with a violent fit of coughing, I said I would awake the rest. ' No,' she said, ' wait a little, the hour is not yet arrived : I wish you would not talk much to me at present.' In a little while she exclaimed, ' O, will my beloved minister not witness the closing scene ? I could wish him to close my eyes : I am sure he would come if he knew how low I am; but O Father, perhaps I am too impatient. Surely I shall see him again in the flesh, if it be for thy glory. After this she fell asleep.

" In the morning I said, ' you are better.' She replied, ' Surely I am. Last night I thought I had come to Jordan's edge, and would be to-day worshipping in the New Jerusalem ; but who would not rejoice in a father's pleasure. O God, give me grace to wait patiently thine approach.' This day she spent chiefly in prayer. Sometimes she was heard to utter, ' Beautify me, beautify me, with thy matchless beauty ; and strengthen me with thy strength : make me wise with thy wisdom ;' at other times, ' O thou incomprehensible God, I am lost in thee ; thy love hath made my soul all tenderness : how doth my finite mind falter as I endeavour to contemplate thee. How am I lost, lost, drowned in thee—in thee, O thou gloriously holy Jehovah !'

" Towards the evening she was heard to say, ' The sun of righteousness will not withdraw his cheering beams : well then, I am not afraid to pass another night of suffering, since he will support me. O no! His spirit shall communicate great strength to my strengthless soul : hallowed be thy name, O thou most High !' "

The Hymn.

O Zion! when I think on thee,
  I long for pinions like a dove;
And mourn to think that I should be
  So distant from the land I love.

A captive here and far from home,
  For Zion's sacred vales I sigh,
Within the ransom'd nations come,
  And see the Saviour eye to eye.

While here I walk on hostile ground,
  The few that I can call my friends
Are, like myself, with fetters bound,
  And weariness my step attends.

But yet we shall behold the day
  When Zion's children shall return,
When all our griefs shall flee away,
  And we shall never, never mourn.

The hope that such a day will come,
  Makes ev'n the captive's portion sweet;
Tho' now we wander far from home,
  In Zion soon we all shall meet.

The Scripture.

GOD is our refuge and strength, a very present help in trouble.

I shall not die but live, and declare the works of the Lord. The Lord hath chastened me sore, but he hath not given me over unto death.

The former troubles are forgotten.

As in water face answereth to face, so the heart of man to man. Iron sharpeneth iron; so a man sharpeneth the countenance of his friend.

I trust to come unto you, and speak face to face, that our joy may be full.

The desire accomplished is sweet to the soul.

O magnify the Lord with me, and let us exalt his name together.

They shall speak of the glory of thy kingdom, and talk of thy power.

The righteous perisheth, and no man layeth it to heart.

Rivers of waters run down mine eyes, because they keep not thy law.

When he was come near and beheld the city, he wept over it.

CHAPTER X.

Our souls inseparable,
Alike enamoured of one glorious form,
Shall walk together to eternity;
And there, beneath the smile of " full eyed love,"
Ever renew our sweet original joy.

AT this period no prospect whatever of our meeting again
existed. She had, in the last letter which you have read,
left, as it were, her farewell blessing; and it seemed only to
remain for me and others who loved her, to resign her willingly into the hands of her Father, sorrowing not, as those
who had no hope, but rejoicing, if I may use the language
of another holy sister, when she heard of the death of a
believer, that one more would now be added to the golden
harps that were sounding the praises of their Redeemer.
Her letters sufficiently unfold with what views and feelings she stood on the very brink of the eternal world, surveying that land where her comfortable hope of purity
would indeed be gratified, swallowed up, so to speak, in the
realized blessedness of her everlasting portion. To the
eye of man she seemed fitted, by the long habit of her
thoughts and feelings, for entering the rest prepared for
the people of God; but God himself alone knows the end
and measure of man's days. Isabella was not yet prepared for her place among the spirits of the just made prefect;
she was yet to be redeemed for a season from death, and
detained in the house of her pilgrimage.

Her friends rejoiced to witness her restoration to comparative ease and vigour, and her progress in the way of
wisdom and holiness, for her faith had only become more

20*

precious in the furnace. To use the language of one well capable of judging, who at this time saw her :—" There was a maturity in the divine life about her, overpower-ingly striking ; already she seemed to breathe the air of the New Jerusalem, and to have caught some of the notes of the just made perfect. The world had receded from her view, and she stood on the very threshold of glory ; and with the eye of faith took a view of the promised rest, and of all the grand and solemn realities of the eternal world. Her countenance beamed with celestial light, reflecting the happy state of her soul, feasted with communications of that love which passeth knowledge. She told us language altogether failed her in speaking of him who was glorious in holiness, ever doing wonders for her, a worm of the dust ; and, while we were amazed at the words which proceeded from her mouth, she turned round, saying : ' Pray, O pray earnestly, that this stammering tongue may be unloosed, that I may speak the Saviour's praise.' "

I also, beyond my hope, was delivered from suffering ; and once more I was able to accomplish, by the good hand of God upon me, a visit to the bedside of my beloved friend. It was an event of no ordinary interest, and productive of a peculiar joy. Upon my return I had written to our friend, Miss ——, a description of her interview, which I here in-sert, as it contains a more vivid picture, and more correct perhaps, than could be furnished by my present remem-brances of her condition at that time.

" You will be most happy to hear that I found her considerably revived, but suffering great pain from the abscess obviously re-forming on her lungs. Her mind, it struck me, was more vigorous than at our last meeting, less under the influence of emotion, and more decided upon points to which formerly her attention was not so easily directed. A greater maturity throughout the whole of the new life was observable. By her intense sufferings, and her own convictions, eternity being, as if consciously so much nearer ; her graces seemed all to have been in most lively exercise, and to have retained what they had imbibed from her visions of the truth, when she thought she was just reaching her everlasting home. Did I say she was less under the influence of emotion? Now this I must modify a little; or at least, accompany with some explanation. It was not because there was any diminution of sensibility in the contemplation of divine things; but the joy, the perfect blessedness, wherewith the renewed soul can be made full, even here, was so realized and made visible before me in our dear friend, that although what she believed and felt was not so indicated as upon some former occasions, by outward expressions of mere emotion, there was in her whole demeanour a nearer likeness to Christ, than I ever saw before. Heaven with its glory and its holiness, seemed more thoroughly wrought into the habits of her thinking; and having been in such immediate prospect of her blessed home, she manifested more of that quietude, which is so much more like completed happiness than mere raptures of feeling. I could not prevent a kind of awe mingling with the joy I felt in the presence of the dying saint; for it seemed as if she had returned to me from the dead; while so perfected seemed the work within her, that the *last* enemy only had now to be destroyed. Then, it was so delightfully visible, that all would be according to the desire of her heart. In the season of her great suffering her confidence failed her not; and many of the blessed promises she more distinctly felt, through the depth of their meaning, than before, while the riches of the Redeemer's love seemed more abundant than ever. It must indeed be an exercise of patience for her to remain, not so much to endure suffering, which is a lesson taught in the beginning of christian experience, but to have a more active share in the employments of heaven denied. Yet, on this point, she was obviously far advanced. I had often checked her longings for heaven, lest these should generate a spirit of impatience: or at least render residence in this world more difficult of endurance: and I observed sometimes she thought me uncompromising and severe.—Now, that the will of God is manifest that still she must abide in the wilderness, her chief anxiety is to get occasions to be useful. She has promised me not to exhaust her strength in speaking so much to christians, but to keep it all for faithful speaking to any poor unawakened visiter that may approach her. I know the sacrifice of delightful feeling she must make, to be silent when others are magnifying her Redeemer's name! but she has, I trust, firmness to have a greater end in view, the saving of one miserable soul, rather than increasing the joys of those that are already secure."

About a week afterwards I visited her again : but a relapse of my malady having rendered my departure to a different country expedient, the hope which we had mutually indulged of communing together on the glorious things of divine love was never gratified. It was the will of God we should see each other's face in the flesh no more. Although however, we never met again, I learned from her sister and others how she continued to feel : and an abundant proof was afforded me of the exercise of her faith and hope and joy. From the friend with whom she had so long corresponded, but whom she had never seen, I received very particular intelligence regarding her condition. There existed between their spirits, throughout their thoughts and feelings, a most intimate and pervading sympathy. Isabella had written, as you see, in the letter found after her death, without the faintest hope of enjoying an interview in this world with this friend whom she so much loved. It seemed to be ordained, that without the exchange of one mortal embrace, they should both expire where they had long endured so much of suffering at the hand of their heavenly Father, and meet first where not a pang mingles with the transports of immortal blessedness.

Although so long and eagerly desired, Isabella had ceased to regard their meeting here as a matter of hope : this, however, was not the case with Miss ——, as appears in the following extract from a letter preserved in Isabella's papers :—

" I have often felt since I read your last note, a hope, that we may yet be permitted to enjoy our long wished for interview : but if not, how much more glorious to meet, as through almighty grace we shall, when this mortal shall have put on immortality, and this corruption shall have put on incorruption, and death be swallowed up in victory."

At last what was so eagerly longed for, was granted to these two friends ; and although myself incapable of witnessing their happiness, I had a lively sympathy with the joyful anticipation made known to me in the following note, equally expressive of the feelings of the one and the other of these friends.

"I am happy, very happy to write to you to-night, for what I am going to tell you will afford such pleasure, and yet I can scarcely believe that I have really the prospect of seeing our beloved friend. I think my being so able for it, is permission from him who preserves my strength, and grants a blessing on the enjoyment he gives. I cannot attempt to describe what I feel at this unlooked for prospect. Our meeting will be a deeply interesting event to me. O what will it be then to behold that friend, who gives to earthly ties all their sweetness, in whose presence is fullness of joy. Indeed, I am almost afraid of desiring the accomplishment of my wishes too eagerly ; so many things may prevent it. And if it should not be, I hope I shall feel quite satisfied. It is what of Christ's image is traced in our beloved friend's soul that makes her so dear—and although I should never see her, I may, by faith, realize to myself something of the glory and beauty of him who is altogether lovely, and enjoy all in him."

They had so long desired this interview, and with so little hope, that the apprehension expressed in this note was very natural, lest their Father, who knows how perilous it is even to his dearest children, to be entrusted with fulness of temporal joy, should prevent the completion of their wishes.

Their friendship was indeed divine and spiritual, and the ties that bound them were not woven of the frail material of earthly relationship, yet still the joy they longed for was but a temporal joy ; for they could not believe that although denied them, the fountain of their true blessedness would be sealed up for a moment, knowing that all 'their well springs flowed as freely as ever from the bosom of their Father ; but it was the highest and purest of temporal joys they panted for, to make divine love their song together in the land of their pilgrimage. It pleased him, however, in whom their souls delighted, to grant the desire of their hearts. The appearance of the day, her own renovated strength, and other favourable circumstances, at last seemed to justify Miss ——— in attempting the long meditated interview with her sister, beloved in the bonds of the everlasting gospel. Conveyed from her room, still unable to walk, her joy corresponded with the expected indulgence, now almost within her very grasp, of so beautiful a hope. It was no romantic feeling that pervaded her soul, as she was carried along those sequestered shores, although so fitted to excite the most exquisite emotions of beauty ; those beautiful waters, with their waving outlines, embosomed amid the picturesque forms of contiguous mountains, faded away before the image of the friend she was gradually approaching ; with whom her heart burned to take sweet and holy counsel, regarding the solemn and lofty things of eternity, that by a sure word of prophesy, to which they had taken earnest heed, they knew they would continue to enjoy, when at the voice of the archangel, proclaiming time to be no more, the visible universe, with all its dwellings of glory and of beauty, should fly for ever away.

She was borne from the carriage to Isabella's chamber, and now, as may well be imagined, the rapture so long thought of, thrilled through their hearts, melting with inexpressible thankfulness beneath this manifestation of their Father's love. The following is extracted from the account which Miss ——— sent me of this memorable and affecting interview :—

" I can at last tell you, that I have been permitted to see Isabella, but this is nearly all I can do, for to describe our meeting would be impossible in writing. Many things combined to make it deeply interesting, and the impressions of this much to be remembered day shall never be forgotten. The time we spent together seemed but a fast fleeting moment. It was, however, a sweet foretaste of a more abiding intercourse. When I went in, Isabella was pale and languid looking; but her countenance soon brightened with a smile, more lovely than any thing I ever saw before, and she was able to speak in the most animated strain during the whole time. On seeing me, she burst into tears, and said, 'Well, I have often imagined myself in your presence, conversing of the wonderful love of Jesus, and now he has permitted me to speak of it face to face.' Sometimes she said, 'Our meeting is a wonderful manifestation of the tenderness of our God; O that he should thus provide such sweet refreshing intercourse, while we are passing through this wilderness, giving us a foretaste of the communion of the saints in glory; and O, that such a theme should even now be given us as the love of Jesus. Truly this is a joy with which a stranger intermeddleth not.' At another time she told me, she had often been called presumptuous for speaking so confidently of her own safety; but she thought it much greater presumption to refuse to rejoice in those blessings God had freely bestowed, and thus to make him a liar. Mary at one time was repeating part of a hymn, beginning 'Farewell, thou vase of splendour.' Isabella interrupted her by saying there were two lines in it most suitable to the present moment,—

> "'We yet shall hold communion .
> In amaranthine bowers.'

"In speaking of Brainerd's life, which she had been reading, she said, 'I was exceedingly cast down with it, for he was so faithful in every good word and work, that I more than ever felt how little I had done in the cause of Jesus. I got no rest in thinking of it till the parable of the sower was brought to my mind, and I was comforted by seeing that different measures of increase were given to the good seed, and that while Brainerd brought forth an hundred fold, though I was conscious of only bringing forth thirty, it might still be to the glory of God. When the time was expired, and I was called away, she said, 'My very soul is stirred up within me: I know not how we shall part. It is the Lord's doing, that we have met, and it may please him to grant us another interview. Pray for me; I am a highly favoured creature, and O that I might show forth his praise! O that men would praise the Lord for his goodness, and for his wonderful works unto the children of men.' "

They thus parted, rejoicing in spirit, that God had counted them worthy to have experienced so much of each
other's sympathy, amid their various tribulations, before
this glad event ; and now, face to face, to strengthen each
other's joy and faith in a crucified Redeemer.

"Our meeting that day," as Miss —— expressed herself, in a
note to Isabella, " was retired from human view, and we had no
witness of our joy ; but surely it is not presumptuous to think we
were regarded with interest, by such beings as have visited our
world, on missions of mercy, yea, and by the God of angels; for
it was his matchless love that supplied us with sweet intercourse,
and not only so, but his blessed Spirit imparted that relish which
made our converse sweet."

> " 'Emmanuel shall be our theme,
>   While in this world we stray :
> We'll sing our Jesus' lovely name,
>   When all things else decay.
>
> When we appear in yonder cloud,
>   With all the ransom'd throng,
> Then will we sing more sweet, more loud,
>   And Jesus be our song.' "

There was indeed a very perfect sympathy between
these two young believers, for after this interview, Isabella
thus gave vent to her feelings.

" MY WELL BELOVED SISTER IN JESUS,

" I would begin by saying, bless the Lord, O my soul, and forget not all his benefits, for surely I am a highly favoured creature;
when, O when, shall I in any measure feel grateful for the goodness manifested unto me, a poor worthless worm. I shall not now,
my dear friend in the gospel, attempt to describe the real joy I
felt, at seeing you. It was almost too much for this poor decaying frame to bear up under ; and such a favour as I never expected to receive in this weary and parched land. Often had I given
thanks to God on your behalf, but never did I so much rejoice
over you, as since I have seen you. And adored be grace, the
time is not far distant, when I shall see you without spot or wrinkle,
or any such thing : when I shall see you for ever basking your

delighted soul beneath the immediate shining of the adorable Sun of righteousness. O what a ravishing sight will it be to see Jesus our friend, our hope, our all; not as a man acquainted with grief, but seated upon a throne, even very highly exalted, having a name above every name, listening with infinite complacency to the grateful adorations of redeemed thousands.—Having, my dear friend, the prospect of such amazing blessedness, may we not, even now, well rejoice? yes, we may surely well rejoice in Jesus, in the Lord our righteousness, and in the Lord our strength. We err greatly, if we do not rejoice, because it is an evidence that we incline rather to trust a little to some of our endeavours, than rest entirely on the gloriously finished work of Christ. O my friend, what shall I say of this vast, this stupendous work? alas! the dear subject is too weighty for such a worm.

> " ' Who shall fulfil the boundless song,
> What vain pretender dares?
> The theme surmounts an angel's tongue,
> And Gabriel's heart despairs.'

" Haste on, O blessed eternity! and let us begin aright the praises of the Lamb. While here, our best attempts to celebrate his praises are most imperfect; but there no impurity shall ever be known. We shall there sing an everlasting farewell to all suffering, and welcome with hitherto unknown delight, unnumbered ages of consummate felicity.—I hope that your soul, my beloved friend, is flourishing in the ways of holiness. The Lord grant you an extensive appetite for the bread of life, that you may be nourished abundantly on that delicious food. Often, often as I think of you with singular pleasure, O, I cannot tell you, how dearly I love you in the truth; but God is my record, how much I long after you in the Lord Jesus. I pray you remember me in secret. I am a poor ungrateful creature. I want to glorify my God more; but when I would do good, evil is present with me. But grace shall one day triumph over all this corruption. I am suffering more at present, than when you saw me, but all is well. It must be needful for me. I hope you were nothing the worse of your visit to me. Give to —— my love, for Jesus sake, while I remain, yours, in the Gospel.

" I. C."

No pleasure certainly is so divine,
As when two souls in love combine;

He has the substance of all bliss,
To whom a virtuous friend is given,
   Add but eternity, you'll make it heaven.

So the poet of a former age thought, but, in a higher sense than he dreamed of, perhaps, their meeting contained the ingredients of an eternal felicity :—they implied the presence of the ever durable substance of all blessedness.

From Miss ———'s memorandum of the second visit to her beloved Isabella, I extract what follows.

" In speaking of the views of the love of God, which she had realized by faith, she said, ' The believer labours to express them; but he finds he cannot, in the language of mortals, and that words seem to rob the subject of its greatness.' When I mentioned, that in the margin of my bible, the verse, ' Praise waiteth for thee in Zion,' is translated ' Praise is silent for thee in Zion,' she replied, ' Well, that is delightful, and quite consistent with Paul's expression, " rejoicing with joy unspeakable." ' We had some conversation, also, on different passages of the Song of Solomon, and in telling me how constantly she had studied this portion of the Scripture, she mentioned in what way it first attracted her attention. She then said, that she had often been refreshed by that passage in the close of the fifth chapter, where the Church, after going from one expression of admiration to another, sums up the whole in the words, ' This is my beloved, and this is my friend, O ye daughters of Jerusalem.' We then proceeded to speak of the first part of the sixth chapter, on which she remarked, that she thought the believer's testimony to what he saw and enjoyed in Jesus, was more likely, than any thing else, to convince sinners of their blindness, and lead them to inquire after the way of salvation. She was very weak, and often said, ' The spirit longs to leave this earthly tabernacle, that it may be set free to serve the living God.' On coming away, she said, ' Surely the Lord himself, by whose permission we have met, has drawn near, and caused our hearts to burn within us, while we communed together. Yes, and very often when my spirit thus revives, I grieve to part; but in glory there shall be no more separation, and we shall be ever with the Lord.' "

The delight which Isabella had from her intercourse

with this beloved friend of her spiritual life, and others, did
not in any way diminish her interest in former and earlier
friendships.

An old man in a contiguous cottage, a most intimate
friend of Isabella's, died about this time. He was, I am
persuaded, a holy man, who walked in great meekness and
humility with God; and the record of what Isabella said
when she heard of his death, as preserved by her sister,
is very affecting—a monument at once of her love, of her
gratitude for his kindness, and the reverence with which
she regarded him as an instrument selected by God to promote her eternal interests.

From their earliest childhood old John had felt a peculiar interest in these girls; and when by his fireside often he
used to say to them, how much better it would be for them
to read their bibles than to spend their time, as they did, in
vain and trifling amusements. Isabella was the greater favourite, and therefore it might be, that he most frequently
addressed his most pointed observations to her. Afterward,
when she, like himself, had seen the love of God in Christ
Jesus to her vain and guilty soul, John rejoiced exceedingly; and many a happy hour the old man and the young
believer spent together. Latterly, although within a few
yards of each other, they could have no personal communion, but from day to day they glorified God in each other:
willing, when he should appoint, to depart in peace—their
eyes having seen a common salvation.

"Well Mary, I am more and more convinced, that the prayers
and cries of that now unspeakably blessed saint have been heard
and answered of God on our behalf; and we have exceeding cause
to feel ashamed, that we have not felt more grateful, for having
such a friend. It did not strike me at the time, but it has often
since, that my first religious impressions might have been in answer to a prayer which he sometimes offered, when his righteous
soul was grieved by beholding me pleasing myself with sinful vanities.' Here she burst into a flood of tears and said, 'O, if the unregenerate would but think, when indulging in what they call

innocent amusements, of the agony, the deep anguish with which some of God's children around them may be filled on their account; could they but witness their tears, and hear their strong cryings; it would interrupt, at least for a time, that mirth, the end of which is heaviness, that cruel madness which, if not forsaken, shall plunge them into the blackness of darkness for ever.' When uttering these words, she raised herself in bed ; and as if unconscious of aught around her, fixing her eyes upon an eternity of bliss and misery, she exclaimed, with a loud voice, ' O, I am in an agony for a world lying in wickedness. If my feeble voice could reach to the utmost ends of the earth, I would now use it in proclaiming, that all beneath the sun is only vanity and vexation of spirit; and that true happiness is only to be found by coming unto the everlasting God, believing him to be what the bleeding wounds of Jesus so loudly proclaim him to be, even a God who delighteth in mercy.' Turning then to me, she said, ' My dear love, will you leave me for a little, I want to pour out my complaint unto God.'

"About this time also, she thus expressed herself in a similar manner:—'O my heart is almost broken, because the name of my God every day is blasphemed amongst men. My own iniquity, and the iniquity of those around me, are bowing me to the dust. It pains my soul, that Christians should have so little compassion upon their fellow sinners; that we should understand so little what it is to sigh and cry over a rebellious world. I believe I am soon to have done with earth : unwilling as I am to run, the Lord has been drawing me tenderly to himself of late, and giving me hope that I shall shortly be enthroned with him above the skies. I have more to grieve me than a world lying in wickedness ; the state of the church is at present awful : when will he come, and try her, and purify her, and make her white. Let us give him no rest until he make Jerusalem a praise in the earth, and till he glorify the place of his glory.' "

What mind has been more deeply affected regarding the everlasting peace of others, or wrestled more vehemently for their salvation, with groanings and sighings that could not be uttered ? Yet in her own estimate how feeble were her feelings, how faithless her prayers, compared with what so great a matter demanded, was apparent on many occasions, of which the following exclamation to one

of her confidential friends, may be inserted as a deeply interesting example :—

"O I cannot tell you what a day of wrestling with God for the
salvation of souls I have had. The ardency of my spirit has almost exhausted my bodily strength. Never, I think, have I spent
such a night, and yet how much have I to lament my coldness, my
insensibility, my want of faithfulness and compassion for poor perishing sinners. O that I were more alive to the awful misery of
their condition ; then would I be more earnest in imploring them
to flee for shelter to the true refuge."

From these, as well as other sayings of hers already recorded, and from her feelings more especially expressed
when she heard of the death of her aged friend, you may
gather her notions of the efficacy of prayer;—how, in fact,
she believed its power to be co-extensive with what is
agreeable to the will of God. In her own experience there
were many remarkable circumstances, not necessary to
mention, which others as well as herself were constrained
to attribute to the especial providence of Him, who is ever
faithful to fulfil his promise to believing supplicants. Since
her death also, the same interposition and the same faithfulness are not a little apparent, by which those obtain the
desires of their heart who delight themselves in God. Often
had she vehemently desired, in the ecstasy of her joyful
gratitude for what she herself had received, that her voice
could reach round the globe, to tell what her Saviour was
able to bestow; and in the solemn words you have so recently perused, may be seen how earnestly she longed to proclaim in every ear the vanity of all things under the sun,
and tell each foolish sinner of the only refuge from the results of his own self-destroying insanity. God had already
wrought great marvels in her, and for her ; and she was
persuaded that the voice of her supplication had often been
heard ; but she knew not, at that moment, that it was in
the divine counsels that this desire of her heart should be
so largely gratified, and that many thousands should yet

21*

know of the agonies which she endured, in her love for souls so intent upon their own ruin, and hear her, although dead, yet thus still lifting up her voice :—

O, I would cry, that all the world might hear;
Ye self tormentors, love your God alone,
Let his unequalled excellence be dear,
Dear to your inmost souls, and make him all your own.

The Hymn.

Oh! never, never canst thou know
  What then for thee the Saviour bore,
The pangs of that mysterious wo
  That wrung his frame at ev'ry pore;
The weight that press'd upon his brow,
  The fever of his bosom's core!
Yes, man for man perchance may brave
The horrors of the yawning grave;
And friend for friend, or child for sire,
Undaunted and unmoved expire,
From love, or piety, or pride—
But who can die as Jesus died?

A sweet but solitary beam,
  An emanation from above,
Glimmers o'er life's uncertain dream,—
  We hail that beam, and call it love!
But fainter than the pale star's ray
Before the noontide blaze of day,
And lighter than the viewless sand
Beneath the wave that sweeps the strand,
Is all of love that man can know,—
All that in angel's breast can glow,—
Compar'd, O Lord of Hosts, with thine,
Eternal—fathomless—divine!

The Scripture.

Give me understanding according to thy word. O let me not wander from thy commandments.

Thy testimonies are wonderful, therefore doth my soul keep them.

Our gospel came not unto you in word only, but also in power, and in the Holy Ghost, and in much assurance.

Let us draw near with a true heart, in full assurance of faith, having our hearts sprinkled from an evil conscience, and our bodies washed with pure water.

Let us hold fast the profession of our faith without wavering; (for he is faithful that promised.)

Our conversation is in Heaven; from whence also we look for the Saviour, the Lord Jesus Christ: who shall change our vile body, that it may be fashioned like unto his glorious body, according to the working whereby he is able to subdue all things unto himself.

Ye that stand in the house of the Lord, in the courts of the house of our God, praise the Lord; for the Lord is good : sing praises unto his name; for it is pleasant.

CHAPTER XI.

Good sister,
How do you find yourself when God is with you?
I feel a gentle flame within my breast,
That seems to alter every nerve about me.
I'm lightsome now; and my whole soul's directed
Up to those heavens, as if I had some friend
Residing there, that never would forsake me.

FROM time to time during the autumn, Isabella continued to be visited by various people of different ranks in society : by some, it is much to be feared, as they would go
to see any object wonderful or extraordinary ; by others,
who did truly delight to witness in this dark and polluted
world any resemblance of the divine image. Whatever
their station, or peculiar claims to regard, Isabella ever
recognised only one distinction, the love of the Saviour.
To any one in whom this existed, springing from the knowledge of his glorious excellencies, her soul went out in
most willing and glad sympathy. Often, when thus enjoying the society of kindred spirits, she would most vividly realize the happiness of heaven, in most blissful anticipation, as by a spirit of prophecy ; and to the feelings
excited in her mind, whenever an opportunity occurred,
she would give vent in language most deeply interesting
to all who heard her. "Something was said," writes one
of her visiters at this season, "with respect to the perfect
union that exists among the redeemed around the throne
in heaven: Isabella instantly seized the idea, her eye at
the moment beaming with an expression of holy delight,

and continued speaking for a long time on the glorious
theme, with an energy and depth of feeling that surpassed
any thing I had ever witnessed before. 'There, in heaven,' exclaimed she, as in a holy rapture, ' all imperfection
shall be done away, and the redeemed will then sing for
ever of redeeming love.' "

Had a stranger, at such a moment, been admitted to her
chamber, he might have been tempted to attribute what
he heard with his ear to feverish excitement, or temporary
emotion ;—but although uttering impassioned and burning
words, a calm, meek solemnity suffused her whole aspect,
nothing forced nor violent, but most perfect keeping and
decorum in all her demeanour, would have met the most
critical and jealous survey of his eye. To use the language of a respectable divine, who, although living at a distance, occasionally saw Isabella, " Her whole conversation
was in heaven. I do not remember of any other topics,
but those which were spiritual, ever occupying us in our
interviews, even for a moment : she seemed intensely anxious to utter the language of heaven, even below. Should
any think that much of her joy was owing to mere enthu-
siastical feeling—most certainly, in her case, there was
nothing but what was solid, rational, and scriptural. It
all originated with, and rested upon Him, who is the rock
of ages, who knew and liberally bestowed what her necessities demanded."

From what has been already told of her reverence for
the holy Scriptures, it must have appeared that her mind
was well defended against any spurious enthusiasm of feeling. She weighed well what they contained, and was
fearful of indulging any emotion but such as they sanc-
tioned. Submission to the divine record is most counter
to the habits of enthusiasts : they must have visions and
revelations of their own, and cannot submit like children
to be guided by what all may know. Isabella, however,

never lost the spirit of a new born babe that desires the
sincere milk of the word. Much as she knew of God and
his purposes, she every successive moment seemed to feel
more deeply, how little of this most valuable knowledge
she had attained. One day she exclaimed, "I am indeed
most brutish in my knowledge"—and again, "O ! thirst
much for revelations of his will : I want to be better acquainted with the word of God, and to hide it in my heart,
that I may not offend him. I am so ignorant of the Scriptures, and often sin because of this ignorance. I do not
expect to live long ; therefore how zealous ouhgt I to be,
to know as much of God in Christ as I can here. I do
think, that in speaking both to believers and unbelievers,
we ought to quote the scriptures always : to the law and
to the testimony if we do not appeal, it is because there
is no light in us."

Such feelings, so expressive of humility and discretion,
grew with her to the very close of her life ; and one of the
last requests to her beloved friend Miss ———, only a few
days before her death, I now copy from a note of Mary's
lying before me.—"Isabella sends her love in the Lord
Jesus, and hopes you will implore of him to illuminate her
mind in the knowledge of his most blessed word."

While many testimonies might be recorded of the scriptural wisdom of her feelings, all who approached her at
this season could with one voice bear witness of the heavenly spirituality and holiness that were visible, throughout her whole humanity. I select the words of an
aged believer, who, during a few weeks retirement at the
head of the Gairloch, saw Isabella for the first time, as a
memorial of the impression her appearance at this period
produced upon her visiters :—

"Her favourite theme seemed to be what the Lord Jesus had
done for her soul ; and her whole soul was wrapt up in the exercise of holy gratitude for his wondrous condescension. She seem-

ed also to have a very lively perception of the sinfulness of sin; and more especially, when her mind got fixed on the glory of that Redeemer, who though he knew no sin became sin for us, that we might be made the righteousness of God through him. Every thing she said breathed a holiness of mind, that made one feel as in the presence of a being that had in a more than ordinary degree the image of the Lord impressed upon her, and who was fast ripening for immortal glory. There was a spirituality in the atmosphere that surrounded her, that was quite refreshing to the soul. The longer you stayed the more unwilling were you to quit her; her earnest desire was to spend her time with God: even a question about her health she seemed to consider an intrusion, for the maxim of her life at that period was, ' to me to live is Christ;' and she soon after experienced that ' to die is gain.' "

In the society of Mr ——, whose testimony you have read, she seems to have had great enjoyment. After his departure he had written Isabella in such a way as to induce her to dictate the following interesting reply :—

" MY DEAR MR. ——,

" It is to me a very pleasant task, for your sake as well as my own, to return you my sincere gratitude for your great kindness. For your sake, because the day is fast approaching when you shall be amply rewarded by the blessed Saviour; and for my own sake, because it has furnished me with another subject for gratitude, and will moreover be particularly useful to me in my present weak and reduced condition. Think not, my dear friend in the Lord, that you have by your kindness in the least hurt my feelings. O no, I desire to look upon it as a great blessing from the Lord, and to thank him much on your behalf.—Your dear letter has also been most refreshing to my poor soul. O, how good is the Lord to me. I am indeed a wonder to myself. In the midst of pain and weakness, how astonishingly does he support this sinking spirit with fresh supplies of his grace; causing me in the midst of bodily distress to sing aloud for joyfulness. Truly, it becomes me to say, that the Lord is good and gracious, and that he is also merciful. My weakness prevents me saying what I would on this deeply interesting subject. I am now considerably weaker than when I had the real pleasure of seeing you. Having already received such a strong evidence of your christian affection and sympathy, I need scarcely remind you to remember me, the least of saints, when you are permitted intimate communion with the Father and the Son, through the blessed Spirit. O pray that I may glorify him in life and in death, and be enabled to say even in the most trying circumstances, " not my will, but thine be done." How animating to think, that we shall not always be the poor sinful imperfect creatures that we now are; but that we shall one day be able to sing, without the least mixture of sin, yea, to sing uninterruptedly, the delightful and soul-ravishing song of ' Worthy is the Lamb.'—Wondrous theme, we shall never, never tire of thee! No, redeeming love is so immensely wide, and high, and broad, and long, that eternity shall be necessary to explain its boundless mysteries. What transports of joy must the disembodied spirit experience when it arrives on the heavenly shore, and beholds with unclouded vision the purities of the glorified state! Then shall we see as we are seen, and know even as we are known. O, how ought such rich prospects to attract us to a throne of grace; that, by frequent intercourse with God, we may receive those influences that will mature us for the blessed society of heaven, where, I trust through grace, you and I shall meet to sing throughout eternity the praises of Jesus. Farewell, my beloved friend in the faith; may the Lord bless you and yours abundantly.

Yours, with much christian love,
" ISABELLA CAMPBELL."

From an allusion in the beginning of this letter, it is apparent how she esteemed the attentions of her benevolent friends. While, as she often said, she could tell to no one the sweetness she felt in living from day to day upon the bounty of Providence, she saw in each kindness, at once a token of love to herself and a proof of love to the Saviour in those who bestowed it. So judging of christian charity, she had cause of rejoicing, when at any time the object of its tenderness. In receiving what others had to give, she thus gave thanks and glory to God on their behalf as well as her own.

The following extracts from the notes of various indivi-
22

duals are pleasing additions to what you have already read of her sayings :—

"I remember well that day we spent with her, when for the first time I saw her. After being silent for a little, she said, ' Is it not good in our heavenly Father thus to permit us to see each other in this wilderness, and to speak to each other of what he has done for our souls.' I said, ' You seem very happy.' O yes, I am happy, and have I not great cause, for I know that when he shall appear I shall be like him; I shall see him as he is, and my soul shall be satisfied in him. I am complete in him; Θ that I could love him more. Can it be possible for one to have been plucked as a brand from the burning, and not feel love in their hearts to such a Saviour? I think it is impossible for a child of darkness to be quickened anew, and not to hear a song of gratitude proceed from his lips.' I asked, ' Do you always rejoice?' ' O no, I feel my own coldness, and lament; but then, sweet assurance! this vile body shall be changed, and I shall have nothing to prevent my constant joy.' Speaking to her of glorifying God, she said, ' O that I could do more for him; that I just could declare his *love* to others! O, what I have experienced of his love! Truly it passeth knowledge.' She was very weak that day, and she said, ' Sometimes I wish I could speak more than my strength will admit; but this is not right. O that my own will were lost in his.' At parting she said, ' Perhaps we may not meet again on earth, but to meet in heaven would be far better: O it is great goodness that has allowed us to meet at all.' "

"After she read my card," says another, "she expressed a wish to see me. Being conducted to her room, she appeared very weak. After a short pause, during which she seemed to be engaged in mental prayer,—' I understand,' said she, ' you are acquainted with Mr. ———, and that through his instrumentality you are come to understand the truth.' ' Yes,' said I, ' I understand the truth more clearly than I did.' ' Well,' said she, ' when the Lord begins a good work, he will bring it to perfection; but tell me, if you please, how you felt before this change, and what was the first thing that led to your conversion, in your conversation with Mr. ———.' ' Before then,' said I, ' I aimed at conformity with the will of God. For many years, I had been much in duty, prayed much, and grounded my hope of acceptance with God upon strict observance of the external duties of religion. I dreaded eternal punishment; and if I got to heaven, or if I could avoid the consequences of sin some way, I never was much concerned about holiness of heart and life; I never understood the doctrine of free grace.' 'That was a fearful state,' said she, 'and exactly similar to my own, and I believe similar to the state of all nominal and self-righteous professors, before conversion; but how do you feel now, or what is the ground of your peace?' 'Formerly I believed that my salvation was conditional; viz. that if I were to perform such and such duties, (enumerating many,) the Lord would give me faith, and an interest in Christ; but now I am fully convinced of the inefficacy of the best human merit in the way of salvation; that it proceeds entirely from the free grace of God. I believe that Christ died for the sins of all who believe in him: I believe in him; therefore, he died for my sins also: I regard his promises as addressed to myself individually. Before, I approached the throne of grace with fear, as coming before a sovereign, whose laws I could not obey, and from whose justice there was no possibility of escape,—now, I regard God as my Father, to whom I am reconciled through Christ. The performance of duty now, proceeds from an ardent desire to glorify God, and my soul is lost in amazement, when I contemplate the love of Christ.' By this time she became animated, and those cheeks, which a little before were pale and emaciated, assumed their natural hue. Such an angelic appearance I never did, and probably never shall behold in this world. 'Well, but my friend,' said she, 'you must not think that now you have got a fund upon which you can draw at pleasure. Remember that you are walking through the rugged path of life; that your spiritual enemies will assume a more formidable aspect than they have hitherto done. You are not to suppose that now you have nothing to fear, because you believe. You may calculate to be assailed in many ways of which you have no idea. Hence the necessity of walking humbly with God. Never think, that because you are a believer, you can do this and that in your own strength. No, my friend,' continued she, 'you must take unto you the whole armour of God, wherewith you may stand against the fiery darts of the adversary of souls. Look unto Jesus,' (at these words, she seemed absorbed in thought,) 'through whom you will be more than conqueror. You imagine, perhaps, just now, that you would do and suffer any thing rather than deny Christ; but remember the case of the apostle Peter. He saw the glory of Christ on the mount; he was fully convinced that he was the Saviour, and declared that though all would forsake him, yet for his part, though he should suffer death, he would never forsake nor deny him; but behold him in a short time denying that ever he knew him. Such is our state when left to ourselves.' 'Glory to God!' exclaimed she, 'that he never leaves, nor forsakes those that trust in him: may he grant you, according to the riches of his glory, to be strengthened with might by his Spirit in the inner man. O the length, and breadth, and height of the love of Christ, which passeth all knowledge!' While speaking of redeeming love, and of the unsearchable riches of divine grace, it was evident that her soul was elevated above all earthly things, and participated in the joys of the saints in light. Though her body was weak, yet her soul was acquiring strength. She could not find language to express the dispositions of her soul.

Upon my sympathizing with her, and expressing my sorrow to see her suffer so much, she calmly replied, there was no cause of sorrow, for it was a token of her Father's love to her, and that though I might suppose that she was secluded from the world, yet she was not alone, for God was with her. She realized his presence, and therefore enjoyed all that she could wish for in this world. She described at considerable length the character of the natural man, and the deceitfulness of the heart; and related a short anecdote of herself before she came to a saving knowledge of the truth, the substance of which is as follows. 'When I was a little girl,' said she, 'I was often concerned about my eternal salvation. I prayed, not only at stated periods, but often during the day. When I happened to visit my friends, I felt very uneasy when I was deprived of my usual solitude, and of an opportunity of prayer in secret. This disposition did not proceed from a desire of being esteemed pious; for I was anxious to conceal, as much as possible, my piety from the world; but all this proceeded from self-righteousness. I was convinced, of course, that I could not render perfect obedience to the law of God; but I believed what I could not do, Christ would do for me. In this manner, I claimed a considerable degree of merit, in my own justifying righteousness; but it pleased the Lord to convince me of this fearful delusion, and according to the riches of his grace, he taught me that Christ is the way, the truth, and the life.' "

After another visit, says the same individual:

"You have already an account of my first visit; the second and last time I visited her, she was very weak ; and, though most anxious to converse with her, I felt very reluctant to say much ; but I soon perceived that her silence did not proceed from her exhausted state, but that she was engaged in devout meditations and prayer to God, before she addressed one whom the Lord sent to her for instruction. 'Well,' said she, 'how are you coming on since you left us?' 'Not so well as I expected,' said I ; 'I see the truth clearly sometimes.' 'You have these glimpses in the contemplation of the love of Christ, and when you lose sight of that, then you have no peace.' 'Yes,' said I, 'that is exactly my state ; and the fears of a wicked conscience terrify me, when I read such a passage as this,—" If any man be in Christ Jesus, he is a new creature." ' 'I see,' said she, 'but it is not our good works or merits that entitle us to eternal life. People puzzle and perplex themselves, by looking into their own hearts, to see whether they have faith. If you heard any good news that you believed to be true, you would immediately rejoice, without waiting to inquire whether you believed or not. The Gospel bringeth salvation ; and it is the fact, that God so loved us, that he gave his only begotten Son to be the propitiation for our sins, that gives us peace and joy. The source of our joy is entirely without ourselves ; it is Christ who is the Lord our righteousness. God hath given us eternal life, and this life is in his Son; in him dwelleth all the fulness of the Godhead bodily, and ye are all complete in him.' Then she referred to the following passages,—" He was bruised for our iniquities ; the chastisement of our peace was upon him, and with his stripes we are healed." " He was delivered for our offences, and raised again for our justification." 'I believe all that,' said I. 'Well,' said she, 'believing it to be true, is one thing, and being personally interested in it, is another.' 'Yes,' said I, 'I believe that Christ died for me, and thereby purchased eternal redemption for me.' 'Remember then,' said she, 'what the Apostle Paul saith,—" The life which I now live in the flesh, I live by the faith of the Son of God, who loved me, and gave himself for me." ' After this, she paused a while. 'Again,' said she, 'whenever your mind is cast down, or when you do not see your interest in Jesus clearly, the reason, I am sure, is plain to yourself, that it arises from losing sight of Christ, and of the love wherewith he loved you. God is love, and eternal life is to know God as our reconciled Father in Christ; and they that know his name or character, put their trust in him. You will meet with opposi-

22*

my consolations much more abound. Well, if you cannot come soon and see me, write me a few lines. I felt much invigorated by your dear note, and was glad to see ——, who I think is in a most hopeful state, and will be glad to see her again. Adieu, my very much loved friend in Jesus. My beloved Mary joins me in earnest Christian affection. O pray for us that our souls may thrive and flourish in holiness; and O, may you enjoy largely the presence of the Prince of Zion, and be filled with the consolations of the Holy Ghost.

" Yours in everlasting bonds."

" My dear sister in Jesus,

" It hath greatly rejoiced my spirit to hear of your joy in the Lord, and to receive another evidence of your love to the brethren in your kind remembrance of unworthy me. I find that, since your last visit at my bedside, my love towards you has been on the increase, and why? because God has enabled me to rejoice over you with no ordinary joy : yes, my well beloved friend, I feel much affection to you, because of your near and indissoluble relation to our blessed Emmanuel. This, my friend, is the grand and substantial tie that unites us—a tie which the combined attempts of men and devils shall never be sufficient to break asunder. O, my dear, dear friend, continue to rejoice in Christ, as all your salvation, your strength, and your desire. You can never, while here, rejoice enough in him, in whom are hid all the treasures of wisdom and knowledge. But our infirmity is, that we look often more to ourselves than this *Incomparable Individual*, and what is the result? It is ever doubting and fearing, mourning and heaviness; and no wonder of it, for the amazing wickedness of these hearts is awfully great, and when we contrast our best attempts to serve God with the pure requirements of his holy law, we may well stand aghast, and admire the unheard-of long suffering of Jehovah. But when Jesus, in whom we are complete, and who shall one day present his dear-bought Church to his Father, without spot, or wrinkle, or any such thing, is discovered by the keen eagle-eye of faith to be all that we need, even wisdom, righteousness, sanctification, and complete redemption, and that it is he who worketh in us, to will and to do of his good pleasure, then our fear vanishes, and we feel that we are not the children of night nor of darkness, and that, where the Spirit of the Lord is, there is liberty. When I would speak of my temporal health, I would say with gratitude to God that I am most tenderly dealt with. O, he is kind, kind to me; I suffer less pain than when you saw me, and although I am weak I am astonishingly happy ; indeed, my dear friend, I would not at this moment be strong, if weakness is my Father's will. I find that Jesus is a most marvellous physician; O what medicines are like unto his medicines ? I hope you will remember Isabella Campbell to Jesus, when he allows you intimate communion with him. God willing, come and see me soon again ; I think of your last visit with much comfort. My sister joins me in Christian love, and hopes your soul is in health.

"Ever yours,

"ISABELLA CAMPBELL."

" Fernicarry, May, 1827.

" MY VERY BELOVED BROTHER IN THE LORD JESUS,

" My dearest Mary has told me that you wished me to write to you. Well, my brother, what thanks can I render to God for you, for all the joy wherewith I joy over you before Jesus, giving thanks to him always in my prayers on your behalf. Grace and peace be much more abundantly multiplied unto you, through the knowledge of God, and our Saviour Jesus Christ. What, my dearly beloved, can I write to you, that will be new to you ? You have long known Jesus : you have seen much of his glorious character ; you have experienced that his blood is precious, and cleanseth from all sins ; and that where the Spirit of the Lord is, there is liberty : yes, a glorious liberty ; for we have not received the spirit of bondage again to fear, but the spirit of adoption, whereby we cry, Abba, Father. But though I can say nothing new on the dear subject of redeeming love, I must say something respecting it, and I believe the time is not far off, when I shall speak of it in loftier strains. Salvation ! O salvation, salvation, even salvation finished by him who thought it no robbery to be equal with God. O what a sound to be proclaimed in the ears of rebellious mortals ! God, in our nature, reconciling a guilty world unto himself, not imputing unto men their trespasses. O, my brother, men may say what they please, but God is love, fathomless love, and he never takes vengeance till man will have done at all of his ways.

Is not love the complexion of the Gospel of his glorious grace ? Did not the mighty scheme of redemption originate in the eternal

love of Jehovah? Was it not that same love which executed the
plan? and is it not because love and mercy to our race did reign
in the bosom of the everlasting God the Father, from all eternity,
that such a message as the following is commanded to be declared
to a rebel universe? "Be it known unto you therefore, that through
this man is preached unto you the forgiveness of sins; and by
him, all that believe are justified from all things, from which they
could not be justified by the law of Moses." O the depth of the
love of God in Christ Jesus! My dear brother, it is not likely that.
I shall ever have the joy of seeing your face in the flesh; but we
shall meet, yes, adored be our God, we shall meet one day before
his throne, and sing together throughout eternity, the praises of
our dear adorable Redeemer. To that blessed land, I am fast,
fast hastening; yes, I shall soon see the glorious face of Emmanuel. I shall soon know that all I have ever yet known of
him was nothing, though I sometimes see as much of him, as
a spirit fettered by the body of corruption can possibly behold.
Yes, Jesus! I have often seen in thee, what has made me forget
all my pains and weakness: what has made me forget for a time
that I dwelt upon earth at all. But, my beloved brother, I cannot
write more, I am so weak, and I fear you will even not be able
to read this. O welcome, welcome, everlasting strength, to praise
my glorious Saviour! I am a monument of his love and mercy.
My love in the truth, to your dear partner: she has been greatly
afflicted, but the Lord is her rock, and her strength. The time
of suffering will soon, soon be ended: let us even suffer cheerfully;
our sufferings are not worthy to be compared to the weight of
glory which shall one day be revealed. Although I know you did
it as unto the Lord, I would offer you both my unfeigned gratitude, for your affectionate and tender kindness to my dearest
Mary. O may she and you shine as bright lights in the midst of
a perverse and dark generation. Now, my dearly beloved, farewell. I am much in prayer for you all. May you, as a Church,
be followers of God, as dear children; and O, do walk in love, as
Christ also hath loved you, and given himself for you, an offering
and a sacrifice for a sweet-smelling savour unto God. O let the
glory of your God and Father, be dear, dear unto you: the consideration will induce you so to walk, as never to dishonour your
holy profession. Again, my dearly beloved brother, Adieu.

"Your affectionate dying friend and sister,

"ISABELLA CAMPBELL."

Although Isabella thus increased the joy of others, and had her own joy increased by such intercourse, she was not ignorant of its being ever true, that those who love Jesus supremely, must have some reproach or other to bear, for his sake, from the world or compromising professors of the faith. The feelings, which the conviction of this excited in her mind, are thus minutely recorded in the journal of her sister :—

" One night, she said, ' O what a service those do us who reproach us for Christ's sake, yet they know not that they do it. They just drive us nearer to himself; how blessed to be hid in his pavilion from the strife of tongues ! Yet their folly often causes me to weep, not for my sake, but for their own ; for I know that all things work together for good to those who love God. O that they would believe what they are doing now ; but as the Jews would not believe, when they were calling Christ a devil, that they were ruining their own souls, neither will they believe. O could they but know the many cries and tears the christian pours forth before God, that they may be forgiven, for they know not what they do; but if they will not be influenced by what God has done for them, nothing will avail. What an awful thing will it be, when we meet them around the great white throne ! Then shall they see, and believe, when it is too late, that we have not followed cunningly-devised fables. Then shall they know, that we are not the poor self-deluded hypocrites which they now take us to be, but shining as stars for ever, being washed and made white in the blood of the Lamb. What dread confusion shall then take hold upon them, though great the change that must pass upon us, before we can behold all this, not only with composure, but with perfect acquiescence in the will of our heavenly Father. Many a tear have I shed upon this bed for them, yet not one for a hundred which I ought to have shed. I do pity them; carried away captive by the Devil at his will. O, the enmity of the heart of man, that cannot endure the image of God, when exhibited in any of his creatures ! I am grieved ; my heart is almost broken at the way in which christians live, at least professing christians. Are they christians ? They can do all that the world will do, and reproach you if you do not follow their example. O can they really belong to him who was despised and rejected of men, and for what cause? because he testified of them that their deeds were evil. Would they enjoy so much of the esteem of the world, did they follow his blessed example—' Whosoever shall be ashamed of me, &c.' Are there not many ways of being ashamed of Christ? and surely it is one of them, to mix from day to day with those who see no beauty in him, why they should desire him, and never mention his blessed name, or commend the great love wherewith he loveth us. O there is much, much wrong among us ; many profess to know God, but in works they deny him. Who are living as pilgrims and strangers? Alas, their number is very few, and were the Lord now to search Jerusalem with candles, many, many, I fear, would be found trusting in refuges of lies, and not in the name of the only begotten Son of God. It is an awful thing to endeavour to serve God and Mammon. Many would startle were you to say this unto them ; but sure I am, their conformity to the world plainly evinces that they consider themselves debtors to the flesh ; and O that they but saw what they are doing, even robbing the great God of his glory, and making infidels to reproach that as religion, which is not the religion of Jesus. ' If any love the world, the love of the Father is not in him.' "

The following letter which I received from Isabella, contains an affecting exposition of her own religious feelings, and such a letter at any time must be cheering for a minister to receive from any of his people.

Fernicarry, August 16th, 1827.

" MY GREATLY BELOVED FRIEND,

" Had I known how to write to you, I would not have been so long of inquiring after your temporal and spiritual welfare, but never having seen dear ——, since your departure, I was ignorant both of your address, and of the most eligible way of conveying a letter to you. I have not, however, forgotten you. O no, my beloved friend, this is impossible. Distance of time nor place can never dissolve the dear bonds which unite me to you. It rejoiced me greatly, to hear from Mr. —— that you were considerably better, and I sincerely trust that, ere now, your are almost quite recovered. O how does the anticipation of you speedy return to Roseheath gladden and refresh my poor soul? for I do long much to see your face once again in the flesh, and to rejoice with you in Jesus, as the Lord our righteousness, and as the Lord our

strength. I hope, my beloved friend, that you have found ample
cause to magnify your God because of this affliction: indeed, I
have myself rejoiced much because of it, feeling fully assured that
our compassionate Father must have some important end to accomplish by your present sufferings. No, my dear friend, he
never grieves us unnecessarily. O no, he loves us too well to do
this: and you, I believe, have already experienced this: you have,
I doubt not, been enabled to glorify him in the fire, and cheerfully
to kiss his rod. Indeed, I could easily conceive your afflictions
to have been so sweet, as to have caused you to glory in tribulation, and to sing sweetly in the midst of pain and weakness. O
my dear, dear friend, I am sure you would not have wanted it for
any consideration. I long much to see you, and to hear you tell
of all his loving-kindnesses. You will have received many proofs
of his fatherly affection since I last saw you.

"You will have had many hours of sweet communion with him;
and you, I doubt not, have esteemed this your chiefest joy. The
Lord water your soul abundantly with the dews of Heaven, that
you may be enriched in the knowledge of His most blessed will,
and be ready at all times to point poor perishing sinners to 'the
Lamb of God, that taketh away the sins of the world.' I trust
your Father has much work for you yet to perform. O that you
may glorify him by bearing much fruit. I have been somewhat
better for three weeks past. I breathe more easily, and endure
much less pain; my cough is also better. O what a miracle am
I in the land of the living! I had expected long ere now to have
been triumphing amidst the redeemed above, to have been arrayed in my spotless apparel, and tuning with alacrity my golden
harp; and, I confess, the thought of remaining much longer in
this dreary vale, was by no means cheering unto me. But I trust
I can now say, 'Good is the will of the Lord.' O it would ill become one who has been so highly favoured, to say otherwise; but
O, often I do. O for a spirit more in unison with a child of grace!
I have of late enjoyed many refreshing seasons of delightful communion with our best Friend. How transporting to behold His
glory in the face of Jesus! There, my dear friend, doth it shine
most gloriously, although the carnal eye cannot at all perceive it.
O, eternal praise be to God for the eye of faith, which entereth
into that which is within the vail, and oft-times feasts itself by
gazing on the beauties of Jesus. O Jesus, what shall we say of
Thee? shall we rather be silent than not give unto Thee that glory

23

which is due unto thy blessed name? No, we shall not, we cannot be mute respecting Thee. We shall here, in much imperfection, begin that new song, which we hope one day to sing, yea, throughout eternity to sing, with pure hearts fervently. O how insipid and tasteless is every thing apart from Jesus! What a sad want does the soul feel, when it wanders from feeding upon this bread of life! O for rapacious appetites, to eat continually of this manna, to live every moment by lively faith upon the Son of God, who loved us, and hath given himself for us. I am sure you will rejoice to hear that I have had the inexpressible pleasure of seeing your dear humble friend Miss ——. O what a dear lovely saint she is! I cannot inform you the real pleasure I had in conversing with her. She has paid me three visits; and I must say, the more you see of her, the more cause will you have for wonder and gratitude. Her faith in Christ, and love to all the saints, have in very deed rejoiced my heart. Why I should be thus rarely favoured, I know not. O for a heart overflowing with gratitude. My dearly beloved friend, pray for me; O pray much for me. You know not half my weaknesses. Mary joins me in christian affection, and longs much after you in the Lord. Hoping soon to hear of your return, I would for the present bid you farewell, by commending you to the unfailing protection of Jesus. Ever yours in the faith of the glorious gospel,

"ISABELLA CAMPBELL."

The following extract exemplifies her deep interest for all her young companions, and shows that she had intended to prepare an address for them.

"'Well it troubles my conscience, a good deal,' said she to her sister, 'that I never yet made you write, for I think it is unkind to them and unfaithful to God, not to testify to them that "Wisdom's ways are ways of pleasantness and all her paths are peace." Formerly she had said, 'O how I do wish to write to all the young women who attended the class with me: I do wish to tell them what I have found, and what they may also find; for God says, 'Whosoever will, let him take of the water of life freely." Now that I have seen my error I am anxious that they also should see theirs: for I do think we were all deceiving ourselves, by supposing that since we paid more attention outwardly to religious things, and since greater pains were taken with us than with many other young people around us, that we were much more meet for the kingdom of heaven than they. But ah! it was a delusion so to think; for I am sure there was little, if any, real godliness among us, as our conduct when we left that place uniformly proved: for instead of talking of Christ as we walked together by the way, our whole conversation was earthly and trifling, as they themselves must remember. O how many Sabbath evenings did we spend in this sinful way, when we might have been glorifying God together! Alas! the remembrance of this season fills me with sore pain. O that I had strength that I might go to every one of them, and say that unless they repent they shall all likewise perish; as I undoubtedly would have done had God allowed me to remain in the state in which I then was. It is grievous to see how people can think themselves going to heaven, and serve the world and the devil while upon earth. If they cannot now delight themselves in God, how do they expect to live and delight themselves with him for ever? I am sure the secret dread, which they have of him, that fear of having one minute to think exclusively of him, ought to convince them that they have not yet known him as a God, as their friend, their portion, their all. O these dear young people! would that the Lord would breathe upon them, that they might live and stand upon their feet, a precious, living company, determined to follow Jesus through good and through bad report, as all his followers must. O that they would but be persuaded to leave this vain and foolish world, and join themselves to those, who though despised and rejected of men, are peacefully pursuing their journey to Emmanuel's happy land!' "

Often did she afterward talk of her early class-mates, and express a desire to write to them, but never was able to accomplish it.

To my friend and brother, who presided at the communion in my absence, she addressed the following note, expressive of those holy anxieties which possessed her soul :—

"*Roseneath, Fast-day.*

"MY BELOVED FRIEND IN THE FAITH OF THE GLORIOUS GOSPEL:

" 'Grace, Mercy, and Peace, from God the Father, and from the Lord Jesus Christ, be multiplied unto you.'

"O my dear, dear friend, I have much, much of the Lord's goodness to tell you of; what of his amazing love in Jesus have I not experienced since I saw you last! When your hear it, I am sure, it will heighten your song of gratitude. O, his ways with me have all been wonders. I can, indeed, say that he is a kind and compassionate master. Do help me to praise him, for well you may. You also have felt much of his love, and known much of the liberty wherewith he maketh his children free. O my beloved friend, on this occasion be strong in the Lord and the power of his might. Remember how it exalts omnipotence to make weakness strong. Do lean much upon Jesus : he possesses all power in heaven and on earth, and we never stumble by believing this, but by forgetting it. I am most desirous that you may, on the ensuing Sabbath, bring much glory to Prince Jesus. I am much in prayer for you, and I believe that these prayers will not be unanswered through him who maketh continual intercession for us. Be faithful, my much loved friend. Care not for man, whose breath is in his nostrils. Greater is he that is with you than all they who can be against you.—Now be strong. O how loath I am to stop, but I can dictate no more now. Mary wishes for you now and always, much of the presence of the King of Zion, and prays that you may be filled with the consolations of his Holy Spirit. Adieu, my beloved friend. Pray much for us, while I remain,

"Your deeply attached friend in the truth,
"ISABELLA CAMPBELL."

From Isabella rallying so wonderfully after the successive crises of her disorder, the hope was not unfrequently cherished that the abscesses wearing themselves out, she might at last recover. The dampness of the house at Fernicarry, however, and its distance from medical attendance, rather diminished the probabilities of this. Some christian friends therefore, anxious that every means should be used for prolonging so interesting and valuable a life, made arrangements for her removal to Helensburgh, where greater attention could be paid to her case by her medical attendant, who resided there. Although she herself had no prospect of recovery, she felt it her duty to yield to the wishes of her friends, leaving the event to the disposal of her heavenly Father. So long as her passion for holiness became stronger, it was not likely that her attachment to life would increase, even when she was most convalescent from the severer attacks of her malady.

" O I am glad at finding you so much recovered," said a visitor one day, ' Yes,' she replied with emphasis, ' all my friends manifest great pleasure at my recovery. I myself long greatly to fall asleep in Jesus. I love to behold him ; I loath myself because of sin ; I am vile ; I am awfully ungrateful; I am doing nothing for my God. When shall the matchless loveliness of our plant of renown completely and continually engross my heart ? It is sin, it is sin, my dear friend, I pant so much to get quit (of. Pray, O pray that I may bear much fruit to our Father's glory.' 'O the glorious meaning,' exclaimed she to another, 'of that word purity ; that is the state the new man pants after. There can be no perfect happiness except in a state of perfect purity. It is the holiness of heaven that constitutes its blessedness ; the presence of God produces entire conformity. When he shall appear we shall be like him, for we shall see him as he is.' "

Meekly, however, and gratefully she acquiesced in the proposed arrangements ; although her heart was far away from this vain and changeful world. Mr. ——, who had long known Isabella, and had interested himself in carrying the arrangements into effect, conducted her to the village from the secluded spot where she had enjoyed such extraordinary blessedness of fellowship with the Father, and with the Son, and with the Holy Ghost. Of this event he gives the following account :

" Isabella's removal to Helensburgh took place on the 1st of October, 1827, about four weeks before she fell asleep in Jesus, so that the hopes that were fondly cherished by her friends in bringing her to this place, were graciously disappointed by Him who doeth all things after the counsel of his own will. The day was favourable, and towards the afternoon, I left the village in a carriage, for accomplishing our purpose. I could not refrain from

23*

silently praying that our heavenly Father would be pleased to bless her removal, in the alleviation of her disorder ; that having her days lengthened out, she might be enabled to testify to many of her Saviour's love. On my arrival, Isabella, being aware of my coming, was in readiness to leave that spot where first she was brought to know the love of God in Christ, but to which she was never more to return. On entering the door, the first object that arrested my attention, was her tall emaciated figure standing at the head of the stair-case, and endeavouring to make her way down to the door without any assistance. On seeing me she smiled, and meekly said, ' So you are come to take me away.' ' Yes, Isabella, and I trust it will be for your benefit.' ' O yes,' she replied, in her usual calm and solemn manner, ' it is all well, the will of the Lord be done.' Having rested a little to recover from the fatigue of walking from her bed-room, she was carried down to the road, and laid in the vehicle, with her mother by her side. At this moment, when writing these lines to you, I see in imagination her form distinctly before me, and hear her subdued voice speaking of the love of God. After being seated in the carriage, there appeared in her countenance an expression of calm and peaceful resignation, which seemed to say to us all standing by, ' Don't weep for me ; Lord, I am thine, make of me what thou wilt ; all is well that thou doest, let me be silent and adore.' When ready to start, I proposed taking my seat beside the driver. ' No, no, you must not do that,' said our dear friend, ' you must come in, there is plenty of room for us all ; and besides, I want to speak with you on the way down. I stepped in, and we proceeded at a slow pace. I confess, when I saw Isabella so lively, and so much stronger than she had been a few weeks before, my hopes of her recovery were considerably flattered. I knew not, or I was unwilling to believe, that the insidious malady which took her away had already completely undermined her constitution.

When a little on our way down, she was asked if she felt the jolting of the carriage unpleasant ? 'Not at all, I feel wonderfully well. O how gracious is my heavenly Father to me ! What has he not done for me, a poor sinner ! The kind attention you have all shown me,—it affects me much, when I think on the kindness of all my christian friends in this place ; for I see it is all of the Lord, it is his doing altogether, and I desire to be humble and grateful.' ' Who can tell, Isabella,' it was observed, ' but your removal to Helensburgh may yet be the means in the hand of God, of restoring you to health again; at least, God has some wise end in view, in allowing you to be taken to the village.' 'There can be no doubt of that,' was her reply; 'yes, God has an end in view in all this, worthy of himself; but, Sir, as to my getting better, I have little hope of that. Yet should it please the Lord to spare me and restore my health, I trust he will also give me grace, to enable me to live to the praise of his glory.' I think it was at this part of the conversation, that I saw her mother struggling with her maternal feelings, and endeavouring to hide from my notice, the tears that filled her eyes. Silence ensued for a little, when Isabella, who was evidently musing on what had just been said, resumed the conversation, exclaiming, ' Well, I cannot help thinking that I see something singular in this dispensation of Providence; indeed, I do see the hand of God in it very distinctly. He doeth all his will in heaven above, and in the earth beneath : his own glory will be promoted by it; I have no doubt of that, and that is enough, you know.'

" The gentle breeze that was blowing in the former part of the day had now entirely subsided, so that the smooth surface of the Gairloch reflected very distinctly to our view the various objects which line its southern margin, presenting, a faint indeed, but certainly a pleasing emblem, of the purity and bliss of heaven; and it suggested a topic on which our dear sister delighted much to dwell, the glory and blessedness of the redeemed there. To give you her language verbatim on this occasion, I will not pretend ; in substance it was as follows :—' How very different will our views of God be in the world of light! here we see through a glass dimly, but there face to face. O, how transporting, how animating is the hope of seeing God as he is in the temple above, and of being made like him there. What manner of love our heavenly Father hath bestowed on us, that we should be called the sons of God ! yet it doth not appear what we shall be ; but we know that when he appears we shall be like him ; for we shall see him as he is. But O, how very little we really know about the joys of heaven ; and I think the reason why we know so little of these joys, is, because there is yet so much sin about us, and in us. " Eye hath not seen, nor ear heard, neither hath it entered into the heart of man to conceive, the things that God hath prepared for them that love him." ' We arrived before dark at Mr.———'s, and in a few moments Isabella was placed in the room, and, I believe, on that bed, from which her happy and glorified spirit took its flight to the regions of eternal glory—to the presence of her Redeemer. 'Blessed are the dead which die in the Lord, from henceforth: yea, saith the spirit, that they may rest from their labours, and their works do follow them.' "

I have not in any way attempted to describe it to you, since your eyes are familiar with the exquisite scenery which Isabella had now looked upon for the last time. Often she had rejoiced in its contemplation, wondering, as she did so, that her heavenly Father lavished so much beauty on a world so scornful of his love, so accursed with its own wickedness. Her feelings are well and truly described by the same friend who was with her during this farewell view of the glories of the Gairloch, upon which she had so often looked from the garden where she was accustomed to retire for prayer.

"Isabella had a taste for the beauties of creation. Although the work of the Redeemer finished on the cross was, of all others, the theme which afforded to her mind the purest and most exalted joy; yet she had a lively sense of the divine wisdom and goodness as exhibited in the works of nature, and could enter into the sentiment of the poet with the feelings of an heir of immortality, as she contemplated these works, and say, 'My Father made them all.' When the conversation happened at any time to turn upon the goodness of the Great Creator, Isabella catching the theme, would express herself in the following manner: 'O yes, all God's works praise him. "The heavens declare his glory, and the firmament showeth forth his handy work." Our heavenly Father hath left distinct impressions of his power, and wisdom, and goodness, in every object above and below, that presents itself to the eye of man; so that the disciple of Jesus has abundant opportunity when abroad, travelling either on his master's business, or for recreation, to hold communion with God, his Almighty friend and benefactor.' She indeed gloried in the cross of Christ; but whilst she did so, she was far from despising those lessons which the picturesque and enchanting scenery, amidst which she spent the most of her days, was calculated to convey to her active and contemplative mind. These objects of creation, I know well, from what I have heard her say on various occasions, she considered as so many mirrors, reflecting to the senses of man the glories of the invisible God; and in which the enlightened Christian may easily trace the operation of a divine hand. Her local situation indeed, was peculiarly calculated to produce and foster in a mind like Isabella's, so devout, and so much given to contemplation, an ardent love for the beauties and sublimities of nature. Far secluded from the hurry and the noise of society, living in a spot where nature exhibits to the eye some of her most beautiful, as well as some of her grandest appearances, Isabella had unceasing opportunities of lifting up her soul to her Father in heaven, while engaged in reading important lessons in the works of his hands strewed around her."

"Beloved Isabella," says one of her young friends, "was very fond of flowers, and I frequently carried her a nosegay. She would examine every flower most minutely, and seemed to rejoice greatly because these his works praised Him whom her soul loved. When presenting it to her, she in general looked up, and then at the flowers, seeming to be lost in wonder and admiration; and cried out, ' Yes, truly his works praise him, they do show forth his handy work.' When the rose of Sharon was pointed out, she seemed as if in a holy transport, and said, ' Yes, Jesus, I am the rose of Sharon, and the lily of the valley.' " " A friend," writes her sister, "having sent her a bunch of flowers, she said, ' They are very beautiful; the new Jerusalem is filled with unfading flowers, even with souls washed in the blood of Jesus, who shall reign with him for ever and ever.' " Going into her room one morning, when the sun was shining beautifully, her sister heard her also exclaim, " O, when shall I be bewildered with the healing, life-supporting ray of the sun of righteousness? When shall I never see any thing but light, nor feel any thing but love? When, when shall I be altogether holy? O Father, I long to be altogether full of affection toward thee; I long to see thy glorious beauty."

With a mind capable of such perceptions and emotions,

it is not difficult to conceive how interesting every object would seem that met her eye during this farewell view of the shores of Roseneath, and all their loveliness; but what increased its effect, must also be obvious to you all. It was on the evening of the thanksgiving day of the communion; and you know how deeply exercised her mind had been during that solemn season, regarding the spiritual interests of the people that dwelt there. Of her continued anxiety on this point, as well as of her feelings after her journey, the following extracts from a letter of Miss ———, (the sister of her beloved friend,) is descriptive :—

"Hearing she had arrived in Helensburgh, I called in the evening to inquire how she felt :—she said, 'I am weak, but the Lord has graciously strengthened me, and I do not suffer unless from fatigue.' She then inquired whether I had enjoyed the services at Roseneath, where I had been that day; and on my mentioning the happy effects which seemed to be produced on certain individuals by some of them, she said, 'I expected to hear good news. It has been greatly impressed upon my mind, that it would be a season much to be remembered. I have had such enlargement in praying that it might be so. O praise the Lord with me, let us exalt his name together; surely this is but as the first fruit of a mighty harvest, to be gathered in to the glory of our God.' Next morning, when I returned, finding her much exhausted, I said— 'I fear you have not rested well;' she answered, 'I had a very happy night; I could not cease from praising the Lord. Before you came in last night, I felt so weak that, had I known of your coming, I should have said that I was unable to see you, but joy made me quite strong—O, I have much for which to praise our gracious Father.' "

To her friend she thus expressed herself :—" O my dear Miss ———, pray that my coming here may be altogether for his own glory. When I think of his goodness in providing so many dear friends, I am amazed; I am a wonder to myself. When I contemplate his spiritual blessings in Christ Jesus, I am lost in a sea of wonders." At this visit, Isabella asked her to tell her about Irving's translation of

Ben Ezra, which had been mentioned to her by a friend. During their conversation upon this subject, she remarked, "Well, when fully understood, the doctrine of the Redeemer's advent is most grand and cheering, and the reception of it opens up many parts of scripture which before appeared obscure." Shortly afterward, when they were speaking of an individual who seemed to have seen the necessity of making her calling and election sure, but had been lulled into quietness without believing the Gospel, she said, "I have been thinking much of that. 'They have healed the hurt of the daughter of my people slightly.' It is a fearful sin, the besetting sin of this day; and I see many just godly ministers guilty of it."

A correspondent says:

"Before leaving Helensburgh I saw her again. This was the last time. I brought her some flowers, of which she seemed very fond. On my giving them, she said, 'Is there a rose of Sharon?' I said, 'No, but there is a lily of the valley.' 'O,' she said, 'He is the lily among thorns. Do not every one of these tender, beautiful leaves, with their delicate colours, plainly show forth the glory of God?' She being rather weaker that morning, I said, 'You do not seem so well.' 'O no,' she replied, 'I have had a good deal of sickness; but while the outward man decays, the inward man is renewed day by day. I do feel, that beholding as in a glass the glory of the Lord, I am transformed into the same glorious image.' I had just heard of the triumphant death of a young lady, and I told her what I had heard. O with what seeming joy she listened. 'Yes,' she said, 'he is faithful, and his promise is, "As the day is, so shall thy strength be." O that, should my sickness be unto death, I may glorify God as she has done.' I asked her if she thought she was to recover.' 'I do not think so; but it is right to use the means; and as my friends are anxious to try every thing, I cheerfully consent.' She then asked me, 'Do you wish I should recover?' I hesitated a little, and said, 'Were it for the glory of God, or the good of souls, I should say yes; but in reference to yourself, I would say no: for while here, you must daily offend your best friend; but there, you shall serve him perfectly.' Never shall I forget the sweet look she gave me, when clasping her to me, she said, 'O it is delightful to think that grace can, and will be perfected in glory, and that to depart and be with Christ is far better.' She spoke much of those who, after saying they believed, gave proof that their faith did not purify their hearts. 'O,' she said, 'what an awful thing self-deceiving is! How shall they tremble when death stares them in the face, because Christ is not their rock! Here we cannot build too securely; but O, to have a name to live and be dead!' I said, 'but you do not doubt of your safety?' No, no, I do not doubt; why should I? for I feel the spirit witnesseth with my spirit, that I am a child of God; he has drawn me, and I have run after him.' We spoke much of feeling joy when we heard of any one asking the way to Zion. I remember she said, 'O what sin has done! for now, when I hear that a sinner has found peace for his soul in believing, I feel much trembling mixed with joy, lest whilst in words he profess Christ, in works he should deny him. I do not doubt if it be real faith, but it shall produce the fruits of the spirit; but I fear lest sinners make to themselves a false Saviour.' She told me much of her own feelings previous to finding rest to her soul in the simple truth; but I dare not say I could remember her words, the substance of them I trust never to forget."

"My next visit to her was after her removal to Helensburgh," writes another. "Having received me in her usual manner, and pausing a little, she said, 'You would not expect when you saw me last, that it would be here we should meet again.' I said, that I did not expect it indeed. She said, 'the Lord's ways are not as our ways.' The conversation turned immediately upon the assurance of faith. She said, 'it is a God glorifying doctrine, and I know it is so from long experience. It is what all may attain to; the invitation is to all: and the more we trust to, and believe in him, the more we honour him. There is not a sin which I myself could so much dread as doubting of my own case, because it would be making God a liar. I have known some of a few months standing in the divine life, who have made farther advances than others who had been twenty years in it, just because they looked more simply to the Lord Jesus.' Talking of the joy and peace of believing, she said, 'There is both joy and peace; and I shall maintain there is not a full reception of the gospel truth without joy and peace.' Speaking of a young man who was at the time coming out in the ministry, she said, with much warmth of feeling, that she hoped he would bring much glory to Jesus."

You will observe that the subject of assurance of faith, which, from various circumstances, had occasioned much discussion in her neighbourhood, is sometimes alluded to in these extracts. The eminent piety and holiness of her life; her unchanging joy in God; the confidence with which she wrote and spoke of her own future blessedness, induced many inquirers to ascertain her opinions regarding the necessity of such an assurance. I insert the answers which she made to various individuals, illustrative of what she thought and felt regarding it.

"If I am really believing," said Isabella, "that Christ hath suffered for me, how can I but have peace and joy? because in believing this, I must be believing that I shall never be called to suffer. It is quite impossible for any soul, believing that God hath so loved it as to give Christ to die for it, not to enjoy confidence towards him, even as a child towards its father."

"When asked, if it was impossible for a believer to doubt? 'No,' she replied, ' for that would be saying the same thing as that a believer cannot sin; but I say, when a believer questions in any measure the love of God towards him, that he has turned away his eyes from beholding the gift of his love, Christ Jesus.' A lady, herself for many years supported amid great sufferings by the consolations of the gospel, (who, although prevented by God's providence from holding any personal communion, had often intermediately rejoiced with her in her joy,) wished to know if she ever doubted? ' I cannot say that I ever doubt,' was her answer. ' A thought sometimes, like an arrow, shoots through my heart; but there is nothing I so much dread as a doubting of God's faithfulness.' To another question of the same lady, regarding her continual joy, she replied, ' I always rejoice in God, although my sorrow for sin is so great that I do not always experience a sensible joy.' "

These sentiments I record without hesitation ; not only as resting upon most unexceptionable authority, but in strict accordance with what pervaded her letters, as well as the whole tone of her feelings during our intercourse, subsequent to her reception of the gospel. The testimony

24

of her sister also, recorded in the following extract from her notes, is ample and explicit :

"When asked one day by a friend, whether she thought it possible for any one to get to heaven without assurance ? she answered, ' I believe there are many now before the throne, who while on earth, were not at all times persuaded of the love of God, who did not at all times rejoice in the finished work of Jesus; but that they must have been assured and rejoiced in Christ Jesus is certain, else they could not have rendered unto God any cheerful obedience, nor known what it is to have any peace with God through our Lord Jesus Christ. Now, if a soul has not known what it is to have peace with God through Christ, I am sure that soul can never have believed the gospel, for it is written, " Therefore being justified by faith, we have peace with God ;" and again, our Lord says to his disciples, " In the world ye shall have tribulation, but in me ye shall have peace." But I can easily conceive of a soul, even after experiencing joy and peace in believing, by making frames and feelings a ground of confidence, getting very disquieted and unhappy. Alas! no wonder they should do so, seeing they have ceased to gaze upon that which first brought peace and joy; I am, however, often deeply grieved that the examples of unbelief we have recorded of many, who I believe were the children of God, instead of reprovers, should so frequently be taken as comforters to those in a similar state of mind. O what comfort ought it to afford me, to hear that others as well as myself were of little faith, and slow of heart to understand the scriptures? It has often struck me, that if sorrow could be experienced in heaven, (but this, I well know, cannot be,) how keenly many would feel, who have got over all their struggles, because of the use which is made of their trials and temptations. O surely, surely it can never be right to take comfort in any thing that is dishonouring to God, and could they now address us from the heights of Zion, their language, I am sure, would be,

" 'Trust in the Lord, for ever trust,
And banish all your fears.' "

Questions, however, were sometimes put to her, both before and after her arrival in Helensburgh, apparently prompted by a vain curiosity ; and the solution of which by Isabella, distinguished as she was for wisdom and holiness in the church of God, could confer no benefit : for example, regarding the possibility of reaching heaven without assurance. Isabella, herself, was sensible of this, and mentioning the subject one day to a friend, she said, " I think it is a successful snare of Satan, by which he keeps people away from the great personal question, whether they are or are not believing on the Son of God. The other day, one asked me, ' If salvation was possible without assurance ?' and I just asked her, if she knew what she meant by such a question ? and said, that I thought if there was any meaning in it, it was this, can I be saved without giving glory to God ?"

The inquiry of greatest importance which the exhibition of Isabella's christianity ought to have prompted was this, whence arose in her such assurance, and such joy ? She would have rejoiced in making it known ; and how she herself ever felt regarding it, all may learn from the words which she used to another friend : " It would be robbing Jesus of his glory, were we to place our assurance in any thing but his finished work, and it would exhibit a self-righteous spirit." So far, indeed, was she from resting it on any high attainment in personal holiness, that she took great delight in exposing such impious presumption and folly, by using the metaphor of an old divine : " who would ever cast an anchor within the ship to hold it secure ? so there can be no safety found for any soul in itself, but just as it is standing on the rock of ages."

Nearly a month had passed away since her arrival, but the hopes of her friends were not encouraged by any appearances of amendment, while Isabella herself meekly waited for the salvation of God, for the time when he should permit her to behold his glory.— Although no decided change was visible, she seemed persuaded that the time was not far distant when the voice of the bridegroom should be heard ; solicitous only like a wise virgin with oil in her vessel, to be in readiness to go forth from her frail and perishable

tabernacle, and share with other ransomed spirits, the holy and blessed solemnities of their spiritual union in the eternal habitations. Under this impression, she used farewell language to her friends when they went out from her chamber. " About ten days before she entered into the valley of the shadow of death," says one of them, when leaving her she looked at me, her countenance assuming a grave and solemn aspect ; peace and serenity, and joy in the Holy Ghost, seemed to pervade the whole of it : she said, " I think you shall never see me again on earth, for I feel such a great weight upon my breast, which I think will soon finish me ; but I am happy." " My salvation," said she to another, as if beholding just before her the last scenes and the consummation of all her sufferings," is much nearer now than when I believed :"—to a third who had been performing some office of tenderness about her, she exclaimed, clasping her in her arms, " I have been taught to love you with that love which eternity tends to heighten. I am dying, but I am glad to go and be with Jesus, which is far better.

> " ' There shall I bathe my weary soul
> In seas of heavenly rest,
> And not a wave of trouble roll
> Across this troubled breast.' "

Of those at a distance also, she spoke under the impression that in the face she should see them no more. " I shall never behold dearly beloved Mr. —— any more on earth ; he is now in the midst of strangers, enduring much bodily suffering. I sympathize deeply with him, as he has often done and still does with me. With him I have spent some of my happiest hours ; yes, Jesus hath often opened to us the Scriptures, and made our hearts burn within us on our pilgrimage road. O, I love him, I love him much in the glorious gospel, and though separate in body we are not in spirit : no, thank God, we never can."

At this time she had received a letter from a friend whose society she had in the previous summer occasionally enjoyed. The letter gave her great delight, and the following reply dictated to her sister, is affecting, as an exposition of her feelings, but still more so as her last exertion to write of the glory and the love of Jesus, to any of her believing friends.

"Helensburgh, 7th Nov. 1827.

" My very dear Mr.——,

"I am long of replying to your kind and refreshing letter—refreshing truly it was to my poor soul. I had, for some days previous to its arrival, been saying to my sister, how much I longed after you in the Lord, and how greatly I desired to see or hear from you once again in this solitary land. Judge then of my joy, and I trust I can say, gratitude, when your letter was put into my hands. I could not help considering it an answer to my prayers. I could not help being overwhelmed with a sense of the Lord's goodness. Well does it become us to say, ' Who is a God like unto our God ?' 'O how great is his mercy to them that fear him, to them that trust in his mercy !'

" At the earnest request of some of my dear friends in Jesus, I have been removed to this village, in order to have more immediate access to medical aid. For some time after my removal, I felt better than when at Fernicarry, but it has since graciously pleased my compassionate Father to revive the heat of the furnace. Adored be his grace for every thing I endure; it is all sent in love, I require it all. O pray, my dear friend in the Lord, that I may be enabled to exercise continual faith in that soothing promise,— ' All things shall work together for good, to them that love the Lord,' &c. O did we firmly believe this, how different, how composed would be our conduct, amid all the cares and trials of this mortal scene. O that we should be so slow to learn, so loath to trust, our true and faithful God—even a God of love. Surely, surely it well becomes me to proclaim this glorious truth to all around me, that God is love.—What of it have I not experienced ? When I review his marvellous dealings towards me, I am constrained to say, ' O Lord my God, full many are the wonders thou hast done ;' and though now my most enlarged conceptions of the scheme of mercy are but narrow and contracted, and my thoughts

24*

of gratitude cold and languid, I rejoice greatly that the welcome day is not far off, when my whole soul shall be absorbed in the contemplation of redeeming love, when Jesus shall be my eternal theme. O how much I long to behold, in the light of heaven, his matchless beauty. Yes, my spirit pants vehemently for a dismissal from this earthly house. O to be entirely freed from corruption, to be led by the Lamb to living fountains of water, to bathe my weary spirit in the full ocean of eternal delight. Thrice welcome, happy morn, when I shall bid an everlasting adieu to sin, when I shall shut mine eyes on vanity. O sin, sin, often hast thou grieved me, often hast thou caused me to hang my harp on the willow; but soon, soon shall I be completely freed from all thy direful influence—soon shall I see my adorable Saviour as he is."

The last agonies prevented her bringing this letter to a close: but two days before her death her sister asked her whether she had any message to leave for Mr. ——, and what she should do with the letter? She said with emphasis, " Send it to him when I am gone, and tell him how much I loved and rejoiced over him in the Lord Jesus. Tell him how happy I was in the prospect of dissolution. Tell him that the Lord was my rock and shield. Tell him that my whole soul was refreshed by the all-satisfying influence of the Holy Spirit: in short, tell him that all was well—nothing, nothing was wanting."

The Hymn.

My soul doth pant t'wards thee,
My God, source of eternal life ;
   Flesh fights with me ;
   O end the strife,
And part us, that in peace I may
                    Unclay
My weary spirit, and take
My flight to thy eternal spring,
   Where for his sake
   Who is my king,
I may wash all my tears away
                That day.

Thou conqueror of death,
Glorious triumpher o'er the grave,
   Whose holy breath
   Was spent to save
Lost mankind, make me to be styl'd
              Thy child ;
And take me when I die,
And go unto my dust, my soul
   Above the sky,
   With saints enrol,
That in thy arms for ever I
            May lie.
              Amen.

The Scripture.

AND the work of righteousness shall be peace ; and the effect of righteousness, quietness and assurance for ever.

He giveth power to the faint ; and to them that have no might he in-
creaseth strength. Fear thou not; for I am with thee; be not dismayed,
for I am thy God: I will help thee; yea, I will uphold thee with the right
hand of my righteousness.

Now lettest thou thy servant depart in peace : for mine eyes have seen
thy salvation.

Precious in the sight of the Lord is the death of his saints.

He will swallow up death in victory. Blessed are the dead who die in
the Lord.

Father, I will that they also whom thou hast given me be with me where
I am; that they may behold my glory, which thou hast given me; for thou
lovedst me before the foundation of the world. Thou hast loved them as
thou hast loved me.

Thine eyes shall see the King in his beauty.

As for me, I will behold thy face in righteousness.

CHAPTER XII.

THE message Isabella sent to her christian correspondent, was triumphantly expressive of the fact, that, in her
great extremity, she found that He in whom she had believed was faithful and gracious. From what you may
have heard, you cannot but be anxious to know more particularly how this was, and how she deported herself in her
last days ; what reason, in fine, she had to adopt the language in which her message was couched. I consider it
a most blessed thing, that a minute and accurate record
has been preserved, which I trust will be most edifying,
not only to you and to your children, but to 'many that
shall yet be born to the family of Christ. Isabella had
often said, " We may contrive to live without Christ, but
without him how shall we die?" and while it was the subject of her own earnest prayer, she also besought the intercession of her friends that she might glorify God in
death. You will now see whether these supplications were
answered—whether in the last pangs she endured as seeing him who is invisible—continuing to hold fast the beginning of her confidence—and that peace, which for so
long a period of suffering, she so meekly and serenely enjoyed.

You have had unfolded to you her history from earliest

childhood. Search and see whether among yourselves, or any other people, a more beautiful example can be found of what the world would call an irreproachable and innocent life ; and then I entreat you deeply to ponder on this record, which, by the permission of God, I now place before you, to discover what originally gave—what continued to give peace to Isabella ; what inspired in her bosom such confidence towards her righteous and holy Creator ; what took away all fear and sorrow, as she finally bade farewell to all things under the sun, when passing from time to eternity, to stand before the judgment seat of the Lord God Almighty.

Read, O my people ; so read, mark, learn, and inwardly digest this true record, that, in your own experience, you may solve the mystery, which her dying hours present to carnal and unregenerated minds—the mystery of increasing grief for sin, with increasing trust in God,—of clearer perceptions of her own guilt and unfruitfulness in her Father's vineyard, in union with more exulting assurance of heavenly purity and glory.

On Saturday, early in the morning, she was seized with agonizing pain, which, having continued for several hours, made her indeed feel that her end was drawing nigh.

"About nine o'clock," her sister writes, " she called me to her, and said, 'do you think the blessed time has come ?' I replied, 'I think I have seen you enduring greater pain than you do at present; I trust the Lord shall spare you to us a little longer :' at hearing which she burst into tears, and said, 'Spare me ! I have been a cumberer of the ground : it is because his mercy endureth for ever that I have not been consumed. O, when I reflect on the days and years of my ignorance, when I lived as a heathen without God and without hope in the world, it is enough to crush my spirit to the dust with a load of sorrow ; and when I think of my still more aggravated transgressions, committed since mine eyes have been in some measure enlightened, I am ashamed and unable almost to open my mouth. I would lie in the dust before him,

and say, O Lord enter not into judgment with me, else this spirit
would fail which thou hast made: show mercy according to the
multitude of thy tender mercies:—

> " ' Poor, weak, and worthless, though I am,
> I have a rich, almighty friend ;
> Jesus, the Saviour, is his name ;
> He freely loves, and without end.

> " ' But, ah ! my inmost spirit mourns,
> And well my eyes with tears may swim,
> To think of my perverse returns ;
> I've been a faithless friend to him.

> " ' Often, my gracious friend I grieve,
> Neglect, distrust, and disobey,
> And often Satan's lies believe,
> Sooner than all my friend can say.' "

Her beloved Miss ——, having been anxious to know
the opinion of Dr. —— of Isabella's case, that morning
accompanied him to see her, without, however, being previously aware of her increased suffering. A friend who
was with them, gives the following account of the interview :

"On our arrival, we heard that she had been in great pain, and
found her so weak that we thought it wrong to remain in her
room, and went with Mary to the adjoining apartment. She soon,
however, requested that the door might be thrown open, and desired that we would say what we thought was the duty of a Christian regarding prayer for the removal of temporal suffering. We
all agreed, that knowing all things shall work together for the
good of those who love God, we would not desire the removal of
what we believed infinite love and wisdom had appointed ; and
that, consequently, we would make no request regarding it, but
that it might be sanctified, that the will of God might be clearly
manifested by the result produced in the use of those means for recovery which he had put in our reach, and that our wills might be
made cheerfully to acquiesce in his. She said this had long been
her view, and that she had found much comfort in being able to
put a blank into God's hand as to all her temporal concerns. Before

coming away, we went for a few minutes where she was suffering great agony, and unable to speak. Miss —— said to her sister, 'her sufferings seem intense :' she smiled, and soon as she was able to utter a word, said, 'He will never send one needless pang, and as my sufferings abound, so do my consolations.' "

Subsequent to the departure of her friend, her sufferings continued to increase, while, to resume her sister's narrative, she thus gave vent to her feelings:

"How great is the God of Jesurun, and yet this great and mighty One, who sitteth upon the circle of the heavens, humbleth himself not only to look upon me, but to dwell in me, and to walk in me ! How it is the marvel of angels that this vile body should be the temple of the Holy Ghost !' Upon asking her about twelve o'clock, whether she would not have any food, she replied, ' Not just now; my Father is feeding my soul with the finest of the wheat. O the inexpressible pleasure which I feel in the prospect of soon sitting down with Abraham, Isaac, and Jacob, where there are rivers of pleasure for evermore.' Some hours after this, when shifting her pillows, my dear mother said with tears, ' O my love, you are suffering much.' ' Yes,' she replied, 'no chastening for the present seemeth joyous, but grievous; but the Lord is sweetly bearing me up, and saying unto me, ' Fear not, for I am with thee;' and I know, and am persuaded, that the afflictions of this present time are not worthy to be compared to the glory which shall be revealed.

> "' To Jesus, the crown of my life,
> My soul is in haste to be gone ;
> O bear me, ye cherubims, up,
> And waft me away to his throne.' "

"Towards evening she said, 'now is my salvation nearer; almost, I think, at hand. O blessed thought ! I shall soon recognise myself amongst yon perfected multitude, who worship him day and night in his temple. O to grace how great a debtor ! And here she paused; then looking upwards, she said,

> "' Let others boast of merit now,
> But merit I have none;
> I'm justified for Jesus' sake,
> I'm saved by grace alone.' "

"Soon after this, her suffering increased so greatly, that for some hours she could only speak a word or two at a time. Once, when the dear Christian friend, in whose house we were living, came into the room to inquire for her, she seemed much affected, and said, ' It is Jesus who hath made you all that you are to me. I pray him to reward you a thousand fold. When he himself was about to suffer those mysterious sufferings which the offended justice of God required of the people, there was none with him—it is said they all forsook him, and fled. How greatly different is it with me, a vile sinner, whose sins pierced and nailed him to the tree. My bed is encircled with the kindest, tenderest of friends, who count no pains too great, so that they may be able to minister in the least degree to my comfort. O what shall I render to the Lord for all his benefits; I am crowned daily with his loving-kindnesses and tender mercies. Most blessed Jehovah, let the spirit be poured out plentifully from on high, that this soul which thou hast redeemed may abound much in thanksgivings towards thee.'

"Feeling somewhat relieved towards midnight, she said, ' Some of you, my dears, may retire to rest. "He who keepeth my soul, slumbers not nor sleeps." My spirit feels so refreshed at present, that I care not whether I sleep or no; indeed, I'd rather be awake, and adore Christ Jesus, my Lord.' When leaving her, she said, ' "When I do thee upon my bed remember with delight," &c. O that I could but tell you the exceeding joy which I have in the Lord through Jesus Christ: truly " Wisdom's ways are pleasantness, and all her paths peace." How much is implied in these words, " The peace of God which passeth all understanding." ' -

THE SABBATH.

" She slept pretty well until six o'clock on Sabbath morning, when she was awoke by violent pain. When I entered her room, she said, ' I hope you have slept to the glory of God.' I did not, at first, comprehend what she meant; which she observing, immediately quoted the following passage--" Whether ye eat or drink, or *whatsoever* ye do, do all to the glory of God." I remarked she was weak, and urged her silence. She replied ' No, I cannot be silent. I'll speak the honours of his name with my last labouring breath. I have long besought him to glorify himself mightily in my death; and now, when he is doing such marvellous things for me, shall I withhold his praise? I cannot—I cannot.' After a few minutes silence, she said, ' I have been imploring my merciful heavenly Father to comfort my dear afflicted mother. She is bowed to the dust with sorrow, fatigue, and anxiety; what a tender parent she has been to me, he only knoweth. O Mary, do all that you think will soothe and cheer her smarting heart. Think of her heavy and continued trials, and see that you neglect not to bring before her blessed truths, the reception of which will soothe her sorrows, heal her wounds, and drive away her fears. But I am so exhausted, that I must now be silent for a minute or two.' Seeming as if she would fall asleep, I left the room; but in a few minutes I heard her begin to pour out her soul before the Lord: the door being ajar, I could hear pretty distinctly. It was deeply touching to hear with what great humility and child-like confidence she addressed the Father of her spirit. Some of her petitions I shall never forget. They were as follows:—

"O most blessed God, thou hast redeemed me, just because it hath seemed good in thy sight. Thou knowest thou hast given unto me the spirit of adoption, crying "Abba, Father." Thou knowest, who knoweth all things, that I have some love to thee. And O thou merciful One, thou knowest how long thou hast borne with the ingratitude of thy sinful creature; how often thou hast healed her backslidings, and loved her freely, and enlarged her when she was in distress. Now, O heavenly Father, permit her to plead with thee, not for her righteousness' sake but for the sake of thy great mercy, permit her to implore that thou wouldst still further magnify the riches of thy grace, by granting to her those supplies of thy spirit that will enable her to quench all the fiery darts of the wicked one. O let her glorify thee in the trying hour—in that hour when human aid must fail, and when only thine arm can support. Hold thou me up, so shall I be in peace and safety still. O my merciful Father, when shall I cease to grieve the Holy Ghost? when shall I awake in glory, and be satisfied with thy likeness? O Jesus, I pant to sing of thee." These are only a few of the blessed things which she uttered. Toward the end she was much distressed with coughing; at last, falling back in the bed, she said, 'O Father, hear Jesus, hear the intercession of thy well-beloved Son; vain would be my sinful prayer, unless he were pleading my cause at thy right hand, and now though I must stop, he ever liveth to make intercession for me. O what love!'

"After this she fell asleep, and slept calmly for about an hour and a half. Upon being asked when she awoke, whether she would not have something to strengthen her weak body? gazing upon us with a look of great pleasure, she replied, ' What meaneth all this kindness? 1 am loaded daily with his benefits.

> "O sweet to know a father's love.
> To feel a father's care."

I have no inclination at all for food; neither do I think I shall again eat the bread of mortals; but, if you please, I shall take a little wine.' When it was given to her, she said, ' Thanks be unto God for his unspeakable gift, through whom all these blessings flow. What a highly favoured creature I am. Don't you all wonder at my Father's care of my body? Truly he giveth meat unto all them that fear him : he will ever be mindful of his covenant.'

" About eleven o'clock, she called me to her, and said, ' I hope you intend going up to the courts of our God this morning?' I answered, ' I'd prefer remaining with you.' ' O no,' she replied, ' I want my dearest mother to-day with me ; and more than one is quite unnecessary. I want to speak to her about Jesus, and the blessedness there is in serving him. I want to devote much of my remaining time to her ; not one of you can feel as she does in the prospect of parting with me. Her tenderness to me from my earliest years, can well demonstrate the great love wherewith she loves me. O that the Lord may fill the blank, which my removal will leave in her heart, with his own fulness!'

" When I returned at one o'clock, I found her suffering more pain, and little inclined to speak. In a few minutes she inquired what part of the word of God was preached from to-day. Upon telling her that it was Hebrews xii. 1, she said, ' Well, these weights are many, and every child of God, I believe, hath some sin which doth more easily beset him, and we have no power at all of our own by which to remove them. But blessed be God, who giveth us the victory through our Lord Jesus Christ ; he hath said he will perfect that which concerns us ; and his promises are yea and amen in Christ Jesus. O then, ought not his faithfulness to be our shield and buckler ; ought we not to say, behold the Lord is my helper?'

" Upon being told, a short time after this, that a beloved Christian friend had sent to inquire for her, she said, ' Truly, whoso loveth him that begat, loveth them also that are begotten of him.

Nothing appears to me a more agonizing proof of the scarcity of vital godliness in our land, than the rareness of this grace of the spirit. How beauteously did it adorn the first Christians, and how God-like did it make them, and how much did it comfort them under their multiplied trials, and sacrifices for the truth's sake! What would Paul think, were he to witness the chilling manner in which many who profess the Christian name meet each other. And what would he think of the still more chilling intercourse which they hold after they have met! O I wish to speak to you all on this subject; it has long grieved my spirit. Remember, I pray you, these solemn words, " Whoso loveth not, knoweth not God; for God is love." '

" About four o'clock in the afternoon she said, ' It is vain in you delaying to send for my dear S——. Be assured this corruptible shall soon put on incorruption; I feel as if a mighty struggle were nigh at hand, and I desire much to recommend Jesus to him, so long as I have strength to speak. O that he knew God.' While she was yet speaking he arrived; on which she exclaimed, ' Blessed be the Lord for granting this interview.' I do not remember hearing what she said to him at their meeting :— I am rather inclined to think I was not in the room at the time, for she requested me a little while before to go and write for a dear minister of Christ, whom she ardently wished to see. What she said when making this request, so far as I remember, was as follows; ,' I particularly want him to be here; he is a man of faith, and his prayers must bring down great showers of blessings.' For some time after this she lay silent, evidently enduring much pain and oppression in breathing, the former of which increased so greatly, as to make her cry out in the anguish of her soul, ' O Lord, help me to bear! O Lord, help me to bear!' The scene was most deeply affecting. None of us could do any thing to alleviate, in the least, her distress. But the Lord soon appeared with deliverance. All at once, she stretched herself in bed, and clasping her hands, exclaimed, ' O what unutterable delight ! a little more of this will destroy this frail humanity. What a sweet foretaste of glory ! I feel no pain, no weakness at all, in this frail frame. I am even refreshed, from the crown of my head to the sole of my foot, with the consolation of Zion.' Some Christian friends having come into the room, observing them she asked who they were, and upon being told, she said, ' Draw near and behold the wondrous works of God. O if I could but tell you the happiness which I experience: I see the Lamb who was slain for my-self, and not for another.' While she was magnifying the exceed-ag riches of his grace, the friend already mentioned, whom she o much wished to see, arrived. I do not recollect any thing of what passed at their meeting, but the following remark:—' How very grateful ought you to be, that instead of being called here to preach the gospel to me, you have been called to rejoice with me in the gospel.' She immediately requested us to go to prayer, that we all might be filled with the spirit, which we did; and I believe all present will long remember it as a time of refreshing from the presence of their Lord and Father. A young christian friend whom she greatly loved, begged to be allowed to remain by her bedside during the night, which hearing, she said, ' No, my dear, dear Miss ——, not to-night; go, praise the Lord for what he is doing for my soul. O it is all mercy, mercy, mercy!'

MONDAY.

"I sat beside her from one o'clock until the morning; for a few hours she slept easily, but towards the dawn awoke in much agony, and requested me to open   window in order to relieve her breathing. When endear   raise her head a little, she looked at me with much comp.   ' said, ' O how thank-ful you ought to be, that I have seen.   s of the Lord in the land of the living, that I have bee.   a brand out of the burning, that I have the prospect .   ing my everlasting light, and my God my glory. O w.   ing of soul I feel. I wish that those, who seek satisfact of time, could understand a little of it. It would sure. a distaste for aught beside, and convince them that relig. from being cheerless or gloomy.' Being evidently much exh ed, she lay silent, I think for about an hour. At length, raisi. herself in bed, and drawing aside the curtains, she said, ' Are you still here?' I answered, ' Yes, have you had any sleep?' With much emphasis, she replied, ' O yes, I have had some sweet sort of sleep. I dreamt that I was absent from the body, and present with the Lord. All that I can recollect of it is, that I felt the most unutterable ecstasy. O worm, ungrateful sinner that I am, and shall I indeed see face to face the Lord my righteousness? Thy mercy, Lord, is in the heavens; thy truth doth reach the clouds.'—In a little while after this, she said, ' I wish you to bring my dear, dear mother. I bless the Lord for having given her a few hours repose; but I must see her now, for I am getting much

25*

worse.' She was immediately seized with excessive pain, and for the first time spoke a word or two rather incoherently. Her mind seemed to have wandered to a dear Christian minister, whom she had seen once or twice during her illness, and with whose conversation and prayer she had been much comforted. Several times she mentioned his name and place of residence, and inquired twice whether something had not that morning come from him to her. The Lord having again graciously relieved her, she looked upon me with much solemnity and said, ' Go and pray that I enter not into temptation. The spirit indeed is willing, but the flesh is weak; yes, very weak now. O pray that that roaring lion, who goeth about seeking whom he may devour, may not be permitted to come in like a flood into my poor soul. I believe the Lord has in a great measure bruised him under my feet, (for ah! many a long day did he harass me with his fiery darts.)—I believe he has already made his last attack; and O a horrid one it was. But you know the Lord will be inquired of for all grace; and it becomes us to cry to him at all times, to save us from the dominion of sin and Satan.' When she was told that we were going to breakfast, but that one of us would remain with her, she replied, ' O no, go all, and leave the door open. I do not think that I shall want any thing; indeed all I want is grace.' Upon urging her a little farther to allow some one to stay by her, she looked upon a relation who had come the evening before to see her, and said ' Well, let dear C—— stay. I am so glad to see her : O it is well that Jesus is ever with me.' I do not know what passed between them ; I rather think she was uneasy, and able to speak little. My sister C—— went in while we were at breakfast, to inquire for her. Fixing her eyes upon her, she said, 'O my love, I do not wonder at your weeping so much about me, because you do not sympathize in my joyful anticipations of eternal blessedness. If you did, would you not at least rejoice in part, that I go unto my Father? O my soul is pained about you; why will ye not believe upon Jesus? why will ye not come to him now, when all things are ready; when Jesus the Lord of Glory hath laboured, and you are invited to enter upon his labours? Believe me, it is as impossible for any soul to be happy or safe, at a distance from God, as it is for any soul to create a world.' About eleven o'clock, she was again seized with sore pain and difficulty of breathing, so much so, that she solicited me to sit behind her in bed, in order if possible to relieve her. Mr.—— said, ' He will not leave you.' Holding out her hand, she replied, 'Leave me,—no. I am engraven upon the palms of his hands: he is now standing by me, as a refiner and purifier of silver; I bless his blessed name, that he will never leave me, never forsake me, though the hills should depart, and the mountains be removed,' &c. In a little while she said, 'O my dear brother, in thanking you for all your christian kindness, let me request you to preach Christ in and out of season, and I hope the Lord will give you many souls for your hire.' Mrs. —— coming in to inquire for her, she looked to me and said, 'O the kindness of that dear person; see how she leaves every thing to serve me. This is just a little of my heavenly Father's tenderness put into the hearts of his children: at that day when a cup of cold water given to a disciple shall be rewarded, she shall doubtless have many rewards to receive.'

"In a little while afterward she said, 'I love the sacred book of God; none other can its place supply. I do not wonder that we are so unholy, when we study this precious revelation so little. It is true we cannot see its glory; but in the light of the Spirit; but then the Spirit is promised, and the Spirit works by means of the word. I may say I have scarcely read any book but the Bible; but had I my life, short as it has been, to live over again, I should confine myself still more exclusively to it. I am persuaded that much of the confusion in the minds of Christians at the present day arises from neglecting to read the scriptures so much as they ought.' Here she broke out into a transport of gratitude, and repeated, without stopping, and with astonishing accuracy, the following passages of scripture;—' For the mountains shall depart and the hills be removed, but my kindness shall not depart from thee, neither shall the covenant of my peace be removed, saith the Lord, that hath mercy on thee. ' Behold, I have graven thee upon the palms of my hands, thy walls are continually before me. But Israel shall be saved in the Lord, with an everlasting salvation. Ye shall not be ashamed nor confounded, world without end. The Lord is my shepherd, I shall not want. The Lord is nigh unto all them that call upon him—to all that call upon him in truth. He will fulfil the desire of them that fear him; he will also hear their cry and will save them.'

"Upon being told that dearest S—— was going home, she expressed a wish to see him once again. After she bade him farewell, she said, 'Well, may the Lord, even the mighty God of Jacob, send home with power what I have been enabled to say to him; for I think I have had some liberty in urging him to come to the blessed Saviour. O that I could but see my dear F—— too, that I might warn him of his danger, and beseech him to be reconciled to God.' On being told that some dear Christians, Miss —— and her sister, proposed to come and see her in the evening, she clasped her hands, and looking upwards, exclaimed, ' " My mouth, the praises of the Lord to publish, cease shall never ;" surely he is kind to the unthankful and the unholy. O how rude and ignorant I have been before him. I have even been a very beast, slow and unwilling to learn his commandments, yet he hath spared me, doth spare me, shall spare me. How great is his goodness, and how great is his beauty. I would lie at his footstool, and cry unclean. How will those angels that have attended me in all my wanderings, admire and adore the riches of redeeming grace, when they know that such a provoking sinner has been purged from all iniquity, and placed amongst the pure multitude who surround the throne of God and of the Lamb !' She spoke much throughout this day, mostly in the language of scripture, and when her own strength failed, solicited us to repeat to her the words of eternal life. Frequently would she interrupt us, and finish the passage herself, and then exclaim, ' How glorious, how strengthening, how fitted to bear me up under the keenest anguish ; yea, I shall be borne up, for God is able to make me stand; left to myself, I would fall a thousand times in an hour. Praised be his name for these words, ' I give unto my sheep eternal life, and they shall never perish, neither shall any pluck them out of my hand.' "

Her friend Miss—— had left her, not expecting to meet again on earth : Isabella, however, had desired Mr. —— to let her know how ill she was, that if possible they might see each other once more. In the evening, when told that Miss —— had arrived, she said, ' Well, ask the Lord that this meeting may be greatly to his glory : our intercourse on earth will soon be ended, and he who knows all things, knows that this often has been sweet and pleasant. O that he would now pour out his spirit copiously upon us, and make this the sweetest of them all.' " Her desire was surely granted," says Mary, " for it was a season of high spiritual enjoyment. She seemed to have quite forgotten

her weakness, and for an hour, talked more like an inhabitant of heaven than one who was yet in the body. Again
, and again, she said, 'Dwell in love: if God so loved us,
we ought also to love one another.' "

This last interview between these friends is more particularly described in the following extract from a letter,
which Miss ——, after her return home, wrote to her sister :

"When we arrived, they thought she could not know us. I
took her hand and repeated her name, but received no answer.
Mary said, ' Do you know who is with you ?' She answered, ' I
know her, I know it is dear Miss ——. Your kindness, my beloved friend, is unwearied; my very soul cleaves unto you.' I
said, ' Unto you who believe, Christ is precious.' ' He is,' she
replied, ' he is, yes, most precious. Is dear Miss —— with you ?
I love her much.' On —— coming in, she could scarcely dis-
cern her, but expressed the warmest affection ; told each of us to
take one of her hands, and added, ' I cannot now see your features.'
I said, ' You cannot now see us, but you still see Jesus.' ' I do,
I do,' she said with great delight, ' He is enough, quite enough.
Let him take what he will, he is enough, and will be through
eternity.' I said, ' It seems as if that prayer were now uttering in
heaven : "Father, I will that those whom thou hast given me
may be with me where I am, that they may behold my glory." '
She repeated the words with me—" my glory." Mr. —— said,
' That glory is just his love, and is it not sweet to feel that even
now it can outweigh every sorrow ?' She replied, ' It can, I feel
no earthly sorrow, I feel no fear, all is sweetness and joy.' Mr. ——
said, ' We prayed in the morning that your comfort might be continued.' ' Now is it increased,' she said, ' by sending these dear,
dear friends. O if you knew but half his love to me, it would amaze
you, and it will amaze you through the endless ages of eternity. I
am always better when I am speaking of him. Last night was
one of the greatest agony I ever endured; but when I thought of
Jesus, I scarcely knew I was in pain.'

" Mary said, 'His name is as ointment poured forth.' ' Yes,'
she answered, ' His love is better than wine; we will remember
him more than it.' Mary rejoined, ' My love, you are very happy.'—' Yes, I am very, very happy. Bless, O bless the Lord with

me. Magnify his name; let us exalt it together. I have been a highly favoured creature. I have seen others favoured around me; but I have even had more bestowed on me. No language can make known his glories.' Mr. —— desired me to repeat the lines she had said to Mary and me the first day I saw her :—

> ' We yet shall hold communion,
> In amaranthine bowers.'

"I began the hymn at that verse—

> 'The love that seems forsaken,
> When friends in death depart,
> In heaven again shall waken,
> And repossess the heart.'

She said, ' Yes, it shall awake in glory.' When I finished that verse, ' The harps of heaven steal o'er me,' &c., she said with a lovely smile—

> ' So sung the parting spirit,
> While down flow'd many a tear,
> Then spread her wings to inherit
> Her place in yonder sphere.'

"After this, having observed H—— weeping, she seemed affected for a moment, and then exclaimed, ' O could you weep for me?' Mary asked her, if I would repeat some of her favourite hymns? She said, ' Repeat them, they refresh and comfort my soul.' I began that one, ' Jesus, I love thy charming name!' At the last verse, where it is said, ' I'll speak the honours of thy name with my last lab'ring breath, she exclaimed, ' That has always been my prayer, that my last words may breathe his praise, but how feeble are my words now !' Then looking to those behind me, she said, ' O you that are in health, speak, speak the praises of his name ; and be not silent to those who see no beauty in my precious Lord.' She was now a little stronger, and conscious of what was doing around her, manifesting the same affectionate interest in the comfort of us all; and frequently, when I was standing to give her a tea-spoonful of wine, or to hold up her head, she would say, ' Cause dear Miss —— to sit down, she is too weak to stand; and expressing strong affection, particularly for H——. Mr. —— said, ' Although she loves us so much, she has been telling us this forenoon that there is none she desired but Christ;' she replied, ' " Whom have I in heaven but thee ? and there is none, none in all the earth that I desire beside thee." ' She again became slightly convulsed and oppressed by sickness, whispering, ' My flesh and my heart faileth.' I added, ' But God is the strength of your heart, and your portion for ever; you shall be satisfied when you awake up after his likeness.' ' Yes, I will be satisfied with my portion.' In repeating part of the hymn—' Ye angels who stand round the throne,' I came to this—

> ' I'm fetter'd, I'm chain'd up in clay.
> I struggle, I pant to be free;
> I long to be soaring away,

she added,

> My God and my Saviour to see."

" At these words in the 48th Paraphrase, ' Behold the pledge of peace below, and perfect bliss above,' Mrs. —— said, ' That peace you now enjoy.' I said, ' You are hastening to the bliss above.' She went forward, saying, ' Who shall separate us from his love ? Death ? No, not Death nor Satan ; we are more, more than conquerors through him who loved us.' When repeating that verse, ' The Lamb that sits amid the throne,' &c. Mr. —— said, ' What a name for God to assume, the Lamb ! The Lamb shall feed you with nourishment divine. That is his love, and when you have learned the song of Moses and the Lamb, you will think we are just children, learning to lisp his praise, but you will rejoice in the wisdom that keeps us here.' I said, ' " We know not what we shall be, but when he shall appear," ' &c. She said, ' Is it not sweet and glorious ?' After this she became very ill, and said, ' Mary, let me lean on you,' not knowing that she was supporting her. Mary said, ' You know the joy of leaning on the bosom of Jesus.' She replied, ' I do, O I am comfortable, quite comfortable.' Being in great pain, she said, ' O if it were my Father's will ! but his will is best.' I said,

> ' I'll welcome all thy sov'reign will,
> For all that will is love ;
> And when I know not what thou dost,
> I'll wait the sight above.
>
> Thy covenant in the darkest hour
> Shall heavenly joys impart,
> And when my eyelids close in death,
> 'Twill warm my chilly heart.' "

She answered, 'It will; how sweet! He that shall come, will come, and will not tarry.' I added, 'Even so, come quickly, Lord Jesus.' Solemnly she said, 'Even so.' Mr. —— remarked, 'You remember of whom it was written, "Being in an agony, his sweat was as it were great drops of blood falling down to the ground."' She said, 'That was His death, but he hath cheered my death-bed with his love, and surrounded it with these dear friends.' Mr. —— resumed, "He cried out, My God, my God, why hast thou forsaken me." 'He has promised,' I observed, "In passing through the waters, I will be with thee." Upon which she said, 'He is, and will be with me.' Once calling out, 'My dear mamma, my dear mamma,' I said, "Though a mother may forget, yet will I not forget thee." 'No,' she continued, 'for he hath graven me on the palms of his hands.'

"When I was obliged to leave her, she was again asked if she knew me. She immediately said, 'I do, I do. It is dear Miss ——, to whom my soul is knit in love.' I said, 'We shall not meet here again. When we next behold each other, "this mortal shall have put on immortality; this corruptible shall have put on incorruption. Death shall be swallowed up in victory, and the days of our mourning shall be ended."' She answered, 'I will meet you; pray much for me; I will meet you in glory.' We parted, and before I was lifted to the carriage, she sent Mary, saying, 'Tell dear Miss —— to rejoice much for me.' On Mary returning to the room, Isabella asked 'What did she say?' 'The answer was, "I do, yea, and will rejoice."' Upon which she said, 'That is enough.'"

Miss —— returned home, giving thanks and praising God for this peculiar mercy, that crowned all the happiness of their friendship, with the privilege of a last and so blessed an interview; and cherishing the sweet assurance that their union was not to be dissolved; but that still after death they might be helpers of each other's blessedness. She has often described it as a season of holy joy, and triumphing beyond all that she could conceive of the Redeemer's faithfulness and love; while the feeling of all present seemed to be, that the Lord had indeed opened the windows of heaven and was pouring down blessings, so that there was not room in their contracted hearts to receive them.

A friend who arrived just as Miss ———— was departing, thus relates what passed while she remained.

"Observing me at her bedside, she fixed her eyes upon me, as if wishing to know who I was. I told her it was I. She said, ' I am dying ; my sight is gone. I see you, but I cannot distinguish your features; but, through grace, I will know you differently yet.' She then said, ' My heart and my flesh faileth, but God is my portion : and O what is that! that a worm of the dust might say of the Lord, he is my portion.' Observing her mother weeping, she said, ' Mamma, look at me, you are weeping, you are weeping; weep not for me, but get an interest in Christ.' To the doctor, who came at the time, her manner was most affectionate; she repeatedly thanked him for his kindness to her, and said, ' My Father will reward you, and I hope none of you present will ever forget the Doctor's kindness to me.' Mr. ———— said, ' Whosoever giveth a cup of cold water to a disciple of mine, shall in nowise lose his reward.' ' Yes,' she said, ' and O what a word is that; it is not said the greatest of my disciples, but the least of them.' After a pause, she said, ' Let all get an interest in Christ before they come to this bed. I would be the most miserable being upon earth this night, if I had not an interest in Christ.' Complaining of a great load upon her breast, Mr. ———— said, ' Your Father knows it all.' ' Yes,' she said, ' In every pang that rends this heart, the man of sorrows hath a part.' ''

" After her friends had bade her farewell," her sister continues, " she asked me to go and request one of them, who was greatly affected, not to weep for her, but to rejoice and glorify God on her behalf. Soon after this she fell asleep, and lay calm for about an hour; when she awoke, and complained of great weakness, and rather a tendency to aberration of mind. ' Go, O go,' she said, ' and pray unto God that he would so preserve my mind as to protect me from saying any thing that would be unglorifying to his great and holy name. O beg him to keep my eyes fixed on the glories of crucified love.'

" After this she became very drowsy, and spoke little during the night, and first part of the morning. Once or twice she was heard to say, O what I shall soon see! Glory, glory, glory, the glory of Christ, the glory of God. Yes, and not only see it, but enjoy it ; I am through mercy an heir of God, and a joint heir with Christ.'

26

TUESDAY.

"About nine o'clock in the morning of Tuesday, she was seized with strong nervous affections, and greatly desired that we would allow her to come out of bed, and sit up for a little. Towards eleven o'clock, we were under the necessity of gratifying her. Several dear friends, whom she regarded as believers in the Lord, had by this time arrived, and the idea of being supported by them appeared to delight her greatly. The removing her so much exhausted her strength, that for almost half an hour she took no notice of any thing around her. Our expressed anxieties at length aroused her, and fixing her eyes upon us, apparently with deep astonishment, she said, 'O, what is the matter with you all? He is with me, he is with me, I feel he is with me. Do not be afraid about me. All is settled—he is comforting me, he is upholding me with the right hand of his righteousness; when I pass through the fire he shall be with me, and through the floods they shall not overflow me.' A friend then repeated that animating hymn, 'My God, the covenant of thy love,' &c. When it was finished, she said, 'That is cheering; "When I know not what thou dost, I'll wait thy light above." 'O that is a blessed line.' She then began to repeat a hymn which had often solaced her—'In all my troubles sharp and strong,' &c.; and looking at the friend who had repeated the first, she said, 'O my dear, give me hold of your hand, I love you much, for Jesus' sake; will you repeat another hymn to me—they are a sweet balm to my spirit.' "

Miss ——'s sister, who had returned to see her about this time of the day, gives the following account of her visit :—

"When told I had arrived, she said, 'I cannot see her, but tell her I love her much, and cause her to sit near me.' At this time Mrs. —— sat with her in her arms, and her feet rested on a chair. I sat down and took them on my knee. She spoke much of oppressive sickness, while the grinding of her teeth, and her agonized expression, intimated a state of the most intense endurance. Once she called out, 'O do not hold my feet; let them rend, let them rend.' We felt alarmed, thinking that her mind wandered; but were immediately relieved, by her adding, 'I wish this flesh to be rended, that Christ may appear.' Some time after she looked at me: Mary said to her, 'Do you know who it is that holds your feet?' 'Yes,' she replied, 'it is dear ————.' 'Do you see her?' Mary said. 'I do, and my soul cleaveth to her.' 'Why is it,' she said, 'that you love her?' 'Because,' she answered, 'Christ hath loved her.' She then said, she wished Mary to take hold of her hand, adding, 'you will often think of me.' Mr. —— observing how good the Lord was, in permitting so large a portion of his little flock to witness her last moments, she said, 'O that he who taught you to love me, would give you grace so to love one another.' Afterwards, being in great agony, she cried out, 'My Father, my Father, O my Father, who art in heaven, what shall I do?' Mr. —— said, 'My dear, cast your care on him, for he careth for you,' or something to the same purpose. 'Yes,' she replied, 'I know he hath engraven me on the palms of his hands; and then, as if fearful that her expressions of distress had led Mary to doubt that in this assurance she could even then rejoice,' she added, 'Mary, fear not, he is with me.' Being shortly after laid in bed, she remained as if asleep for some time. Supposing that was so, Mary and I stood by the bedside, talking, when she interrupted us by saying, 'Leave that to my God; leave that to my Father.' Mary inquired what she meant she should leave to God? She replied, 'All that ails me.'"

"Shortly afterward," (to resume Mary's narrative,) "seeing my mother much distressed, she laid her hand gently upon her face, exclaiming, 'My very dear mother, I know you love me; O love Jesus, and we shall meet again, never more to part. I am going to him: yes, I am going home; do not grieve about me—all is settled.'

"To her sister J——, who was weeping, she said, 'My dear love, go to Jesus, and he will bind up your broken heart. Believe me, there is no barrier between you and durable happiness but unbelief. God hath given to you, and all who hear his word, a record, the belief of which is salvation, and the rejection of which is damnation. O think of this ere the evil days come, and the years draw nigh, when thou shalt say I have no pleasure in them; and may the Divine Spirit renew your perverse will, and enable you to receive Jesus as your all-in-all.'

"After being silent for a little, she said. 'Nothing but the fear of man thinking ill of us prevents our speaking of the gospel: but to one situated as I now am, on the very brink of eternity, it appears a small matter—the opinion of man is nothing now to me. O that it ever should have been any thing : that I should ever have thought it better to obey man than God. Had I my life to live over again, I would through grace strengthening me act differently; and now, I would beseech you all with my dying breath, to speak of Christ ; no matter who disapproves the theme. Do, I implore you, deliver your own souls; speak to them, whether they will hear or whether they will forbear. Could you be placed for one half hour in the solemn circumstances in which I stand, you would see the amazing importance of what I say. O may the Lord grant you to be more faithful than I have been.'

"During the whole of this evening she appeared much inclined to sleep ; but it was easy to perceive, that her sleep was far from being pleasant. Once she was heard to say, ' I am losing my eyesight, I cannot know any of them now; but O how blessed ! these are not the eyes with which I see Jesus, who hath delivered me from the wrath to come.'

"Towards morning she became very restless, and once said, ' I endure much agony, but it is all well : why should a living man complain for the punishment of his iniquities. I have been tenderly dealt with, most tenderly ! Truly his left hand is under my head, and his right hand doth embrace me. Such pity as a father hath unto his children, like pity shows the Lord to such as worship him in fear. Yes, he remembers that we are dust; he remembers that I am now very frail dust, and he will not afflict me above what I am able to bear. O what is pain, when the Lord fills the soul with himself, causing it to rejoice with joy unspeakable and full of glory. Sweet is the rod, when we know who hath appointed it. But my strength is gone, and the Lord is revealing wonderful things unto me—things of which I shall never speak in time, but which I shall sing of throughout eternity. O eternity, I am swallowed up in thee : every thing connected with this world appears to me now as a dream that is past and gone. O that I have done so little for my blessed Saviour, during my stay in it. Mercy has been shown to me, and yet I have not shown mercy. I am vile, I am very vile, and yet I can look up to God through Jesus, and say, doubtless thou art my Father, though Abraham be ignorant of me, and Israel acknowledge me not. Now do I in some measure understand the blessedness contained in these words, " The blood of Christ cleanseth from all sin :" yes, other refuge have I none.'—She was going on, but was interrupted by a violent fit of breathlessness.

"After a few minutes she looked at me, and said with much apparent difficulty, 'The last enemy which shall be destroyed is Death. O Death, where is thy sting; O grave, where is thy victory! I have the victory, I have the victory, I have the victory in my glorious Saviour; thou, O Christ, art all I want.'

WEDNESDAY.

"In the morning, she seemed not to know those who approached; but about eleven o'clock, when Mr. —— went into the room, we discovered that the nervous affection had entirely left her. He said, 'I must leave you, for I know you would not have me neglect the work of the Lord.' 'O no,' she replied, 'I would not. Be instant in season and out of season. Farewell my dear brother in the Lord, we shall soon meet in glory; I am fast hastening thither.' In a little after this, she said, 'The time will not be long now. O how I do wish to be holy; sin is a most hateful, soul-harassing thing. You know how long I have felt it a burden, almost too heavy for me to bear. I am exceedingly weak now. The agony of yesterday and last night has almost carried away any little strength I had. All of you, except my dear mother, must sit in the next room to-day; for I can neither talk, nor bear much talking now. But this one thing I know, and praise the Lord for it, that I know in whom I have believed, that the Holy Spirit is supporting me mightily.

"She spoke little during the greater part of this day, but seemed sweetly composed, and several times said, 'Jesus my Lord, I know his name; it is all my boast.' Once, when the Doctor's name was mentioned, she said, 'O how grateful I and all of you ought to feel to him; he has been so singularly kind and attentive to me. May the Lord bless and reward him.' Some time after, she looked at me, and said, 'Grief as well as joy is deceitful. See that ye be not deceived by it. See that ye grieve not the Holy Spirit by indulging in overmuch sorrow on my account. If you loved me as you ought, you would rejoice that I am so soon to have done with sin, and consequently with sorrow. Have you not often prayed, that I might be holy as God is holy; and now that he is about to make me so, will you repine? I believe the time of my departure is nigh at hand, and grateful shall it be to my longing soul. O my Saviour, when shall I be permitted to leave this vain world, and enter into the fulness of thy joy!'

"Looking upwards, she said, ' 1 should like to pray for an increase of faith; but I am so ignorant I know not what things I should pray for as I ought. I replied, ' The spirit is promised to help your infirmities.' ' Yes,' she said, ' and to make intercession for us, with groanings which cannot be uttered ; and well it is for me that this is the case, for I do groan, being burdened, waiting for the adoption, to wit the redemption of my body. O this sore struggle between the flesh and the spirit; but it will soon all be over, and I shall be freed eternally from all that would interrupt my delight in God. Yes, thanks be unto God, who giveth us the victory through our Lord Jesus Christ :—

> " Soon shall I sing of battles won,
> And garments rolled in blood,
> And vanquished foes through Jesse's son,
> The bleeding Lamb of God." '

" At another time she said to me, ' Well, how little of the life of faith do any of us know. I am amazed, that I should have any thoughts at all but holy thoughts. I am wearied of sin. Blessed Father! how shall my soul adore thee, for the sweet prospect of purity, which thou hast been so graciously revealing to me these some days past. O the wondrous song of gratitude, that I shall soon sing :

> " Who shall fulfil that wondrous song,
> What vain pretender dares ?
> The theme surmounts an angel's tongue
> And Gabriel's heart despairs.' "

Shortly after she said,

> " ' Weaker than a bruised reed,
> Help I every moment need."

—Yes,' she added, with much emphasis, ' short as my journey to Zion now seems, I could not hold out in it, if left to myself for one single moment. O the danger of thinking that because we are believers, we can do any thing without the spirit ; we can just do as little as we could before we believed, even nothing.' I said, ' But you shall soon be strengthened.'—She answered, ' I know I shall :

not for any thing in me, but because of his great mercy. I shall
be strengthened by his spirit in the inner man. You know I have
all grace in Christ.' Looking at her, I said, ' You are very happy.'
' Yes,' she said, ' he is working in me mightily ; giving me to believe that the closing scene shall be the brightest. Then, then
shall this which is in part be done away. Come, Lord Jesus, come
quickly.'

THURSDAY.

" When we left her, about 11 o'clock, she seemed easy, and
soon fell asleep ; but in a few hours afterward, my mother sent us
a message, saying, that she had awoke in great pain. When we
went in, she caught hold of my hand, and said, ' Mary dear, the
important season is very near now ; but I fear no evil. The Lord
is my Shepherd, and the valley of the shadow of death shall not be
dark, for Jesus the son of righteousness shall be with me even
there. My pain is great ; none but my Father, my blessed Father, knoweth how great. O pray that I may wait with patience ;
for sometimes I am like to weary.'

" Then seeing my mother weeping, she said, ' Do not weep my
dearest mother, but look to Jesus. O come to Jesus ; think how
kind he has been to me. Many a long day you have heard me
speak of him.' Then catching hold of my brother's hand, she said,
with much difficulty, ' O, I would give a good deal to be able to
speak. I see much, and I think I would be able to say something
which would glorify God ; but every word I utter is a dart piercing my soul.' Fixing her eyes upon S., she entreated him, in
the most solemn manner, to believe upon Jesus. I do not exactly
recollect her words ; but one thing I remember, which was as follows ; ' Believe me, you can never be happy until you come to
the Saviour, for there is not happiness for any creature out of him.'

" She now became very ill, so ill that no one present thought
she could stand the struggle for any length of time. This awful
suffering continued nearly for two hours, when she was considerably relieved, and able to speak a few words at distant intervals,
which she did in a slow solemn tone of voice. About half-past
six o'clock, she took hold of my hand and said, ' Come nearer me,
my dear.' When I had done so, she pressed it gently, and whis-
pered ' Farewell.' Seeing me agitated, she said, 'O bear in mind
that our separation will be but short. Live alone to God.—Farewell."

" After this her principal attention was directed to S.—She could not think that he should be absent from her for a moment, and often when she could not speak, would she gaze upon him with a look of affectionate meaning. About 8 o'clock she requested that her bed might be removed into the parlour; and that S. might carry her. She stood the removal well : and after having reclined for a little, begged we would allow her to sit in a chair by the fire, which we did. A stranger, to have seen her at this time, would have supposed her in comparative health, so great was the change in the short space of two hours. But ah ! it was only of short continuance ; in about half an hour, she again asked us to lay her in bed, which we had no sooner done than we perceived that her powers of articulation were almost gone. Once or twice she endeavoured to say something, but we could not understand her. At last, taking hold of my mother's hand, she said, 'I want my dear brother in Christ, Mr ———, to be present, and engage in prayer when my spirit flies to glory. Will you send for him now ?' These, I think, were amongst the last words which she uttered.

" A beloved christian friend whom she had long wished to be present on this occasion, entering about this time, she gazed upon her evidently much delighted, and made several attempts to speak, but could not. Once, when looking upward, we thought she said, ' Saviour, Saviour,' but were not quite certain. It was now about 12 o'clock : during the two following hours of her life she appeared to suffer but little. She kept her eyes for the most part fixed upon my mother and brother ; a sweet smile played upon her countenance, and the calm composure, with which she awaited the approach of death, was truly a practical fulfilment of the words of the Psalmist, ' The latter end of the righteous is peace.'

" About 10 minutes before she fell asleep in Jesus she became so weak, and her breathing so imperceptible, that almost all present conceived she had left an earthly for a house not made with hands, eternal in the heavens. In this state she continued for perhaps more than five minutes ; when to our astonishment and comfort, she opened her eyes suddenly, and clasping her hands looked upwards with a look of such inconceivable transport as made many present exclaim, ' Surely God is here !' Such an expression of delight I never beheld. Her whole countenance seemed to shine, and all present confessed they had never pictured to themselves an object half so lovely.

"It was evident she had now turned her eyes away for ever from viewing vanity. Once or twice she tried to utter something, but still kept looking heaven-ward. Her admiration seemed to rise higher and higher every moment. At length, as if wishing to get nearer to the King in his beauty, she clasped her hands closer, and attempting to put herself more in a waiting position, expressed higher rapture than ever. The chastened smile which sat upon her lovely countenance was deeply impressive, and seemed to speak what she often inculcated; 'O let us contemplate continually the unparalleled agonies of Jesus, and see in them how very awful a thing sin is, in order that we may be kept humble.' I think she was not with us more than a minute and a half after this. Her happy spirit winged its triumphant flight almost unobserved to any present, without a struggle or a groan, or a single movement of any of her features, to the land of everlasting blessedness, on the forenoon of the 1st of November, 1827, she having somewhat exceeded the twentieth year of her age."

Although it is not needful to add any thing to complete the portraiture, by her sister, of the last moments of the holy and blessed Isabella, lest any of you should be desirous of knowing particularly what impression a scene so remarkable produced upon other eye-witnesses, I subjoin an extract from a letter of one of the youngest and dearest of Isabella's christian friends:

"Her spirit is now landed safe upon the peaceful shores of Canaan: now is Isabella playing mightily upon the golden harp, to the praises of Him whom she had long known and loved to follow.

"I remained with her two days before her death. O had you but witnessed the closing scene—it was a solemn, although magnificent and glorious sight. For about the space of an hour she did not seem to recognise any of us. Her eyes appeared to be half-shut; but at that moment, when her spirit was about to wing its flight, she opened them fully, fixed as if on the glorious Jesus. Her whole countenance became full of animation; really, her face had the appearance as we may suppose that of an angel—quite unearthly. I dare say, if our sister had been permitted to speak, she would have said, 'I see the heavens opened, and the Son of Man sitting at the right hand of God.'

" Thus did dear Isabella soar on high, leaving her fellow-travellers behind, filled with admiration—struck dumb, I may say, with astonishment at her triumphal ascent to glory. Death was truly a welcome messenger to her—was indeed a joyful summons, for it summoned her to her Father's house, and to her beloved Jesus, at whose feet she longed to cast her crown. The Lord was truly glorified in her death. She and Mary had often made it a subject of earnest prayer. Mary, according to Isabella's request, set seasons apart for this purpose. The Lord has indeed heard the words of their supplication, and showed himself to be the hearer and answerer of prayer."

As with one accord, the eye-witnesses of this most memorable scene might have used the language of a beautiful hymn, often indeed sung by some of them, while thinking of the beloved Isabella :

> " Dear as thou wert, and justly dear,
>   We will not weep for thee;
> One thought shall check the starting tear,
>   It is—that thou art free.
>
> " And thus shall Faith's consoling power,
>   The tears of love restrain,
> O! who that saw thy parting hour,
>   Could wish thee here again.
>
> " Triumphant in thy closing eye
>   The hope of glory shone,
> Joy breath'd in thy expiring sigh,
>   To think the fight was won.
>
> " Gently the passing spirit fled,
>   Sustain'd by grace divine,
> O! may such grace on me be shed,
>   And make my end like thine."

In this christian household, death, and the thoughts of death, seemed to have lost all power for a season, to excite the recoilings of nature. The glory of Isabella's departure, so divinely harmonizing with the triumphs of a long period of suffering, excluded anguish and painful sorrow from the first hours of bereavement. She was not :—but yet she seemed more truly to be than ever. By the rending of her mortal frame, the spiritual loveliness of her soul became as it were, more distinctly visible before her surviving kindred and friends. Joy prevailed against grief in the chamber of the dead, and hosannahs were sung to Him who had blessedly constrained them to acknowledge, that even here death can be swallowed up in victory.

Happily there is perserved a letter, written by a young woman to her friend, pleasingly descriptive of such feelings, as are seldom witnessed in a house of mourning, or experienced by the children of men, when bereaved of those they tenderly love.

"Miss Isabella Campbell is dead. I never saw her while in life, but I was informed that she continued to the last to give the most convincing proofs of the power of Christianity, not only to support and comfort their life, but even to make it to rejoice and triumph in death.

"I was with them for two or three days after she died, assisting to make their mournings, and truly I thought them most wonderful people. Instead of mourning, Miss Campbell, and some of her friends, who came to visit her, seemed to be rejoicing in spirit; and I actually heard them say, that they thought it ought to be white, instead of black, that Mary should wear for her. Certainly they have no cause to mourn on her account, and it shows their want of selfishness when they can rejoice in her happiness, instead of mourning their own loss. I was, indeed, sometimes almost ready to think that I had never been among real Christians before, and that I myself was only one in name. They can talk with such frequency of their rapturous feelings of joy which they experience, their faith seems to carry them so far, that, when speaking of the joys of the heavenly world, one would think that faith is almost swallowed up in sight. When the name of Jesus is mentioned, they are filled with raptures of love, and their love to one another seems to burn with fervency; and, in a word, they seem to be altogether lifted above the world, and to live only for God. This is perhaps too highly a coloured picture of their character, but it is the kind of impression which it made on my mind at the time, and I could not but contrast it with the coldness or lukewarmness of my own heart. But let us not despond; although we may not experience such high-toned feelings, and although we may not have arrived to such high degrees of holiness, let us trust in the Saviour, for we have not an High Priest who cannot be touched with a feeling of our infirmities, and we are encouraged to come boldly to the throne of grace, that we may obtain mercy, and find grace to help in time of need, and with us it is always a time of need."

In a few days, the last offices were performed, with becoming solemnity, to our departed friend. The body was conveyed by water to Lochgoilhead, to repose by her father and brother in the burial ground of her ancestors. The day was not apparently the most favourable for such a service; Isabella however had desired that even her funeral, as well as her death, might be glorifying to God; and the inclemency of that day gave most happy occasion to the preaching of the glorious gospel of his love. All sought shelter below—and then did the Rev. ———, in whose parish she had died, with a most faithful and loving boldness, unfold and press upon their acceptance, the great salvation; that they might live and die in the Lord like her, and have, to use her own words, "through eternity, the comfortable hope of purity, gratified in contemplating the incomparable beauty of the glorious Emmanuel."

I rejoiced when I heard that the same dear brother and fellow labourer in the ministry, on the following Sabbath, conducted your devotions in the solemn assembly; preaching a sermon suitable to so memorable an occasion from the words, "They glorified God in me." I trust that the exposition of her character which he then gave—of her assured confidence towards God—of her holy devotedness to his service, and conformity to his will—of her singular of Jesus, and of the souls whom he came to save—of her meek, thankful, and heroic endurance of all that was appointed her in the days of her suffering,—has not yet faded, and never will fade from your remembrance, ever stirring you up to glorify God in her. I trust, indeed, that the example of such a life, and of such a death, has led you often to acknowledge, that there is a great, a most blessed reality in spiritual things; and vehemently to pant after conformity to so lovely a manifestation of Christian faith and holiness; that like her you may manifest some resemblance of that " primary and exemplary temple," which, in the beauty of holiness, God has unveiled to the eye of man.

What she was each of you may be. He, who bestowed his gifts so liberally upon Isabella, is no respecter of persons; and whatever was admirable in her piety is to be attained from the same divine source, by you and your children. The stream of his love is continually flowing around the hearts of you all :—O let not any exclude such a holy felicity, or remain in disquietude and misery while their joy, like hers, may be full.

What remains for me now, my beloved people, but to pray, that not only you, but all to whom her name shall become known, may live the life, and die the death of this righteous one, this holy and single-minded believer on the name of the Son of God. She was of lowly condition indeed, according to the estimate of men in this false and foolish world; but can you doubt of her high and holy lineage ? She was verily of a chosen generation. Search and see if any more decisive tokens can any where be found, of the thoughts and feelings peculiar to the seed royal of heaven, the redeemed children of the Lord, the kindred of him who is the King of glory, the first-born of the high and lofty One that inhabiteth eternity.

27

In the form of an address to the people among whom she had dwelt from her childhood, and by whom she was carried to the grave, I have thus sought to convey to others, in as simple a manner as I could, the history of the life and death of my dear Isabella, now I doubt not seeing " Him as he is," of whom her soul delighted to think with such holy reverence and love in the house of her pilgrimage. Presuming on the knowledge of my people, I have perhaps omitted circumstances usually inserted in similar narratives, but none, I trust, that would have added to the moral effect intended, through God's good blessing, by the faithful delineation of so holy a character. I have said nothing, for example, of her personal attractions, although of such exquisite beauty, that few went from her presence, without feeling that they had never seen a countenance of such divine loveliness of expression. Nor have I described her demeanour, although of such grace and dignity as are not often found even in higher conditions of life—so like an emanation from a mind familiar with such thoughts as that in the prayer of " the holy Herbert :"

> " Though elements change and heavens move,
> Let not thy higher court remove,
> But keep a standing majesty in me."

I have inserted also little of her family—of her sorrowing relations—little even of Mary, so capable of sympathising with her in all her feelings during life, of even being joyful as she was translated to her incorruptible, undefiled inheritance. Of Mary, however, I may say, that she has never recovered the exhaustion and debility induced by her exertions during Isabella's sufferings, and is now unable to leave her pillow, affected by a malady similar to that which so long tried the patience of her sister. I have said she was capable of joy in thinking of Isabella's redemption from suffering. That such a joy could mingle in the same bo-

, som with all the most exquisite tenderness of natural affection, is very apparent from the following extract of a letter she wrote to Miss —— upon reaching Fernicarry after the funeral—with which I bring this memoir to a close :—

"O my Isabella, my Isabella ! I shall feel thy loss, I shall feel the want of thy dear society, so long as I sojourn in a strange and foreign land. Ah, yes ! thou art gone, to be seen no more of mortals ; the grassy turf now defends thy lovely form from the fury of the wintry blast, and though by the busy multitude thou shalt soon be forgotten, and though over thy grave they can tread with as much indifference as though nothing that was precious to Jehovah lay beneath, yet thy brethren and sisters in Jesus shall remember thee still. By thy life and thy death they shall be encouraged to trust in the Lord for ever, and banish their every fear ; and if in the providence of God, any of them are ever permitted to visit the dear spot where thy precious dust lies unnoticed, they will lift up their hearts with their vbices, while they sing, ' This body which corrupted fell, shall uncorrupted rise.' I do indeed feel a blank which nothing in this world can ever fill. The eyes are closed in death, which wept when I wept, and always beamed with transport when I was glad ; the lips are now closed, which so frequently said, ' O Mary ! live above the smiles and the frowns of this world ; and then you will make me happy. The arms in which I have been so frequently locked, which used with peculiar fondness to press me to a heart warm with the love of Jesus, now lie motionless, fast returning to their original nothing. But shall I murmur ? No, Lord Jesus ! the river which maketh glad the city of our God is still flowing plenteously from on high, and thou art thyself a satisfying portion."

THE END.

۴